What the experts say about some of Marc Dawson's previous books

Cricket Extras (1993) – "Probably the most complete set of cricketing quirks and coincidences ever to be collated in one volume." – **former England Test captain David Gower**

Cricket Extras 2 (1994) – "Hundreds of eye-openers. Riveting stuff." – **David Frith, *Wisden Cricket Monthly***

Quick Singles (1995) – "A fascinating book." – **ABC cricket commentator Jim Maxwell**

Cricket Curious Cricket (2007) – "Splendid anthology of unusual facts and feats from the summer game." – **Rob Shaw, *The Examiner***

The Cricket Tragic's Book of Cricket Extras (2010) – "Lavishly and beautifully produced and illustrated. An outstanding publication. What is most remarkable is that so much has been packed into the book, with everything set out with such clarity of detail."
– **Indian cricket statistician Rajesh Kumar**

Outside Edge – An Eclectic Collection of Cricketing Facts, Feats & Figures

Featuring a foreword by Australian Test legend Geoff Lawson Which first-class cricket team contained two players who would later be murdered? Who was the Australian-born Test cricketer who became a cage fighter? Which former England all-rounder set a world record for eating the most peas with a cocktail stick? Which pair of brothers share the most century partnerships in Test match cricket, and who was the bowler who took Test wickets with consecutive balls, seven years apart?

The answers to all these questions can be found in *Outside Edge* – an irresistible, addictive and routinely astonishing collection of cricketing facts, feats and figures from the game's early days through to the era of ODIs and Twenty20.

Opening the door on areas such as cricket and politics, cricket and music and cricket and films, royalty and cuisine, the book transcends cricketing trivia. *Outside Edge* amounts to a wholly original compendium of the most unusual stories from across the whole breadth of the global game's rich history and culture.

Featuring a foreword by Australian Test legend Geoff Lawson

OUTSIDE EDGE

OUTSIDE EDGE

AN ECLECTIC COLLECTION OF CRICKETING FACTS, FEATS & FIGURES

Marc Dawson

Foreword by
Geoff Lawson

Pitch Publishing
A2 Yeoman Gate
Yeoman Way
Durrington
BN13 3QZ
www.pitchpublishing.co.uk

A CIP catalogue record is available for this book from the
British Library

ISBN 978-1-90917-855-7

Typesetting and origination by Pitch Publishing.
Printed in Great Britain by CPI Group (UK) Ltd, Croydon, CR0 4YY

Contents

Foreword

AMERICAN ACTOR Robin Williams infamously, erroneously and tritely labelled cricket as 'baseball on valium', but he is obviously not cognisant of the fact that the USA actually played the first ever 'one-day international' – a thriller versus Canada back in the 19th century. Williams's ignorance can be enlightened if he thumbs through Marc Dawson's new opus *Outside Edge*. It will surely give him the info and the edge on his fellow countrymen.

Outside Edge chronicles facts, feats and figures of the wondrous game. Marc compiles, labels and catalogues thousands of cricket factoids, statistics, phenomena, coincidences and opinions. Some seem obvious and logical, others definitely do not. As an avid reader of cricket literature and miner of cricket statistics I found surprises coming thick and fast like a Stieg Larsson plot. *Outside Edge* is a 'page turner' in every respect. I found myself flipping the next while still halfway through the final sentence on the previous. Seeking that extra page to find out just what obscure or obvious fact I would be presented with … the umpire killed who? … and why? … Salman Rushdie said what about Imran Khan?

The volume raises curious occurrences and wonderful accomplishments and often eyebrow-raising relationships … what do Jermaine Lawson and Geoff Lawson have in common, besides the obvious that they were both fast bowlers?

Cricket has been forever a game that produces, digests and often spits out statistics. In Marc Dawson's virtual gastro-intestinal tract you can check how the runs, wickets and catches are not the only figures that cricket produces – the vital statistics of Liz Hurley, Errol Flynn and the yellow Wiggle appear. Rowan Atkinson's character Blackadder uses the expression 'as about as feminine as W.G. Grace' or even Merv Hughes, if you get the gist. The very cunning Baldrick got the point.

Tendulkar, Hobbs, Bradman and Ranji all are featured but I bet you don't know how many century partnerships the Waugh brothers, or the Chappell brothers or the Crowe brothers or the Flowers have made together.

Ducks! There are plenty of them, often consecutive and well roasted. But who has made the most after making a hundred, between hundreds and before getting a hundred? The Chris Martin batting stat is guessable, but read it anyway!

Club, school and village cricket records and peculiarities get a serious run. The stats are far from ordinary and will win many a trivia quiz besides raising your interest and eyebrows. The CIA gets a mention, yes – *The* Central Intelligence Agency, as does Barack Obama, David Cameron, John Major and Kevin Rudd.

Cricket has traditional roots and the not so traditional. Kenya could almost be described as having a foot in both camps but the Maasai Warriors XI wearing tribal garb didn't impress their trainer much besides bringing a new interpretation to the term 'leg cutter'. The explanation is in these pages.

There is absolutely no question that Marc Dawson is well researched, thorough, intense, a finder of cricket nooks and an examiner of cricket's crannies. You can read *Outside Edge* anywhere, anytime. The interest is a fascination. Clearly Marc needs to get out of the house a bit more. Read this and then loiter around the bookstore for the next instalment.

Geoff Lawson

Geoff Lawson
former Australian Test cricketer

Wielding the Willow

- Hot on the heels of scoring an unbeaten 189 in a one-day international in 2009, Zimbabwe's Charles Coventry became the first batsman to follow a score of 150-plus with a duck. Coventry was out for nought just two days later at the same venue, Bulawayo, and against the same opposition, Bangladesh.

  Two months on from Coventry's 189 – at the time the highest undefeated innings in a one-day international – a team-mate hit an unbeaten 178 against Kenya at Harare. Hamilton Masakadza made 156 in the first match against Kenya, and with subsequent scores of 66, 44, 23 and 178, aggregated a record 467 runs, becoming the first batsman to achieve two innings of 150-plus in the same series.

- When Australia hosted Pakistan at the MCG in 1976/77, one batsman from each side scored a duck and a century. Both batsmen – Rick McCosker (0 and 105) and Sadiq Mohammad (105 and 0) – made exactly the same number of runs. In the early part of 2005, England's Andrew Strauss and Pakistan's Younis Khan both brought up identical knocks of 147 and a duck in a single Test – Strauss against South Africa at Johannesburg, and Younis against India at Kolkata.

- In a three-match Test series in England in 2007, West Indies batsman Shivnarine Chanderpaul raised an average of 148.66, overtaking a record for an overseas batsman set by Don Bradman in 1930. In five innings, Chanderpaul hit 446 runs while Bradman scored a record 974 in seven innings for an average of 126.50.

- After scoring a century on his one-day international debut, Zimbabwe's Andy Flower didn't score another until his 150th match. With an unbeaten 115 against Sri Lanka at New Plymouth in the 1992 World Cup, Flower became just the third batsman to score a century on debut. And despite an unbeaten 99 along the way, he had to wait a record eight years to score a second hundred, an undefeated 120, also against Sri Lanka, at Sharjah in 2000/01.

- To celebrate Test cricket's 105th ground, one batsman from each side scored 119. The Rose Bowl in Southampton became the newest of Test venues hosting England and Sri Lanka in 2011, with Ian Bell hitting an unbeaten 119 and Kumar Sangakkara dismissed for the same score. With an innings of 55, Alastair Cook produced a sixth consecutive Test match half-century, equalling the England record held by Patsy Hendren, Ted Dexter and Ken Barrington. Bell topped the averages in the three-match series, scoring 331 runs at 331.00, while Cook topped the run-scoring with an aggregate of 390 at 97.50.

  With 766 runs in the 2009/10 Ashes, Cook topped the thousand-run mark from two consecutive series. But, in England's next series, India seemed to have the better of Cook, dismissing him for scores of 12, 1, 2 and 5, before he came back with a record 294 at Edgbaston. His average of 5.00 in the first two Tests of the series was one of the lowest for a batsman who came back with a double-hundred.

ALASTAIR COOK

Highest Test Score
at Edgbaston
294
Previous Best
Peter May 285*
1957 v West Indies

- During the course of his first half-century for Australia since giving up the captaincy, Ricky Ponting became the second-highest run-scorer of all time in one-day internationals. In the opening ODI of a five-match series against Sri Lanka in 2011, Ponting scored 53 and shared a 101-run stand with the new skipper Michael Clarke, who also made 53, unbeaten. Along the way, Ponting overtook the recently-retired Sanath Jayasuriya's tally of 13,430 one-day international runs to sit behind the highest scorer, Sachin Tendulkar. Ponting (90*) and Clarke (58*) put on a second successive century-run stand in the second one-day international at Hambantota.

- When Yorkshire hosted Surrey in 2008, Mark Ramprakash raised his bat for the 100th time in first-class cricket with a historic innings of 112 not out. After an agonising ten innings without even a fifty, Ramprakash broke his drought with his 100th first-class hundred at Headingley, becoming the 25th batsman to complete the feat. The Surrey number three blamed the long wait on losing his favourite cricket bat: **"After scoring the 99th, I broke the bat I'd been using for the past two years. I've used five bats since and I've not played that well."**

INNINGS NEEDED FROM 99TH TO 100TH HUNDRED IN FIRST-CLASS CRICKET

Don Bradman	1	W.G. Grace	3	Frank Woolley	10
Tom Graveney	1	Graham Gooch	4	Mark Ramprakash	11
Colin Cowdrey	1	Len Hutton	5	Dennis Amiss	16
Geoff Boycott	1	Phil Mead	6	Andy Sandham	21
Zaheer Abbas	1	Denis Compton	6	John Edrich	22
Viv Richards	1	Les Ames	7	Walter Hammond	24
Graeme Hick	1	Glenn Turner	7	Tom Hayward	47
Patsy Hendren	2	Jack Hobbs	8		
Herbert Sutcliffe	2	Ernest Tyldesley	9		

- Australian one-Test wonder Chris Rogers launched his stint in the 2010 County Championship by becoming the first Derbyshire batsman to score a double-century and a century in the same match. Opening the batting against Surrey at The Oval, Rogers hit 200 in the first innings and an unbeaten 140 in the second. For the opposition, Mark Ramprakash scored 102 – his 109th first-class century – and a duck. The following month, Ramprakash matched Rogers by scoring a double-century and a century in the same match for the first time in his career, doing so with 223 and 103 not out against Middlesex, also at The Oval. His second-innings hundred was his sixth for Surrey against Middlesex, beating the five he had scored for Middlesex against Surrey.

- During the Zimbabwean summer of 2009/10, Vusi Sibanda struck a record number of first-class centuries in a season outside England.

The skipper of the Mid West Rhinos team, Sibanda hit nine tons in ten first-class matches, including twin centuries in consecutive games. During the scoring of his seventh century, he became the first batsman to top 1,000 first-class runs in a Zimbabwean season, overtaking Grant Flower's tally of 983 in 12 matches in 1994/95. Remarkably, as many as five batsmen reached 1,000 runs in the season, with Sibanda the only one to go past 1,500. In 14 matches, Sibanda scored 1,612 runs at 73.27.

Sibanda's nine tons took him past a gaggle of big names, including none other than Don Bradman, who had scored eight first-class centuries in a season outside of England. Bradman scored his eight in Australia in 1947/48; Denis Compton – who holds the overall record of 18 hundreds in a season in England in 1947 – scored eight in South Africa in 1948/49. The others who did so were Australians Neil Harvey and Arthur Morris in South Africa in 1949/50, Martin Crowe in New Zealand in 1986/87, Asif Mutjaba in Pakistan in 1995/96, V.V.S. Laxman in India in 1999/2000 and Michael Bevan in Australia in 2004/05.

- During a first-class match at Montego Bay in 2000/01, both West Indies B openers scored unbeaten maiden first-class double-centuries. Leon Garrick reached 200 in the second innings of the match against Jamaica with Chris Gayle scoring 208 in a record first-wicket stand of 425. It was the first quadruple-run opening partnership in the Caribbean, bettering a 390-run stand between Leslie Wight (262*) and Glendon Gibbs (216) for British Guiana against Barbados at Georgetown in 1951/52. Garrick later opened up with Gayle in his only Test match, scoring a duck and 27 against South Africa at Kingston.

- In consecutive first-class appearances at Headingley, Lancashire opener Paul Horton twice took part in a record third-wicket stand of 258. In 2007, the Sydney-born Horton (149) and the Brisbane-born Stuart Law (206) added 258 against Yorkshire, with Lancashire winning the match by an innings and 126. Fast forward to 2008, and it was déjà vu for Horton – batting with the Lahore-born Mohammad Yousuf (205*) this time, Horton scored 152 – the second time he had done so – and again shared a third-wicket partnership totalling 258.

- Eric Rowan created history with the bat in his final Test series, by top-scoring in South Africa's final five innings against England in 1951. The 42-year-old opener hit 57 in the second innings of the third Test at Manchester, 236 and 60 not out at Leeds and finished with 55 and 45 in his final Test at The Oval. This was the first time that any batsman had made the highest score for his country in so many consecutive innings, Rowan ending the five-Test series with 515 runs, average 57.22.

- Batting against Zimbabwe in 2001/02, Sri Lanka's Chaminda Vaas became the first player to achieve an average of 150.00 in a Test series of three matches or more without the aid of a century. His scores of 74 not out in Colombo, 72 not out at Kandy and eight in Galle gave the number eight a series average of 154.00.

- Bangladesh opener Tamim Iqbal celebrated his 21st birthday in 2010 by smashing 85 off 71 balls on the opening day of a Test against England. He came close to becoming the first batsman since Pakistan's Majid Khan in 1976/77 to score a century before lunch on the first day of a Test, hitting 13 fours and a six in the first innings of the match at Mirpur.

  England's Jonathan Trott opened the batting for the first time in his Test career in the match, taking 33 balls to get off the mark in the first innings, one fewer than Tamim needed to reach his fifty. Tamim added another half-century in the second innings, hitting 52.

- In 43 first-class matches for Northamptonshire, Mike Hussey scored as many as six double-centuries, which, at the time, was a record number for the county. Dennis Brookes – who appeared in a Test for England in 1947/48 – also scored six double-centuries for Northants, but in 492 matches. Hussey's six included three triples, all of which were undefeated, with one in each season.

SIX OF THE BEST

Score	Balls	Mins	4s	6s	Opposition	Venue	Season
329*	444	614	48	1	Essex	Northampton	2001
232	298	512	34	0	Leicestershire	Northampton	2001
208	358	433	30	0	Somerset	Taunton	2001
310*	433	653	38	2	Gloucestershire	Bristol	2002
264	264	436	35	2	Gloucestershire	Gloucester	2003
331*	471	651	38	5	Somerset	Taunton	2003

In his final half-a-dozen matches for the county – in 2003 – Hussey bowed out in spectacular style with five centuries, including a county-record triple, and a further two half-centuries (13 and 100 v Hampshire at Southampton; 331* v Somerset at Taunton; 115 v Derbyshire at Derby; 187 v Durham at Northampton; 147 and 50 v Glamorgan at Cardiff; 4 and 79 v Worcestershire at Northampton). His unbeaten 331 against Somerset broke his own record of 329 not out against Essex at home in 2001 as the club's record score in the first-class game. The year 2001 also saw the West Australian become only the third Northants batsman – after Norman Oldfield in 1949 and Brookes in 1952 – to score 2,000 runs in a season.

- South Africa opening batsman Pieter van der Bijl only appeared in five Tests, all against England in 1938/39, achieving a batting average in excess of 50.00. He set an odd record in his first five innings by being dismissed in a different fashion each time – lbw, bowled, caught, hit wicket and run out.

- When Tony Nicholson scored 50 in the 1974 County Championship it brought to an end one of the longest waits for a half-century in first-class cricket. The Yorkshire medium-pacer scored his only fifty – against Middlesex at Lord's – in his 272nd first-class match. The following month, another medium-pace bowler, Northamptonshire's Bob Cottam (62*) also brought up his maiden first-class fifty, in his 261st match.

MOST MATCHES TO SCORE
MAIDEN FIRST-CLASS FIFTY

306	Roy Tattersall (58)	Lancashire v Leicestershire	Manchester	1958
298	Harry Elliott (50*)	Derbyshire v Northamptonshire	Northampton	1932
283	Kevin Cooper (52)	Gloucestershire v Lancashire	Cheltenham	1993
277	David Hunter (58*)	Yorkshire v Worcestershire	Worcester	1900
272	Tony Nicholson (50)	Yorkshire v Middlesex	Lord's	1974
261	Bob Cottam (62*)	Northamptonshire v Gloucestershire	Northampton	1974

- Rohan Kanhai celebrated the West Indies winning the 1975 World Cup at Lord's with a half-century in what was his final one-day international. He scored 55 in the match against Australia, having scored 55 on his ODI debut, against England at Leeds in 1973.

- In a 312-run one-day win over Bhutan in 2012/13, Oman opener Zeeshan Maqsood was run out for 199. Playing in the Asian Cricket Council Trophy 50-over competition, Maqsood made a duck in his next match, then a 50, followed by another duck.

- Relieved of the Kenyan captaincy, Steve Tikolo scored a pair of 150s and took part in a 300-run stand in a first-class match against Canada in 2009. In the first innings of the Intercontinental Cup match in King City, Tikolo struck 158, and with 169 in the second innings put on 330 for the third wicket with a batsman half his age, the 19-year-old Seren Waters (157*), who struck his maiden first-class century.

- In 2008/09, teenage batsman Fawad Hussain scored a century in his second first-class match, a full year after scoring a century on his first-class debut. In the only innings of his first match, Fawad scored an unbeaten 103 for Rawalpindi against KRL, and then hit 108 in his second innings, 12 months later, against Islamabad.

- When Leicestershire hosted Glamorgan in the 2010 County Championship, the highest match score of 113 was achieved by two

Australian imports. Leicestershire's Victorian all-rounder Andrew McDonald brought up a maiden Championship century, a score matched in the fourth innings by Glamorgan's Tasmanian import Mark Cosgrove (113*). The following week, McDonald scored a second century, a career-best 176 not out and, with a 20-year-old James Taylor (206*), added a record 360 runs for the fourth wicket in the match against Middlesex, also at Grace Road in Leicester.

- Hampshire pair Neil McKenzie and Michael Carberry produced their county's first-ever 500-run partnership in 2011, beating the previous best which had stood since 1899. In the County Championship match against Yorkshire at Southampton, Carberry scored a maiden triple-century of 300 not out while McKenzie made 237, adding 523 runs in partnership. At the end of their union, the McKenzie–Carberry stand became the third highest in the history of the County Championship and the ninth highest in all first-class cricket. It was Hampshire's best for any wicket, overtaking a 411-run partnership by Robert Poore and Teddy Wynyard against Somerset at Taunton in 1899.

- After becoming the first Zimbabwe batsman and, at the time, the youngest ever to score a century on his Test debut, Hamilton Masakadza had to wait a record ten years before scoring his second hundred. With 119 as a 17-year-old against the West Indies at Harare in 2001, he then scored 104 a decade later, against Bangladesh at the same venue in 2011.

In 2011/12, he became just the fifth batsman to cop three consecutive ducks when opening the batting in Tests. Reinstated as an opener against New Zealand at Napier, Masakadza fell for a pair, having made a duck in his previous Test innings at the top of the order, way back in 2002/03, against Pakistan at Harare.

MOST CONSECUTIVE DUCKS BY OPENING BATSMEN IN A TEST SERIES

#	Batsman	Scores	Matches		
4	Pankaj Roy (I)	35 and 0	1st Test v England	Lord's	1952
		0 and 0	3rd Test v England	Manchester	1952
		0	4th Test v England	The Oval	1952
3	Victor Trumper (A)	4 and 0	3rd Test v England	Adelaide	1907/08
		0 and 0	4th Test v England	Melbourne	1907/08
3	Dennis Amiss (E)	0 and 0	5th Test v Australia	Adelaide	1974/75
		0	6th Test v Australia	Melbourne	1974/75
3	Graeme Wood (A)	0 and 0	2nd Test v New Zealand	Perth	1980/81
		0 and 21	3rd Test v New Zealand	Melbourne	1980/81
3	Kraigg Brathwaite (WI)	57 and 0	1st Test v Australia	Bridgetown	2011/12
		0	2nd Test v Australia	Port-of-Spain	2011/12
		0 and 18	3rd Test v Australia	Roseau	2011/12

- Australian pair Bill Lawry and Keith Stackpole scored over 1,300 runs while batting together in Tests without ever sharing a century partnership. In 34 innings, the duo scored 1,379 runs at 43.09, with a best stand of 95, unbeaten, against India at Kanpur in 1969/70. Australia's Graeme Wood and John Dyson also scored over a thousand Test runs while batting together without a three-figure stand.

- The diminutive Aravinda de Silva was a big hit at the 1996 Singer World Series in Colombo, becoming the first batsman to score 200 runs in at least four matches of a one-day international series and remain undefeated. With a total of 334 runs, the Sri Lankan scored 49 not out against India, 83 not out against Australia, 127 not out against Zimbabwe and 75 not out, also against Australia, in the tournament final. Pakistan's Javed Miandad (106*, 3*, 119*, 6*) matched de Silva's feat with 234 runs in a series against India in 1982/83, while India's M.S. Dhoni (87*, 35*, 15*, 75*) became the third batsman to achieve the feat, with 212 runs against England in 2011/12.

- During the Derbyshire–Glamorgan match at the County Ground in 2011, both teams extracted a century partnership for the tenth wicket. Just the third instance in first-class cricket – and a first in England – Jonathan Clare and the last man Mark Turner added 104, a record for the last wicket in Derbyshire–Glamorgan matches that lasted for just a day. Glamorgan's James Harris and Will Owen then put on a tenth-wicket stand of 121.

- The first batsman to score a double-century in domestic limited-overs cricket began his List A career with centuries in his first three matches. After making an unbeaten 132 on his debut in 1966/67, Graeme Pollock then scored 102, 169, 43, 47 and 111.

  In 1974/75, Pollock pummelled an unbeaten 222 for Eastern Province against Boland at East London, the first double-hundred in List A cricket. A year later, fellow South African Alan Barrow became the second player to achieve the feat with 202 not out for Natal against an African XI at Durban.

- During a County Championship match in 2011, Essex all-rounder Graham Napier became the first batsman to have hit 15 sixes in an innings in both first-class and Twenty20 cricket. Napier clubbed 16 during a knock of 198 in the Championship match against Surrey in

Croydon, matching the first-class record established by Queensland's Andrew Symonds for Gloucestershire in 1995. In 2008, Napier had struck a record 16 sixes in a Twenty20 innings against Sussex at Chelmsford, beating Brendon McCullum's 13 in a match in the IPL two months previously.

New Zealand's Jesse Ryder became the third batsman to hit 16 sixes in a first-class innings, during his 175 against the Australia A side at Allan Border Field in Brisbane in 2011/12.

- Unable to get a gig with the West Australian Sheffield Shield side, Dean Brownlie moved to the country of his father's birth and made a century on his first-class debut. The former West Australia Under-19 batsman scored an unbeaten 112 in his first innings for New Zealand side Canterbury, against Northern Districts in 2009/10, and said: "**I don't think I was that close. I was scoring a few runs, but given the quality of players in WA, probably didn't score enough runs to demand a spot. It was more a cricketing decision** [to move to New Zealand]**. I just wanted to give it a go and see what happened.**"

Brownlie made his Test debut for New Zealand in 2011/12, scoring a half-century in each of his first three matches and becoming only the third Kiwi – after legends Bert Sutcliffe and John Reid – to do so. Following a 63 on debut against Zimbabwe at Bulawayo, he then made 77 not out against the country of his birth, at the Gabba, and 56 in a historic seven-run win against the Australians, in Hobart. Brownlie's first-innings 56 at Bellerive was matched by Ross Taylor in the second innings, providing a relatively rare example of one team achieving the same highest individual score in both completed innings of a Test.

- After three fifties in his first three Tests, New Zealand's John Reid fell into a hole with a pair of 11s and ten consecutive single-figure scores. In Tests against the West Indies and South Africa in the early 1950s, Reid had innings of 0, 3, 6, 1, 9, 7, 6, 0, 3 and 1 before bouncing back with a maiden century of 135 at Cape Town in 1953/54. His average of 3.60 is the lowest for any batsman in ten Test innings before scoring a century.

- After falling two runs short of his maiden first-class century, South Australia's Tom Cooper got to 200 the following day. Appearing in his 13th first-class match, Cooper was dismissed for 98 by New South Wales in suburban Sydney during the 2011/12 Sheffield Shield, and with South Australia following-on, saved his team with a massive, unbeaten 203. He also shared a 260-run stand for the fifth wicket with Dan Christian (96).

- Following a tricky start to his Test career in which he made a duck, Australia's Phillip Hughes came up with the goods in his second Test by posting a pair of centuries. His 275 runs (115 and 160) against South Africa at Durban in 2008/09 represented the most runs in a batsman's second match, beating, by one, the previous best by Pakistan's Zaheer Abbas in 1971. Zaheer made his 274 runs in one innings, against England at Edgbaston, and it ended up being the best score of his 78-match Test career.

- Don Bradman and the batsman known as "The Black Bradman" opposed each other in one Test series and both scored over 300 runs and two centuries. During the five-match Australia–West Indies series in 1930/31, Bradman hit 447 runs, while George Headley made 336. Both scored a century in the third Test at the Exhibition Ground in Brisbane – Bradman 223, and Headley an unbeaten 102.

- Bangladesh batsman Habibul Bashar appeared in 50 Test matches and batted in 99 innings. The only time he was not required to front his opposition was in the second innings of a rain-ruined second Test against Zimbabwe at Bulawayo in 2003/04. In one-day international cricket, South Africa's Gary Kirsten appeared in 185 matches and batted in all 185 innings. West Indies opener Desmond Haynes batted in all but one of his 238 one-day internationals, with rain ruining what would have been a perfect record, at Sydney in 1984/85.

- After Bangladesh's Tamim Iqbal had played Zimbabwe at Harare in 2011, he became the first batsman to appear in 100 one-day internationals in which he had been dismissed in all 100 innings. It was not until his 106th ODI that he survived a match without being dismissed. After reaching 62 in a historic victory over the West Indies at Chittagong in 2011/12, Tamim remained unbeaten on 36.

- Australian Twenty20 specialist David Warner came of age during a tour of Zimbabwe in 2011, bagging three centuries and topping the 500-run mark. After beginning the Australia A tour with a score of one in the opening match, Warner ended his sojourn with a maiden first-class double-century (211). Following a 289-run opening stand with Aaron Finch (122) against Zimbabwe A at Harare, Warner finished the tour with 666 runs, in eight matches, at an average of 74.00.

    On the back of his impressive first-class numbers, the 25-year-old then got the nod to play Test cricket, and appearing in just his second match – against New Zealand at Hobart in 2011/12 – carried his bat for a century. In a 317-minute and 170-ball innings, Warner hit an unbeaten 123, becoming the first batsman to carry his bat for a hundred in the fourth innings of a Test match.

Warner's opening partner in the two-match series also made history by losing his wicket in the same manner in each of his four innings. Phillip Hughes was dismissed for scores of 10, 7, 4 and 20, all caught at second slip by Martin Guptill off the bowling of Chris Martin.

> **"If Hughes is shaving tomorrow and gets a nick, Martin Guptill will appear out of the medicine cabinet with a band-aid."**
>
> ABC cricket commentator Kerry O'Keeffe

- Mark Ramprakash scored his first and his 100th first-class century on the same ground. His maiden ton of 128 came at Headingley for Middlesex against Yorkshire in 1989. His 100th – 112 not out – was scored at the same ground in 2008, but this time for Surrey.

- Two of the biggest scorers of first-class centuries made their Test debuts in the same match in 1991 and both made identical scores in each innings. A first by a pair of specialist batsmen, Graeme Hick scored six and six, while Mark Ramprakash made 27 and 27 in the first Test against the West Indies at Leeds.

- When Virender Sehwag scored 175 against Bangladesh in the 2011 World Cup, he became the fourth batsman to make such a score in one-day internationals. His opening partner Sachin Tendulkar had scored 175 against Australia at Hyderabad in 2009/10, while South Africa's number three Herschelle Gibbs also made 175 against the Australians, at Johannesburg in 2005/06. The first to make such a score was India's fast-bowling captain Kapil Dev who hit an unbeaten 175 at number six against Zimbabwe during the 1983 World Cup at Tunbridge Wells.

  Sehwag later passed 175 again in the same calendar year, reaching 219 against the West Indies at Indore. Never before had a batsman made two scores as high in the same calendar year, with Sehwag doing so within the space of a dozen matches.

- In a first-class match blighted by bad weather at the Grace Road ground in 2012, Leicestershire's Wayne White cracked a 12-ball fifty, while Ned Eckersley hit 70 off 19 deliveries. Facing a wad of declaration-style bowling from Essex to bring on a result, Ramnaresh Sarwan went from an overnight score of 61 to 98 in a matter of minutes, with White reaching his fifty in 11.

- Batting against England at Georgetown in 1997/98, Shivnarine Chanderpaul followed a first-innings century with a first-ball duck.

Fast forward to 2008/09, and Chanderpaul became the first-known batsman to achieve this unusual double twice, scoring an unbeaten 126 and a golden duck against New Zealand at Napier.

Fellow West Indian Garry Sobers did something similar during his Test career, but in reverse. He also followed a first-innings ton with a first-ball duck – 132 and nought against India at Port-of-Spain in 1970/71 – but had earlier followed a first-baller with a century in the same match – nought and an unbeaten 113 against England at Kingston – in 1967/68.

- India's Dilip Vengsarkar appeared in three Tests at the home of cricket and marked each with a century. Although he made a duck in his debut innings at Lord's in 1979, he came back with 103 in the second innings, and returned with scores of 157 in 1982 and 126 not out in 1986.

- West Australian bowler Michael Hogan made history in 2012/13 by taking part in two half-century partnerships for the tenth wicket. In the match against South Australia at Adelaide, he put on 69 and then a match-winning, unbeaten 68, only the second occasion in Sheffield Shield history that a team's highest partnerships in both innings were both for the tenth wicket.

- During the 1912 Ashes, England's number three contributed just three runs in the three Tests. In a series won by England (1-0), Reggie Spooner scored one in the first Test at Lord's, one at Manchester and in the last of his ten Tests made one and a duck at The Oval, for a series average of 0.75.

A hundred years on, Australia's number three Shaun Marsh was on the winning side of the ledger in the 2011/12 Test series against India, but made just 17 runs at an average of 2.83. In six innings, he scored 0, 3, 0, 11, 3 and 0.

THE TOP FIVE WORST BATTING AVERAGES BY TOP-ORDER BATSMEN IN A TEST SERIES

Qualification: five innings

Avge	Batsman	Inns	Scores	Series	
0.16	Mohinder Amarnath	6	0, 0, 1, 0, 0, 0	India v West Indies	1983/84
1.71	Ken Rutherford ‡	7	0, 0, 4, 0, 2, 1, 5	New Zealand v West Indies	1984/85
2.83	Shaun Marsh	6	0, 3, 0, 11, 3, 0	Australia v India	2011/12
3.16	Alec Bannerman	6	0, 0, 13, 5, 1, 0	Australia v England	1888
3.40	Ricky Ponting	5	0, 6, 0, 0, 11	Australia v India	2000/01

‡ *Ken Rutherford's first Test series*

- Assam opener Dheeraj Jadhav scored five centuries in the 2011/12 Ranji Trophy, the most by any batsman in the season. He hit his five in the only five matches he played, aggregating 704 runs at an average of 176.00.

- Amateur UK batsman Simon Davis struck a purple patch in 2011 with three centuries in a week including a record-breaking triple. Opening the batting for Tudhoe against Mainsforth in the Durham County League, Davis scored 328 not out with 20 fours and 32 sixes, his last 100 runs coming off just 28 balls. Coming into the game, Davis had already reeled off scores of 132 and then 162, off 61 balls. He said: **"The thing that worried me before the Mainsforth match was over-confidence."**

- In a first-class match against Zimbabwe A at Harare in 2004, Sri Lanka A batsman Thilina Kandamby scored a half-century made up entirely of boundaries. A first in first-class cricket, his 52, off 41 balls, contained ten fours and two sixes.

    In a County Championship match in 2006, Essex's Mark Pettini scored a century in contrived circumstances in which Leicestershire's wicketkeeper and an opening batsman opened the bowling to hasten a possible result. Pettini's unbeaten 114 was made up entirely of fours (12) and sixes (11) scored off 29 balls in 24 minutes.

- In a one-day international at Napier in 2012/13, Ross Taylor scored exactly 100 against England. It was the first ODI century by a New Zealander against England since Jamie How hit 139 at the same venue, exactly five years previously to the day, in 2007/08. Two weeks after Taylor's ton, How scored the first List A double-century by a Kiwi, spanking 222 for Central Districts against Northern Districts at Hamilton.

- Just two matches on from a record-breaking triple-century, West Indies opener Chris Gayle bombed, falling to the first ball of a Test against the same opposition. In the opening Test of the three-match series against Sri Lanka in 2010/11, Gayle had regaled all at Galle with a monster innings of 333; in the second Test, he made 33 runs. In the third, he was out to the first ball sent down at the game's newest venue. Bowling first at the Muttiah Muralitharan Stadium in Pallekele, Suranga Lakmal dismissed Gayle lbw, with the ground becoming only the third – and the first outside India – to witness a wicket to its first ball in a Test match.

- After bagging a pair in a Test against England in 1929/30, West Indies opener Clifford Roach struck back in his next innings with a double-century. His two ducks at Port-of-Spain were followed by a career-best 209 against England at Georgetown. Prior to his pair, Roach had topped 199 runs in the previous Test, with innings of 122 and 77 against the tourists in the first Test at Bridgetown. South Africa's Jacques Kallis did a similar thing in 2011/12 with his first-ever pair – against Sri Lanka at Durban – followed by an innings of 224 at Cape Town.

- Although he never scored a Test century, Australia's Alan Fairfax managed a Test average in excess of 50. In ten Tests between 1929 and 1931, Fairfax scored 65, 14, 14, 20 not out, 49, 53 not out, 41 not out, 15, 9, 16, 54 and 60 not out for a career average of 51.25. For batsmen who have played at least ten Test innings, he remains the only one to command a 50-run average without the aid of a century.

  Australia's Ian Chappell possesses a similar record in one-day internationals. In 16 one-dayers, Chappell scored 673 runs for an average of 48.07, but never scored a century. He passed 50 on eight occasions in 16 innings, with a highest score of 86 against New Zealand at Christchurch in 1973/74.

- When Virender Sehwag and Sachin Tendulkar went in first against Sri Lanka at Perth in 2011/12, it represented the first occasion of double-centurions opening the batting in a one-day international. Their sum total of 419 runs was made up of Sehwag's 219 against the West Indies scored two months previously and Tendulkar's unbeaten 200 against South Africa two years previously.

- With an innings of 137 at Abu Dhabi in 2011/12, Alastair Cook became the first England batsman to out-score his opposition in a one-day international. With Pakistan all out for 130, Cook became the 40th batsman to achieve the feat in ODIs. England's number three Jonathan Trott was out for a first-ball duck in the same match, as was Pakistan's Asad Shafiq, providing only the second such instance of the number threes from both sides being out first ball. In 2005/06, England's Andrew Strauss and Pakistan's Younis Khan suffered first-ball ducks batting at number three in a one-day international at Rawalpindi.

- Bangladesh bowler Abdur Razzak went past 40 in a Test innings for the first time in 2011, recording one of the fastest knocks of all time. Batting at number eight against Zimbabwe at Harare, Razzak clocked 43 not out – with five fours and three sixes – off 17 balls at a strike rate of 252.94.

- Two batsmen carried their bats on the first two days of a first-class match in Pakistan in 2010/11, with one doing so on his first-class debut. After Punjab opener Taufeeq Umar remained unbeaten on 106 in the match at Lahore, Baluchistan debutant Zain Abbas carried his bat for 71.

- Martin Guptill had an unlucky first-class debut, out for a duck in the first innings and for 99 in the second. Opening the batting for Auckland versus Wellington in 2005/06, his partner Richard Jones (92) also fell in the nineties in the second innings after a first-wicket stand of 148.

- After a 16-year break from the game, and fast approaching 50, former New Zealand batsman Martin Crowe staged an ill-fated comeback in 2011/12. With 392 runs needed to pass the important first-class milestone of 20,000 runs, Crowe padded up for the Cornwall club in a reserve-grade match in Auckland.

  After concluding his first day back with an unbeaten 15, his first premier match ended after three balls, and so his dream of a first-class renaissance: **"I said from the start it would end in tears with an injury. While getting off the mark, I pulled a thigh muscle running a normal single. So three balls into my first premier match back, it's over."**

- New South Wales fast bowler Trent Copeland opened his batting account in Test match cricket by hitting the first balled he faced on his debut to the boundary. Although scorecards haven't always noted such feats, Copeland reportedly became the first Australian since Stan McCabe, at Nottingham in 1930, to do so. Batting at number ten on his debut, against Sri Lanka at Galle in 2011, Copeland scored 12 – made up of three boundaries – in the first innings and an unbeaten 23 in the second.

- The Oval Test match in the 2009 Ashes series contained, for the first time, six batsmen who had scored a century on debut. Four came from the England side – Alastair Cook, Andrew Strauss, Matt Prior and Jonathan Trott; the others were Australia's Michael Clarke and Marcus North.

- Pumped up for his first first-class match at the WACA in Perth, David Warner bludgeoned the fastest-known Test century of all time by an opening batsman, reaching three figures with a six. On the opening day of the third Test against India in 2011/12, Warner got to his ton off just 69 balls, proceeding to 180 off 159, an innings that contained 20 fours and five sixes. Warner became one of the rare ones to out-score his opposition (161 and 171) twice in the same Test – he also became the first batsman to score a century batting second on the first day of a Test match in Australia.

  Warner and Ed Cowan, the two Paddington-born batsmen, brought up a century partnership off 84 deliveries, just shy of a 79-ball effort by Sri Lankan pair Sanath Jayasuriya and Marvan Atapattu against Bangladesh in Colombo in 2001. After India had been dismissed for 161, Warner and Cowan (74) carried the score to 214, just the second occasion that Australia had surpassed an Indian total with all ten first-innings wickets in hand – in 1967/68, Bob Simpson (109) and Bill Lawry (100) had added 191 for the first wicket at Adelaide after India made 173.

- After waiting two years for a Test century, Ricky Ponting came back to life during the 2011/12 Test series against India scoring two hundreds in three matches. With a drought-breaking 134 at Sydney, the former Australian captain then scored 221 in Adelaide. Batting with his successor, Ponting and Michael Clarke (210) became the first pair since Don Bradman and Bill Ponsford (388 and 451) in 1934 to achieve two stands of 250 in a single Test series.

With a fourth-wicket unison of 288 at the SCG, the two put on a record 386 in Adelaide. It was Australia's fourth-highest partnership of all time, and all above them featured Bradman. The biggest-ever stand in a Test in the South Australian capital, it bettered a 345-run partnership by South Africa's Eddie Barlow and a 19-year-old Graeme Pollock in 1963/64. After a 334-run stand between Clarke and Mike Hussey at the SCG, it represented just the second time

The Adelaide Oval scoreboard during the record-breaking stand between centurions Ricky Ponting and Michael Clarke against India in 2011/12

Australia had two triple-century partnerships in a Test series, after the aforementioned stands between Ponsford and Bradman in the 1934 Ashes.

- India's Virat Kohli scored his first century in a Test on the back of a record eight hundreds in one-day internationals. On India's Republic Day, and Australia Day, Kohli hit 116 in the fourth Test against Australia at Adelaide in 2011/12, an innings laced with 11 fours and a six.

> **"They** [the Australians] **sledge when they get frustrated. Obviously it was hot out there and constantly they were sledging the players so they could spoil our concentration. In Sydney, they were after me because I wasn't scoring and today they were pissed because I got a hundred."**
>
> Virat Kohli

MOST ONE-DAY INTERNATIONAL CENTURIES
BEFORE MAIDEN TEST CENTURY

#	Batsman	M	Runs	Maiden 100		
8	Virat Kohli (I)	74	2860	116 v Australia	Adelaide	2011/12
6	Saeed Anwar (P)	45	1504	169 v New Zealand	Wellington	1993/94
5	Adam Gilchrist (A)	76	2376	149* v Pakistan	Hobart	1999/00
5	Shoaib Malik (P)	115	3023	148* v Sri Lanka	Colombo	2005/06
5	Andrew Symonds (A)	154	3863	156 v England	Melbourne	2006/07

- Following a sterling Test series against India in 2011/12 in which he topped 500 runs, Ricky Ponting suffered a slump in the one-day internationals that followed and was given the flick. In a tri-series involving Australia, Sri Lanka and India, Ponting made 2, 1, 6, 2 and 7, the first time in his international career he had been dismissed for single figures in five consecutive innings. With an average of just 3.60 after five matches, Australia's most successful one-day international cricketer was dropped.

  With just 18 runs in his final one-day international series, Ponting possessed one of the worst batting averages of all time from his final five innings. At the time of his sacking, the least impressive set of numbers belonged to Namibia's Louis Burger, who appeared in six ODIs during the 2003 World Cup. After an innings of four not out on his debut, he then scored 0, 5, 0, 1 and 1 for a total of seven runs in his last five innings at 1.40.

- When South Africa's Jacques Rudolph scored a double-ton at Chittagong in 2002/03, he became the first Test debutant to feature in a triple-century partnership. With an unbeaten 222, he and Boeta Dippenaar (177*) piled on an unbroken third-wicket stand of 429 against Bangladesh.

- After his first five one-day internationals, South Australia's Tom Cooper had scored a record total of 374 runs. The New South Wales-born batsman began his ODI career for the Netherlands in 2010 with innings of 80 not out, 87, 67, 39 and 101 to beat England's Allan Lamb, who made 328 runs (35*, 99, 118, 27, 49) from his first five matches, beginning in 1982.

- Australia's Bob Cowper went through the highs and lows of Test cricket in the mid-1960s with two ducks and a triple-century sandwiched in between. Following a second-innings nought against England in the third Test at Sydney in 1965/66, Cowper found redemption with 307 in his next innings at Melbourne. In his next Test – the first against South Africa at Johannesburg in 1966/67 – Cowper suffered another duck and then a second-innings score of one. He became the first

Australian to follow a triple-century with a duck in his next innings, and just the second after England's John Edrich.

SOMETHING BIG THEN NOTHING AT ALL

Don Bradman (A)	299* v South Africa at Adelaide 1931/32	0 v England at Melbourne 1932/33
John Edrich (E)	310* v New Zealand at Leeds 1965	0 v South Africa at Lord's 1965
Bob Cowper (A)	307 v England at Melbourne 1965/66	0 v SA at Johannesburg 1966/67

- In 2011/12, South Africa's Jacques Kallis scored nought, nought, a century, nought and a century in consecutive Test innings. His first-ever pair at Test level came against Sri Lanka at Durban; he then brought up his highest score to date in his next innings in his 150th Test, one of 224 against the same opposition at Cape Town. In his next Test, against New Zealand at Dunedin, Kallis copped another duck and then made a second-innings century (113).

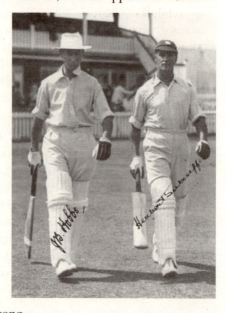

- During the 1926 Ashes series, England's Jack Hobbs and Herbert Sutcliffe achieved six 50-run stands in consecutive innings. They then made it seven in a row in 1928 with a century partnership (119) against the West Indies. South Africa's opening pair of Neil McKenzie and Graeme Smith also strung together half-a-dozen half-century stands on the trot, in 2007/08. Their highest was a record-breaking 415 against Bangladesh at Chittagong.

- After going 18 one-day internationals from his debut without a century, David Warner made a splash with two in a row in 2011/12. With 163 at Brisbane and 100 at Adelaide against Sri Lanka, Warner became the first batsman to score two centuries in the finals of a tri-series in Australia.

The normally explosive Warner's century in Adelaide came off 140 balls, the seventh-slowest ODI hundred by an Australian batsman. He also took part in a major partnership of 184 with Michael Clarke (117), the first 150-run stand in a final to come in a defeat. On the other side, Sri Lanka's captain Mahela Jayawardene (80) and former captain Tillakaratne Dilshan (106) set the tone with a match-winning opening stand of 179, the highest first-wicket partnership in the series. Dilshan also became the first player to open both the batting and bowling in a one-day international, bowl ten overs, score a century and take both a wicket and a catch.

- When Sachin Tendulkar scored his 49th Test match century, it came two months after the 20th anniversary of his first Test ton at Old Trafford in 1990. With an innings of 214 against Australia at Bangalore in 2010/11, Tendulkar became the first batsman to have scored Test centuries spanning a 20-year period. The previous longest span had been 19-and-a-half years by Don Bradman, who scored his first Test century in 1928/29 and his last in 1948, a period interrupted by the Second World War.

  Tendulkar's historic 50th Test century came at the appropriately-named venue of Centurion in South Africa. Unbeaten on 111, Tendulkar hit 13 fours and a six in the second innings of the first Test against the South Africans in 2010/11. A.B. de Villiers (129), though, stole the show with a record 75-ball century for the hosts, while Jacques Kallis posted his maiden Test match double-century (201*).

- Batting in his 34th innings since making his 99th international century, Sachin Tendulkar brought up his hundredth hundred in 2011/12 during the Asia Cup. With one of his slowest-ever one-day international centuries – he got to his hundred off 138 balls – Tendulkar hit 114, his first ODI century against Bangladesh. At the time of his historic ton, only three batsmen had ever reached 50 international hundreds – Ricky Ponting, with 71, Jacques Kallis 59 and Brian Lara 53.

  Although the tension was palpable as he sought the milestone, it wasn't his longest streak without a century. In 2007, he went 34 innings *sans* a hundred, but was nevertheless in tip-top form, scoring 15 fifties, which included three 99s and another four innings in the 90s.

- While Pakistan's captain Saeed Anwar was scoring his ninth hundred in one-day internationals, his number three Shahid Afridi was scoring his first. In the sixth match of the 1996 KCA Centenary Tournament in Nairobi, a teenage Afridi scored the fastest-ever ODI hundred – off 39 balls – in his debut innings. Anwar made 115 off 120 balls with a strike rate of 95.83 in the match against Sri Lanka, while Afridi got to 102 off 40 with a strike rate of 255.00 – a record difference of 159 between two century-makers in a one-day international innings.

- During a run of ten one-day internationals in 2006/07, Bermuda's Lionel Cann struck a six in a record nine consecutive innings. Passing

40 in four consecutive matches, his biggest haul was five sixes in an innings of 42 against Canada at St John's. Cann ended his 26-match ODI career in 2009 with a record strike rate of 117.06. He scored 590 runs – with 29 sixes plus 46 fours – off 504 balls in 25 innings.

- Representing the Police Sports Club in Sri Lanka in 2010/11, Tharanga Indika became just the fifth batsman to score a pair of centuries on his first-class debut. Batting at number four against Seeduwa Raddoluwa in Colombo, the 22-year-old Indika hit 158 and 103 not out, becoming the first Sri Lankan to achieve the feat.

TWO CENTURIES ON FIRST-CLASS DEBUT

148 and 111	Arthur Morris	New South Wales v Queensland	Sydney	1940/41
152 and 102*	Nari Contractor	Gujarat v Baroda	Baroda	1952/53
132* and 110	Aamer Malik	Lahore A v Railways	Lahore	1979/80
130 and 100*	Noor Ali	Afghanistan v Zimbabwe XI	Mutare	2009
158 and 103*	Tharanga Indika	Police SC v Seeduwa Raddoluwa	Colombo	2010/11
126 and 108	Virag Awate	Maharashtra v Vidarbha	Nagpur	2012/13

- Graeme Smith opened his account in the 2010/11 South African Supersport Series with a double-century and a triple-century partnership. With 217 for the Cape Cobras against Lions, Smith shared a 333-run stand for the first wicket with Andrew Puttick (111) – it was Smith's fifth triple-hundred partnership in first-class cricket, but his first outside Tests.

- Chasing a victory target of 172 in a 1983 World Cup match, the West Indies' opening pair did so on their own, soaking up a record 45.1 overs in the process. Desmond Haynes made 88 not out off 136 balls and Faoud Bacchus an unbeaten 80 off 135 in the 60-over match against Zimbabwe at Edgbaston.

- After single-digit opening stands in the first Test against Sri Lanka in 2007/08, Alastair Cook and Michael Vaughan gave England their first century first-wicket partnership in 15 matches in the following Test. Stands of 0 and 4 at Kandy were followed by stands of 133 and 107 at Colombo, only the eighth time in Test history that an opening pair had shared two century partnerships in a Test.

England's Len Hutton and Cyril Washbrook are the only pair to achieve the feat on two occasions, both times coming against Australia, in 1946/47 and in 1948.

FIRST-WICKET CENTURY STANDS BY SAME PAIR IN EACH INNINGS OF A TEST

Partners	Stands	Match	
Jack Hobbs and Herbert Sutcliffe	157 and 110	England v Australia	Sydney 1924/25
Bob Catterall and Bruce Mitchell	119 and 171	South Africa v England	Birmingham 1929
Len Hutton and Cyril Washbrook	137 and 100	England v Australia	Adelaide 1946/47
Len Hutton and Cyril Washbrook	168 and 129	England v Australia	Leeds 1948
Geoff Boycott and John Edrich	107 and 103	England v Australia	Adelaide 1970/71
Mark Greatbatch and Rod Latham	116 and 102	NZ v Zimbabwe	Bulawayo 1992/93
Taufeeq Umar and Imran Farhat	109 and 134	Pakistan v South Africa	Lahore 2003/04
Alastair Cook and Michael Vaughan	133 and 107	England v Sri Lanka	Colombo 2007/08

- The first hundreds scored by Pakistan's Saleem Malik in a Test and in a one-day international were exactly 100 and both came against the same country. His first Test century (100*) came on his debut, against Sri Lanka at Karachi in 1981/82, while his first ODI century (100) also came against Sri Lanka, at Faisalabad in 1987/88.

  England's Nick Knight followed suit in 1996 with scores of 113 against Pakistan, with M.S. Dhoni joining the list in 2005/06. After scoring his first century in a one-day international – 148 – against Pakistan at Visakhapatnam in early 2005, Dhoni then hit his maiden Test ton of 148 against the same opposition ten months later at Faisalabad. For Dhoni, both of his maiden centuries came in his fifth match in each format. Knight's two maiden centuries came in the same month of August in 1996 – 113 in the second Test against Pakistan at Leeds and 113 in the second one-day international at Edgbaston.

- Playing for Sussex in 2011, Ben Brown and Joe Gatting became only the third pair of batsmen to each score a century before lunch on the first day of a first-class match. By the break, Sussex had surged to 216 without loss in the match against Oxford MCCU, with Brown and Gatting matching two other pairs who had achieved the feat in Currie Cup matches in South Africa – Transvaal's Syd Curnow and Alfred Langebrink against Orange Free State at Johannesburg in 1929/30 and Border's Ossie Dawson and Keith Kirton against Rhodesia at East London in 1954/55.

  Brown went on to make 112 and Gatting 106, with the pair sharing a first-wicket stand of 224. Further down the order, Matt Machan made 99 in what was just his second first-class match.

- South Africa's Daryll Cullinan scored 14 centuries in Test match cricket, all of which came batting at number four. The most centuries scored at different batting positions is six, a record shared by England's Colin Cowdrey (2, 3, 4, 5, 6, 8) and the West Indies' Garry Sobers (2, 3, 4, 5, 6, 7).

- On his Test debut in 1989/90, Indian spinner Ventakapathy Raju was sent in as a nightwatchman and saw off a record number of team-mates. Promoted up the order on day two of the first Test against New Zealand at Christchurch, Raju made 31 – the highest score of his 28-match career. Surviving 83 balls, he came in at 88/3 and was the last man out at 164. During his stay, Raju witnessed the fall of six wickets – Navjot Sidhu, Sachin Tendulkar, Manoj Prabhakar, Kapil Dev, Kiran More and Atul Wassan.

- New Zealand fast bowler Neil Wagner made history as a batsman in 2012 when he became the first player to bat as a nightwatchman in both innings of his Test debut. The South African-born Wagner – who claimed a world-record five wickets in an over in a first-class match in 2010/11 – scored four and 13 against the West Indies in Antigua. He also got the gig in the second innings of his second Test, giving him three stints at nightwatchman in his first four Test innings.

- India's Rahul Dravid achieved a world first in 1998/99 when he followed a pair of centuries in a Test match with a century in a one-day international. After scoring 190 and an unbeaten 103 against New Zealand at Hamilton, he then made 123 not out in a ODI a few days later at Taupo.

  Pakistan's Mohsin Khan had previously come the closest to achieving the feat in 1982/83 against India, with 94 and 101 not out at Lahore followed by 117 not out in a ODI at Multan.

- After adding a Test-record 576 runs in partnership at Colombo in 1997/98, Roshan Mahanama and Sanath Jayasuriya were then both dismissed with the score on 615. After coming together at 39/1, Mahanama made 225 and Jayasuriya 340. Curiously, a decade later, another pair of Sri Lankans came within a whisker of being at the crease when the team total ticked over to 615. After putting on 437 for the fourth wicket against Pakistan at Karachi in 2008/09, Mahela Jayawardene (240) and Thilan Samaraweera (231) were both toppled with the score on 614.

PARTNERS IN A 400-RUN STAND FALLING ON SAME TEAM SCORE IN A TEST

	Partners	Score	Fall	Match		
576	Roshan Mahanama	225	615/2			
	Sanath Jayasuriya	340	615/3	Sri Lanka v India	Colombo	1997
437	Mahela Jayawardene	240	614/4			
	Thilan Samaraweera	231	614/5	Sri Lanka v Pakistan	Karachi	2008/09
405	Don Bradman	234	564/5			
	Sid Barnes	234	564/6	Australia v England	Sydney	1946/47

- In the same match that Sri Lanka's Marvan Atapattu made a pair on his Test debut, three of his team-mates also failed to score in each innings. Rumesh Ratnayake (0 and 0), Graeme Labrooy (0 and 0) and Jayananda Warnaweera (0 and 0*) were all part of a thrashing by India at Chandigarh in 1990/91. In Sri Lanka's first-innings 82, Asanka Gurusinha (52*) was responsible for 63.41 per cent of his side's total, a record in the subcontinent.

- When Steve Waugh and Ricky Ponting added 239 runs against India at Adelaide in 1999/2000, it represented Australia's fourth double-century stand in consecutive Tests. In the preceding Test series, against Pakistan, the Australians had produced a 200-run stand in each of the three matches. The highest of 327 at the WACA featured 197 from Ponting, a score that had followed three consecutive ducks.

MOST DOUBLE-CENTURY PARTNERSHIPS
BY ONE TEAM IN CONSECUTIVE TESTS

#	Stand	Wkt	Pair	Match	
4	269	1st	Michael Slater-Greg Blewett	Australia v Pakistan, Brisbane	1999/00
	236	6th	Justin Langer-Adam Gilchrist	Australia v Pakistan, Hobart	1999/00
	327	5th	Justin Langer-Ricky Ponting	Australia v Pakistan, Perth	1999/00
	239	5th	Steve Waugh-Ricky Ponting	Australia v India, Adelaide	1999/00

- The Pakistan-born Shahbaz Bashir struck a century on his first-class debut in 2012, becoming the first batsman to do so in a match for the Netherlands. Bashir hit 102 against the United Arab Emirates at Deventer, while fellow debutant Sebastiaan Braat scored 23 in the same innings batting at number 11.

- Surrey stalwart Mark Ramprakash was handed a one-match ban in 2011 after a run-in with the umpires in a County Championship match at Cheltenham. After scoring 141 in the first innings, the then-41-year-old became just the 22nd batsman in the history of first-class cricket to be dismissed obstructing the field. Out for 35 when he got in the way of Gloucestershire's Ian Saxelby, Ramprakash returned to the field to remonstrate with the umpires. He later said: "**Very disappointed to be banned given the circumstances. I don't agree with the umpires.**"

  Ramprakash ended his first-class career in 2012 as the only batsman to score 15,000 first-class runs for two counties – 15,046 at 50.48 for Middlesex and 15,837 at 67.96 for Surrey.

- During the calendar year of 2011, Tom Stray made three scores in the 130s in second-XI cricket. He began the year with 130 for the Victorian Under-23s, sharing in a 347-run opening stand with Ryan Carters against New South Wales at Junction Oval in Melbourne. After two first-class matches for his state, the up-and-comer strayed across the border and made two hundreds for the South Australian Under-23s – 135 against Western Australia and 139 not out against Tasmania. He then made his first-class debut for the Redbacks, scoring 19 in his first innings, after a string a failures (0, 8, 1, 6) for the Bushrangers.

- W.G. Grace celebrated his 22nd birthday by hitting a first-class century for the Gentlemen against the Players at Lord's in 1870. He got another first-class ton on his 29th birthday, hitting 110 for a Gloucestershire-Yorkshire XI against an England XI, also at Lord's, in 1877.

- When Pakistan's Aamer Sohail struck 77 against Sri Lanka at Gujranwala in 1995/96, it was his first half-century at home since making his debut in 1990/91. His first ODI fifty in Pakistan after making 17 overseas, Sohail shared in a 156-run opening stand with 19-year-old Saleem Elahi, who won the match with an unbeaten 102 on his debut. Elahi, who had never previously appeared in a first-class match on home soil, brought up his ton with a six and also shared a 78-run stand in ten overs with Rameez Raja (44*).

- After scoring a half-century batting at number 11 and a century at ten in consecutive Tests in 1998/99, South Africa's Pat Symcox was dropped. The right-arm spinner, who began his career as a top-order batsman, scored his one and only Test century – 108 – against Pakistan at Johannesburg.

- Yasir Hameed, who appeared in 25 Tests for Pakistan, achieved his two highest scores, and his only two centuries, for his country on debut. Batting at number three against Bangladesh at Karachi in 2003, the right-hander scored 170 and 106, becoming the first Pakistani Test debutant to achieve the feat of twin tons, and only the second batsman after the West Indies' Lawrence Rowe (214 and 100*) against New Zealand at Kingston in 1971/72. With his first 1,000 ODI runs coming in just 22 matches, Hameed's highest score in all first-class cricket is a neat 300.

• After South Africa had followed-on at Durban in 1938/39, Eric Rowan played a three-and-a-half-hour innings against England without scoring a single boundary. Rowan got to 67 as South Africa went down in the third Test by an innings and 13.

In 1981/82, one of the game's biggest hitters of all time occupied the crease for the same time, bar a minute, also making a fifty without a boundary. In England's first innings of the fifth Test against India at Chennai, Ian Botham hit 52 off 156 balls in 207 minutes.

RECORDED TEST MATCH FIFTIES WITHOUT A BOUNDARY

Score	Mins	BF	Batsman	Match		
67	208	-	Eric Rowan	South Africa v England	Durban	1938/39
59	124	111	Farokh Engineer	India v England	The Oval	1971
58	139	-	Bill Woodfull	Australia v West Indies	Sydney	1930/31
56	-	-	Warren Bardsley	Australia v South Africa	Nottingham	1912
53	168	-	Bobby Peel	England v Australia	Melbourne	1894/95
52	219	167	Chetan Chauhan	India v West Indies	Mumbai	1978/79
52	207	156	Ian Botham	England v India	Chennai	1981/82

• When Shivnarine Chanderpaul scored a pair of unbeaten half-centuries at Cape Town in 2007/08, he became the first batsman to achieve such a distinction twice in Test cricket. His undefeated 65 and 70 against South Africa followed two unbeaten fifties (128* and 97*) against England at Lord's in 2004. He did it a third time in Tests a few months after his Cape Town double, with 107 not out and 77 not out against Australia in Antigua.

• All out for under 220 in both innings of a Sheffield Shield match at Hobart in 2011/12, Queensland's number nine top-scored each time with a pair of unbeaten half-centuries. The only Queenslander to pass 50 in the match, fast bowler Ben Cutting scored 79 not out – with seven fours and four sixes – in the first innings and 66 not out – with seven fours and three sixes – in the second.

In Queensland's opening Shield match the following summer, Cutting broke through with his maiden century in first-class cricket, scoring 109 at number eight against South Australia at the Gabba. In the same innings, Usman Khawaja scored 88 on his debut for Queensland.

• During South Africa's tour of England in 2012, Hashim Amla passed 300 for the first time in a Test match and also reached 150 for the first time in a one-day international. The first South African to record a Test match triple-century, his unbeaten 311 at The Oval saw him top the run-scoring charts with 482 runs at 120.50 in the three-match series. He then scored most runs in the ensuing one-day internationals with 335 at 111.66, including 150 at Southampton. During the series, Amla got to the milestone of 3,000 ODI runs in the fewest innings (57) and also became the first batsman to make the highest score for his country in six consecutive one-day internationals.

92	2nd ODI	New Zealand	Napier	2011/12
76	3rd ODI	New Zealand	Auckland	2011/12
150	2nd ODI	England	Southampton	2012
43	3rd ODI	England	The Oval	2012
45	4th ODI	England	Lord's	2012
97*	5th ODI	England	Nottingham	2012

He also appeared in two of the three Twenty20 internationals and top-scored both times, with 47 not out at Manchester and 36 at Birmingham. With 83 runs at 83.00, Amla came out on top in all three forms of the game on the tour, scoring the most runs and commanding the highest averages in the Tests, ODIs and Twenty20 internationals.

HASHIM AMLA AGAINST ENGLAND 2012

Tests

M	Inns	NO	Runs	HS	Avge	BF	SR	100s	50s	0s	4s	6s
3	5	1	482	311*	120.50	819	58.85	2	0	0	54	0

One-Day Internationals

| 5 | 4 | 1 | 335 | 150 | 111.66 | 355 | 94.36 | 1 | 1 | 0 | 33 | 2 |

Twenty20 Internationals

| 2 | 2 | 1 | 83 | 47* | 83.00 | 57 | 145.61 | 0 | 0 | 0 | 13 | 0 |

"I'm not even the second-best batsman in my team."

Hashim Amla

- Graeme Smith had different opening partners in the Leeds Test against England in 2012, sharing identical partnerships in each innings. For the first time, openers put on identical century stands in each innings of a Test, with both partnerships ending at exactly the same spot. In the first innings, Smith and Alviro Petersen added 120 for the first wicket, while Smith and Jacques Rudolph put on 120 in the second innings. Both partnerships were ended at the 37.2-over mark.

- Hampshire's Arthur Hill appeared in three Tests for England during which he improved his best score each time he batted, ending his career with a century in his final innings. After being run out for 25 on his debut, against South Africa at Port Elizabeth in 1895/96, he then hit 37 in the second innings, 65 at Johannesburg and 124 at Cape Town.

Pakistan opener Shakeel Ahmed also appeared in three Tests, batting five times, bettering his score each time – 0 against the West Indies at St John's in 1992/93 and 5 and 7 at Bulawayo and 29 and 33 against Zimbabwe at Harare in 1994/95.

- During the third Ashes Test at Adelaide in 1932/33, Walter Hammond and Bill Ponsford were the top-scorers for each side with both dismissed for the same score with both batting at the same position. A unique occurrence in Test match cricket, Ponsford made 85 at number five for Australia in its first innings, while Hammond also hit 85 at five in England's second innings.

- India's V.V.S. Laxman cruised through the 2007/08 Pakistan series with just one dismissal in five innings. With 209 runs and a highest score of 112 not out, he topped the batting averages for both countries with 209.00, and for good measure, topped the bowling averages as well. With one wicket – 1-0-2-1 at Kolkata – Laxman finished the three-match series with an average of 2.00 and a difference of 207 between bat and ball.

"Even if it's before he has to go in to bat, you see Laxman under a table catching up on sleep. It always boggles my mind that amid the noise and clutter of the dressing room, here is a man, who needs to go in to bat in a short while, sleeping calmly."

Rahul Dravid, 2008

"I can guarantee that in 125 of his 134 matches he went to shower just before the batsman ahead of him went in."
Sourav Ganguly on the retirement of V.V.S. Laxman in 2012

- Within the space of just three Sheffield Shield matches in 2008/09, Tasmania's Brett Geeves was twice left stranded on 99 in search of his maiden first-class century and had the same team-mate to blame. The first instance occurred during the match against Victoria at the MCG, when the number 11 Tim McDonald was dismissed for one with Geeves perched on 99 and a heartbeat away from his first-ever hundred in first-class cricket. Just two matches and two-and-a-half months later, Geeves was again left high and dry on 99, this time when McDonald was last man out in the first innings against New South Wales at Newcastle. Ninety-nine not out remained his highest first-class score, the only batsman to make two such scores in Australian first-class cricket.

- In the second one-day international against New Zealand in 2012, Jamaicans Chris Gayle and Marlon Samuels became the first pair of batsmen to score centuries in the same match in Kingston. With 125, and nine sixes, Gayle became the first West Indies batsman to score 20 ODI centuries, overtaking Brian Lara's 19. Samuels hit an unbeaten 101 – his third century – in a 129-run stand with Gayle. He said: **"Chris has been a part of life for a large part of my life. I always enjoy batting with him."**

  Back in the West Indies whites for the first time since 2010, Gayle's fertile limited-overs form spilled over into the Test arena scoring a big century against the Kiwis in Antigua. In the first Test at the Sir Vivian Richards Arena, Gayle hit 150 in an opening stand of 254 with Kieran Powell, who struck a maiden century of 134. It was the first time a West Indies Test innings had contained centuries from its openers since Adrian Griffith (114) and Sherwin Campbell (170), also against New Zealand, at Hamilton in 1999/2000.

  Gayle galloped off to the most scintillating of starts, hitting consecutive boundaries off the last four balls of the first over he faced, after making a duck in his previous Test, against Sri Lanka at Pallekele in 2010/11. He topped 200 runs in his comeback Test, scoring an unbeaten 64 in the second innings.

- Kumar Sangakkara scored exactly 200 runs against Pakistan at Galle in 2012, becoming only the second batsman after Zimbabwe's Andy Flower to be left stranded on 199 in a Test. Along the way he became the fastest to reach 2,000 Test runs against a single opponent, passing the milestone in his 26th innings against Pakistan. He said: **"It's also my dad's birthday today and he's been coaching me since I was 14, so I might not have to buy him a gift."**

  In the following Test in Colombo, Sangakkara again missed out on a double-century, becoming just the second batsman after Pakistan's Mohammad Yousuf to be dismissed in the 190s three times in Test cricket. With 192, he overtook Sunil Gavaskar as the highest run-scorer against Pakistan and shared a 225-run stand with Tillakaratne Dilshan (121) who completed his innings with exactly 5,000 Test runs. After a 287-run partnership between Pakistan's Mohammad Hafeez (196) and Azhar Ali (157), the match provided only the second instance of a double-century stand for the second wicket by both sides in the same Test. It was also the first time that two batsmen had been dismissed in the 190s in the same match – the three 190s in a single Test series that didn't contain a double-hundred was also a Test first. The Sri Lankan innings also provided the first instance in Test cricket in which the first five in the batting order had scored either a century or a duck – Tharanga Paranavitana (0), Dilshan (121), Sangakkara (192), Mahela Jayawardene (0), Thilan Samaraweera (0).

● In the first innings of five consecutive Tests in 2012, Kumar Sangakkara scored 0, 0, 199 not out, 192 and 0. He also scored another first-innings duck in his final Test of 2011.

1st inns	2nd inns	Match		
0	14	1st Test v England	Galle	2011/12
0	21	2nd Test v England	Colombo	2011/12
199*	1	1st Test v Pakistan	Galle	2012
192	24*	2nd Test v Pakistan	Colombo	2012
0	74*	3rd Test v Pakistan	Pallekele	2012

● When Otago's Bert Sutcliffe scored a triple-century in a Plunket Shield match in 1952/53, no other batsman went past 50 in the innings. Sutcliffe hit 385 in Otago's 500 against Canterbury at Christchurch, with Alan Gilbertson's 29 the next best score – the difference of 356 runs is the third highest in first-class cricket.

In 1943/44, Vijay Hazare also scored a triple-century in a first-class innings in which no other batsman made 50. He scored 309 in the Bombay Pentagular Tournament final against Hindus, while the next highest contribution to the innings was 21 by his brother Vivek.

BIGGEST DIFFERENCE BETWEEN TWO SCORES IN A FIRST-CLASS INNINGS

396	Hanif Mohammad (499)	Wallis Mathias (103)		
		Karachi (722/7d) v Bahawalpur	Karachi	1958/59
385	Brian Lara (501*)	Keith Piper (116*)		
		Warwickshire (810/4d) v Durham	Birmingham	1994
356	Bert Sutcliffe (385)	Alan Gilberston (29)		
		Otago (500) v Canterbury	Christchurch	1952/53
349	Graeme Hick (405*)	Steve Rhodes (56)		
		Worcestershire (628/7d) v Somerset	Taunton	1988
337	Don Bradman (452*)	Alan Kippax (115)		
		NSW (761/8d) v Queensland	Sydney	1929/30
308	Bill Ponsford (437)	Stork Hendry (129)		
		Victoria (793) v Queensland	Melbourne	1927/28
301	Naved Latif (394)	Misbah-ul-Haq (93)		
		Sargodha (721) v Gujranwala	Gujranwala	2000/01
300	Brian Lara (375)	Shivnarine Chanderpaul (75*)		
		West Indies (593/5d) v England	St John's	1993/94

● During the 1958 series against England, New Zealand opener John D'Arcy and number 11 batsman Johnny Hayes made the two highest scores in an innings in two consecutive Tests. On his Test debut at

Edgbaston, D'Arcy top-scored with 19, while Hayes made the next best score of 14 in New Zealand's first-innings total of 94. The pair made history by repeating the feat in the second Test at Lord's, with D'Arcy contributing 33 and Hayes 14 in their second-innings 74.

- Chris Broad and Steve Windaybank got their first-class careers off to a record-breaking start by posting a century stand while opening the batting together on debut. Going in first for Gloucestershire against Cambridge University in 1979, the two put on 126. Only the fourth pair of county debutants to open the batting in a first-class match, they then added 89 for the first wicket in the second innings.

- After centuries from Alastair Cook in two matches against Pakistan in the United Arab Emirates in 2011/12, his opening partner Kevin Pietersen scored hundreds in the other two. After going three years and 37 ODIs without a century, Pietersen produced two (111* and 130) in consecutive matches, both at Dubai, after Cook had made 137 and 102 at Abu Dhabi. In a surprise move, Pietersen then announced his retirement from limited-overs international cricket – albeit short-lived – which saw Ian Bell replace him at the top of the order. Bell responded immediately with a century, scoring 126 against the 2012 West Indians at Southampton. After the two centuries from Cook, the two from Pietersen and Bell's ton, it signalled the first time that one of the openers from the same team had scored a century in five consecutive one-day internationals. They then made it six in a row with Cook scoring 112 in the second ODI against the West Indies at The Oval.

- When Chris Martin scored an unbeaten four against the West Indies at North Sound in 2012 it represented the 50th innings he had played since previously reaching double figures in a Test. A record gap for any player in Test match cricket, the only time the New Zealand fast bowler had got past ten in a Test had been in 2007/08, with 12 not out against Bangladesh at Dunedin.

  Martin once went more than three years without scoring a single run in Tests. In 11 matches between the end of 2000 and early 2004, Martin contributed scores of 0 not out, 0, 0, 0, 0, 0 not out, 0, 0 and 0 before making a pair of one not outs against South Africa at Wellington in 2003/04.

- With a Test-best score of 27 and an average of 9.80, Tino Best went bonkers at Birmingham in 2012 by belting the biggest score by a number 11 batsman in Test history. Just one blow away from becoming the first number 11 to achieve a Test century, the West Indies fast bowler fell for 95 in the third Test against England in a last-wicket partnership of 143 with Denesh Ramdin (107*) – the only century stand in their innings. It was also the highest tenth-wicket partnership in West Indies history and the third highest of all time. Playing in his first Test in three years, Best became just the third number 11 to reach 50 in a Test against England, after Australia's Fred Spofforth (50) in 1884/85 and South Africa's Bert Vogler (62*) in 1905/06. With a six and 14 fours in his 112-ball knock, he accumulated the highest number of boundaries by a number 11 in a Test innings.

- In the first five matches of the 2011 World Cup, Virender Sehwag hit the first ball of the innings to the boundary. The Indian opener became the first batsman in ODI history to achieve such a feat.

World Cup fever 2011 – fans show support for India during the final against Sri Lanka, and wild scenes on the streets of Delhi after their victory

• In 2012/13, Chris Gayle became the first batsman to hit the first ball of a Test for six when he took to the bowling of a debutant off-spinner. Bangladesh's Sohag Gazi became just the third spinner in 100 years to send down the first over in a Test – at Mirpur – but was done twice by Gayle, who scored another six off his fourth ball. Gayle's opening partner Kieran Powell also made the record books with a pair of centuries (117 and 110), becoming just the second West Indies opener after Gordon Greenidge to achieve the feat in a Test.

In the same match, 38-year-old Shivnarine Chanderpaul scored an unbeaten 203, equalling his highest score in Test cricket. He had previously made 203 not out in 2004/05, against South Africa at Georgetown. Curiously, Pakistan's Shoaib Mohammad's highest score in Tests was 203 not out – achieved twice – against New Zealand at Karachi in 1990/91 and against India at Lahore in 1998/99. Chanderpaul later set another unusual record, when he became the first player to score a double-century and then bat at number 11 in the same Test.

In the second Test, at Khulna, the West Indies was stunned by a first-day century from Abul Hasan. After hitting 113 – the highest score by a player batting at number ten on his Test debut – he then gave away 113 while bowling, becoming the first debutant to score a century and concede 100 runs in an innings.

HIGHEST SCORES FOR EACH BATTING POSITION ON TEST DEBUT

1	166	Khalid Ibadulla	Pakistan v Australia	Karachi	1964/65
2	201*	Brendon Kuruppu	Sri Lanka v New Zealand	Colombo	1987
3	222*	Jacques Rudolph	South Africa v Bangladesh	Chittagong	2003
4	145	Aminul Islam	Bangladesh v India	Dhaka	2000/01
5	287	Tip Foster	England v Australia	Sydney	1903/04
6	155	Doug Walters	Australia v England	Brisbane	1965/66
7	132*	Romesh Kaluwitharana	Sri Lanka v Australia	Colombo	1992
8	128*	Azhar Mahmood	Pakistan v South Africa	Rawalpindi	1997/98
9	71	Balwinder Sandhu	India v Pakistan	Hyderabad	1982/83
10	113	Abul Hasan	Bangladesh v West Indies	Khulna	2012/13
11	45*	Warwick Armstrong	Australia v England	Melbourne	1901/02

• After going for a duck in his first Test innings, Sri Lanka's Dimuth Kuranaratne scored a half-century in his second and hit the winning runs. On his Test debut – against New Zealand at Galle in 2012/13 – both he and his opening partner Tharanga Paranavitana made a duck, but made amends in the second innings with an unbeaten 93-run first-wicket partnership. With a knock of 60 not out, Kuranaratne became the first Sri Lankan debutant to hit the winning run in a Test.

- When 23-year-old Ravindra Jadeja scored a triple-century against Gujarat in 2012/13, he became only the second batsman in the history of first-class cricket to take part in two 500-run partnerships. With an unbeaten 303 against Saurashtra at Surat, Jadeja shared a record Ranji Trophy third-wicket stand of 539 with Sagar Jogiyani (282) as Gujarat piled up a massive 716/3.

  In 2008/09, Jadeja and Cheteshwar Pujara had put on 520 runs against Orissa at Rajkot. Previously, Frank Worrell had been the only batsman to reach such dizzy heights, with two 500-run stands for Barbados in the 1940s.

BATSMEN TO TAKE PART IN TWO 500-RUN STANDS IN FIRST-CLASS CRICKET

Frank Worrell	John Goddard	502*	Barbados v Trinidad	Bridgetown	1943/44
	Clyde Walcott	574*	Barbados v Trinidad	Port-of-Spain	1945/46
Ravindra Jadeja	Cheteshwar Pujara	520*	Saurashtra v Orissa	Rajkot	2008/09
	Sagar Jogiyani	539	Saurashtra v Gujarat	Surat	2012/13

Three weeks after scoring his unbeaten 303, Jadeja made 331 against Railways at Rajkot. He became the first Indian batsman to score three triple-centuries in first-class cricket and the fourth batsman to score two in a season after W.G. Grace (1876), Bill Ponsford (1927/28) and Don Bradman (1935/36).

- After scoring 213 on his first-class debut in 2012/13, Punjab opener Jiwanjot Singh hit 158, to become the first batsman to make a double-century and a century in his first two innings. In his first match – an innings victory over Hyderabad at Chandigarh – Singh took part in a 288-run first-wicket stand with Karan Goel. His second match resulted in another innings victory, this time over Bengal, at Chandigarh. The 22-year-old then scored at least 40 in an innings in his next five first-class games, with another two centuries (110* and 103).

- On the same day that Sachin Tendulkar retired from one-day internationals in the Indian summer of 2012/13, two Haryana bowlers hit the headlines by scoring a maiden double-century in the same innings of a Ranji Trophy match. Amit Mishra (202*) and Jayant Yadav (211) got together for a 392-run partnership, the highest for the eighth wicket in the competition's history and just shy of the world-record 433 by Arthur Sims and Victor Trumper against Canterbury in 1913/14.

- Two batsmen came unstuck in the 190s during the same innings of a Ranji Trophy match in 2012/13. A first in the competition, Hyderabad opener Akshath Reddy made 196, while number three Hanuma Vihari hit 191 in the first innings against Mumbai at the Rajiv Gandhi

International Stadium. They were both caught and bowled and shared a stand of 386, a record for Hyderabad in the Ranji Trophy.

In the same season, Kerala's V.A. Jagadeesh became the first batsman to remain unbeaten on 199 in the Ranji Trophy. Jagadeesh was stuck one run shy of what would have been his maiden double-century, in the match against Services in Delhi.

• In a first-class match in South Africa in 2012/13, two openers failed by six runs in scoring a double-century. Andrew Puttick opened with 194 for the Cape Cobras, while a 19-year-old Quinton de Kock also made 194, with the Lions following-on in the Sunfoil Series match at Potchefstroom.

• 2012 was a crowning year for Michael Clarke, with the "Pup" becoming "Top Dog". He began the year with the scoring of 500 Test runs, and nearly 600, before the end of January. With the help of a record-breaking triple-century (329*), and a double (210), Clarke topped 500 in a Test series for the first time in his career, scoring 626 runs in four matches against India at an average of 125.20, with 594 coming in January.

He ended 2012 with a record harvest of 1,595 Test runs at 106.33, in 11 matches, the most in a calendar year by an Australian, beating Ricky Ponting's 1,544, at 67.13 in 15 in 2005. In eight Tests on home soil, Clarke struck 1,407 runs at the bumper average of 156.33, obliterating the record for the previous aggregate in Tests at home in a calendar year – 1,126 by Mohammad Yousuf in six matches in Pakistan in 2006.

HIGHEST TEST BATTING AVERAGES IN A YEAR

Qualification: 1000 runs

Batsman	Year	M	Inns	NO	Runs	HS	Avge	100s	50s
Garry Sobers (WI)	1958	8	13	4	1299	365*	144.33	6	3
Don Bradman (A)	1948	8	13	4	1025	201	113.88	5	2
Michael Clarke (A)	2012	11	18	3	1595	329*	106.33	5	3
Ricky Ponting (A)	2003	11	18	3	1503	257	100.20	6	4
Mohammad Yousuf (P)	2006	11	19	1	1788	202	99.33	9	3

• After 79 consecutive Tests from his first one in 2005, Mike Hussey left the game with the most number of runs by a batsman who debuted when over the age of 30. At the end of the third Test against Sri Lanka at the SCG in 2012/13, "Mr Cricket", aged 37, had scored 6,235 runs at 51.52, with England's Patsy Hendren second on the list with 3,525.

Cricket on Stage and Screen

- Sri Lankan batsman Tillakaratne Dilshan made his acting debut in his country's first cricket film released in 2011. *Sinhawalokanaya* (*The Cricket Film*) revolves around cricket in 1948, the year of the country's independence from Britain.

- The life of an England fast-bowling legend was brought to life in a stage play in 2011 premiering at the Nottingham Playhouse in the UK. *The Ashes* by Michael Pinchbeck told the story of the famous 1932/33 'Bodyline' Test series in Australia and the central part played by Harold Larwood.

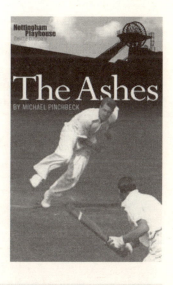

"I responded to something Douglas Jardine – the England captain at the time – said, 'Cricket is battle and service and sport and art'. This got me thinking, this was part of Jardine's call to arms like a director giving notes to his actors. Equally, it reminded me that the artistry of cricket is still applauded: a balletic catch in the slips, the shaping away from the batsman by a seamer, a well-executed cover drive, they are all things a crowd appreciates much like a performer on stage."

Michael Pinchbeck

- Bollywood actor Shahrukh Khan was handed a five-year ban from Mumbai's Wankhede Stadium in 2012 following a skirmish with security guards. Shahrukh was accused of trying to walk on to the ground after an IPL match and of being drunk and abusive, claims denied by the Kolkata Knight Riders co-owner. Earlier in the season, a complaint was filed in court against Shahrukh after he'd been spotted smoking during a match in Jaipur. With smoking banned in public places, the actor had previously been served with legal papers after he was sprung smoking at a match in Mumbai.

- A TV character that shares the name of Australia's greatest cricketer is included in an episode of the long-running American police drama *Law and Order: Special Victims Unit*. In a season-11 episode 'Shattered' – first broadcast in the US in 2010 – Bradman is the name of a criminal who kidnaps an eight-year-old boy on the streets of New York.

- A promotional film on cricket that features Don Bradman is regarded as one of Australia's first 'talking pictures'. Directed by Ken G. Hall to promote cricket and its importance to the British Empire, *That's Cricket* was released in 1931.

- A Don Bradman instructional film, *How I Play Cricket,* was sold to a wide overseas market in 1932. The negative of the film left Australia by air, reportedly becoming the first film to be transported overseas in such a way.

- The story of a Test cricketer who lost his fiancée in a train accident in New Zealand later became the subject of a stage play and a movie. During the second Test against South Africa in Johannesburg in 1953/54, Bob Blair went out to bat just hours after learning that his girlfriend had died when her Auckland-bound train plunged into the Whangaehu River.

  In 2009, Jonathan Brugh – an Auckland actor, playwright and amateur cricketer – turned the story into a one-man play called *The Second Test* which premiered at a theatre in Takapuna. He also appears in a 2011 TV movie based on the event called *Tangiwai*, the site of the accident that claimed 151 lives.

New Zealand actor Ryan O'Kane as Bob Blair in the 2011 telemovie
Tangiwai – A Love Story

- Pakistan all-rounder Imran Khan was once offered a role in a major Bollywood film directed by one of India's best-known actors. Dev Anand – who appeared in films between 1946 and 2011 – wanted Imran to play the part of a cricketer in his film *Awwal Number*. Imran responded: **"You have bowled me over Dev ... but I don't think I'm a good actor."**

- In the same year that he retired from Test match cricket, West Indies legend Clive Lloyd appeared in an Indian movie. Lloyd, who scored 72 in his final Test innings, against Australia at the SCG in 1984/85, played himself in the 1985 Hindi romance film *The Kabhi Ajnabi*, which also featured Indian Test cricketers Sandeep Patil and Syed Kirmani.

- Simon Hughes, who appeared in over 200 first-class matches in the 1980s and 1990s, is the son of a leading UK actor. Peter Hughes appeared in a number of major British films, including *Hope and Glory*, *Evita* and *A Passage to India*, with TV credits including *Bergarac*, *Some Mothers Do 'Ave 'Em* and *The Bill*.

  Hughes, a right-arm medium-pacer, was a key part of a successful Middlesex side in the 1980s that won four County Championships. He later found a niche as a broadcaster, journalist and writer, winning a major award in 1997 for his cricket book *A Lot of Hard Yakka*.

- Two cricket documentaries were recognised at the Grierson Awards held by the British Film Institute in London in 2011. *Out of the Ashes*

– that documented the rise of the Afghanistan cricket team – won the Best Newcomer award, while *Fire in Babylon* – on the rise of cricket in the West Indies in the 1970s and 1980s – won the Best Historical Documentary category.

- Two major Hollywood films released in 2008 include references to cricket. *The Deal*, starring William H. Macy and Meg Ryan, contains a scene of cricket plus a line in the script. *Fool's Gold*, an action comedy with Matthew McConaughey and Kate Hudson, includes a reference to a cricket bat in the script.

- Muttiah Muralitharan rates a mention in an Australian movie released in 2010, the year of his retirement from Test match cricket. In *Animal Kingdom* – starring Ben Mendelsohn – the Sri Lankan spinner's name pops up in the script during a scene of a cricket match on television. Another Australian film from the same year mentions cricket, with Don Bradman's name included in the romantic comedy *I Love You Too*.

- Former England batsman-turned-cricket commentator Geoff Boycott hung up his phone during a live radio interview in 2012 so he could watch his favourite TV show. While discussing the issue of sportsmanship with the BBC's Mark Chapman and Michael Vaughan, Boycott suddenly terminated the interview: "**That's all I've got to say, I'm going to watch *CSI*. Thank you very much.**"

- During the filming of the 1977 war classic *A Bridge Too Far*, part-time actor David English organised his own cricket team that included the likes of Laurence Olivier, Dirk Bogarde and Sean Connery. Many a game was played to soak up the boredom between takes, but one of the critical scenes in the movie had to be re-shot when a vision of the actors playing cricket was caught on film.

  As a thank you for his introduction to the game, Hollywood heartthrob Robert Redford, who played the part of Major Julian Cook, presented English with a bayonet used in the film. English – whose TV CV includes appearances in *Ripping Yarns* and *It Ain't Half Hot Mum* – later went on to form the Bunbury Cricket Club.

- British actor Hugh Laurie, who starred in the US medical drama *House*, was hit in the head with a cricket bat in an episode of the half-hour comedy *Blackadder Goes Forth*. Cricket gets a number of mentions in the episode 'Corporal Punishment' that first went to air in the UK in 1989. Laurie played the part of George in the third and fourth series of the award-winning historical sitcom that also starred Rowan Atkinson and Stephen Fry. The 1989 'Major Star' episode opens with George polishing a cricket bat. The script also includes references to an England captain and the lbw law.

- Cricket gets a good run in the long-running TV series *Doctor Who* with mentions in 'The Eleventh Hour', an episode that debuted in 2010.

Matt Smith, who plays the part of the Doctor, gets knocked out with a cricket bat in the hour-long episode, while an oblique reference to cricket can be found in 'The Lodger'. When the Doctor briefly mistakes football for another game, he asks: "Football … that's the one with the sticks, right?"

Doctor Who has included notable scenes of cricket matches down the years, most famously in the 1982 series *Black Orchid*. The Doctor – played by Peter Davison (pictured) – wins a cricket match almost single-handedly with both bat and ball. In the 'Volcano' episode from *The Daleks' Master Plan* – first aired by the BBC in 1965/66 – the Doctor's TARDIS lands on the pitch at Lord's during an Ashes Test match.

Other on-screen cricketing moments include a scene from the 1979/80 series *The Horns of Nimon*, in which the fourth Doctor – Tom Baker – uses cricket as an inspiration to avoid the destruction of the TARDIS. Cricket references are also contained in the series *Four to Doomsday* from 1982 and in the episodes 'Human Nature' and 'Time Crash' from 2007.

- In a 2011 episode of the BBC TV show *Bargain Hunt,* contestants from both sides purchased cricket items. In a show where teams of two purchase three objects which are later auctioned, the first team chose a cricket kit, while the second purchased a set of cufflinks. A village cricket kit comprising a bat, three caps and a bag was bought for £45, but made just £28 at auction, while a pair of modern silver cufflinks in the shape of cricket bats and balls, snapped up for £28, made £18.

● American actor Vincent Price, famous for his appearances in horror films, once recorded a piece to camera on how to play cricket. Price used various props, including bottles and keys, to explain stumps and bails, the pitch and batsmen for his US audience: **"Cricket, though relatively unfamiliar to Americans, is more or less the baseball of England, the national sport."** Price's first venture into the horror genre was in the 1939 film *Tower of London* which starred the cricket-loving Boris Karloff.

Boris Karloff displays his bowling technique for the cameras

"Wonderful. I think I'm dead and gone to Heaven."

British actor Boris Karloff on watching cricket at The Oval

● Former Indian all-rounder Kapil Dev transferred his talents to television in 1999, appearing in a two-part episode of a leading crime show. Kapil played himself in two episodes of *C.I.D.*, a long-running Indian detective show.

- The climax of a major Hindi film released in 2004 takes place on a cricket field. The scene in *Mujhse Shaadi Karogi*, starring Bollywood superstar Salman Khan, features an array of Indian cricketers including Kapil Dev, Harbhajan Singh, Parthiv Patel and Irfan Pathan.

  Kapil has appeared in a number of other films, including *Cricketer*, a Hindu film from 1983, *Aryan: Unbreakable* from 2006, *Iqbal,* released in 2005, and *Stumped,* from 2003.

 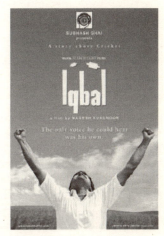

> **"The 1983 team was movie stars playing cricket."**
>
> former Indian captain Sunil Gavaskar noting that the 1983 World Cup winning team contained players, including himself, who had acted in films

- India's two favourite pastimes – cricket and cinema – formally came together in 2011 with the launch of the Celebrity Cricket League. The Chennai Rhinos won the inaugural Twenty20 tournament, beating the Karnataka Bulldozers by 23 runs in the final.

> **"The idea was to combine two popular Indian religions, Bollywood and cricket, to produce great entertainment for the Indian audience."**
>
> Indian film star and Mumbai Heroes player Salman Khan

- A leading Bollywood actor put cricket practice ahead of his job in 2012 when he skipped rehearsals for an upcoming film. Riteish Deshmukh also postponed his honeymoon to play for the Mumbai Heroes Twenty20 team in the CCL. He said: **"Cricket's always been my favourite sport. As a child, I'd dream of joining the Indian cricket team. I think being one** of the men in blue is on the wish-list of every Indian at some point. I think this love for the sport truly unites us in a way, and cuts through all barriers just like our films do."

Celebrity Cricket League

- An Australian actor who shares the same name as a West Indies fast bowler played the part of a cricketer in a popular mini-series of the 1980s. Colin Croft played England's Sir Stanley Jackson in *Bodyline*.

- A cricket-themed story won a major prize at the 2001 Australian Tropfest short film festival. Featuring a Richie Benaud impersonation throughout, the five-minute *Just Not Cricket* – written and directed by Matt Wheeldon – came in second.

- Australia's Brett Lee once appeared in a movie that was directed by a childhood friend. The Australian fast bowler had a small role in a short film called *Dream Date*.

- Michael Clarke's wife is a former TV weather girl. After studying acting at the Australian Theatre for Young People, Kyly Boldy appeared on the reality show *Temptation Island* and picked up presenting roles on Foxtel's Weather Channel and home shopping network TVSN.

- Irish cricketers Niall O'Brien and William Porterfield went Bollywood in 2012 with an acting role in a romantic drama. While abroad in 2011, O'Brien received a request from a film director for the pair to appear as extras in a movie called *Unforgettable*: **"She needed some people and asked us if we'd be keen and after some consideration … we decided why not? I was only in three scenes but they were quite pivotal scenes. I found it quite strange they'd put someone who's never acted before into three important scenes. It wasn't a massive part but an important part."**

"I'd like to be the next Colin Farrell but I don't think I'm going to be. Already there's been a bit of interest in India. I might not be the next Colin Farrell but there are opportunities."

Ireland wicketkeeper Niall O'Brien

- During an appearance on NBC's *Late Night with David Letterman* show in 1988, John Cleese – of *Fawlty Towers* and *Monty Python* fame – was called on to explain cricket. Cleese had some knowledge of the game, having played for the first XI at Clifton College.

John Cleese: **It's a very weird game and I know that Americans can't really understand it. I used to know the England captain and he said it's the only game that's ever been invented where the adrenalin cannot run the whole time, which is an understatement. But it's more a kind of cultural phenomenon.**

David Letterman: **But is it still thriving and flourishing? Are the youth of Great Britain eager to grow up to be cricket stars?**

Cleese: **Yes … that's right … after a time, a few years ago, they decided that people were beginning to lose interest in these five-day games so they now pack all the action into these special one-day games.**

Letterman: **Ah, shortened down to about 12 hours.**

"I always think, 'Well, what was my role in *Python*?' And I always think of myself as the wicketkeeper, because the wicketkeeper has a very important role. You always know which way the ball's turning. You're not star batsman, star bowler, but your influence on the game, if you're reading it properly, can be very instructive."

Monty Python's Eric Idle

- US comedian Jerry Seinfeld dressed up in cricket gear for a scene in a TV advertisement shot for American Express. The star of *Seinfeld* is comprehensively bowled in the 1990s ad, declaring: **"That was a wicked googly!"**

- American actor Jason Alexander issued an apology in 2012 after saying that cricket is "gay". On CBS's *Late Late Show*, the former *Seinfeld* star told the host Craig Ferguson that aspects of cricket, such as bowling, make it a "gay game" compared to other sports. He later released a statement in which he admitted that his comments were wrong and hurtful: **"I should know better. My daily life is filled with gay men and women, both socially and professionally. I** am profoundly aware of the challenges these friends of mine face and I have openly advocated on their behalf. So, I can only apologise and I do. In comedy, timing is everything."

Craig Ferguson: **Have you ever played cricket?**

Jason Alexander: **I've watched cricket.**

Ferguson: **Cricket's an amazing game.**

Alexander: **It's a gay game. There's a lot of people wearing whites. People wearing helmets for no discernible reason ... people not wearing helmets that look like they should have a helmet. Everybody breaks for tea in the middle. And then ya hit it and you just kinda run back and forth without any rhyme or reason.**

Ferguson: **It's a cross between baseball and** *Downton Abbey*.

- from *The Late Late Show with Craig Ferguson*, 2012

- The British actor Tom Felton, who played the part of Draco Malfoy in the *Harry Potter* films, has played the occasional game of competitive cricket as a right-arm medium-pacer. Felton – who shares a passion for the game with fellow *Harry Potter* star Daniel Radcliffe – used to play for the Leatherhead club in Surrey.

"I really enjoy [Ian] Bell. I like to watch a good forward defensive and a cover drive. If batsmen can play orthodox strokes like those, I love them."

British actor Tom Felton

Watching cricket in bed...again. England out the world cup..again Losing hope in British cricket..again Oh well we'll win the ashes...again!

TomFelton
Tom Felton

- When Pauline Chase, a famous American stage actress of the early 1900s, attended her first cricket match in England she appeared baffled by some of the participants. Upon noticing the umpires, she reportedly asked: **"What are the butchers for?"**

DEEPAK VERMA'S DREAM TEAM

Sunil Gavaskar (I)
Rahul Dravid (I)
Ricky Ponting (A)
Sachin Tendulkar (I)
Viv Richards (WI)
Ian Botham (E)
Mahendra Singh Dhoni * † (I)
Glenn McGrath (A)
Shane Warne (A)
Wasim Akram (P)
Malcolm Marshall (WI)

British actor Deepak Verma

- One of the lead actors in the Emmy award-winning British TV drama *Downton Abbey* captained his school cricket team. While a student at Tonbridge in Kent in the 1990s, Dan Stevens captained a third-XI team with a highest innings of 53 not out.

- British comedian Tim Brooke-Taylor captained his cricket team at school which included a future Indian Test captain. Brooke-Taylor – star of the BBC favourite *The Goodies* – had the Nawab of Pataudi in his team, and Richard Jefferson who later played first-class cricket for Surrey.

Brooke-Taylor played at Lord's in 1975, representing the MCC President's XI against a Lord's Taverners XI: **"The ball went high in the air at one point and I said to myself, 'Please let me catch it'. I did so and the whole ground groaned ... I'd caught Denis Compton. He walked past and said, 'Thanks for that, I was knackered'."**

Actor Dan Stevens with a makeshift cricket bat on the set of the period drama Downton Abbey

Actor John Alderton – of *Upstairs, Downstairs* fame – also played in the match as did an array of Test cricketers, including Graeme Pollock, Geoff Boycott, Richie Benaud, Mike Procter, Ted Dexter and Ken Barrington.

- Sachin Tendulkar declared he was an actor and not a cricketer in 2011 to reduce his taxation burden. After an appeal to the Indian Tax Tribunal, board members accepted Tendulkar's claim that acting in commercials was his overriding profession.

- A much-hyped Indian movie released in 2012 has a Sachin Tendulkar connection. The cricket-themed *Ferrari Ki Sawaari* had scenes shot at Lord's and includes a Ferrari once owned by Tendulkar.

- An Australian horror-comedy released in 2008 took out two awards at international film festivals the following year. In *I Know How Many Runs You Scored Last Summer* a young cricketer is hospitalised by bullying team-mates, returning 20 years later to wreak a bloody revenge. It won awards as 'Best Australian Film' at the 2009 A Night of Horror Film Festival and for 'Best Opening Title Sequence' at the South African Horrorfest.

MASS MURDER, IT'S JUST NOT CRICKET

- A film about a father whose son wants to become a famous cricketer like Mahendra Singh Dhoni premiered in India in 2012. *Dhoni* was directed by Prakash Raj, who also takes on the film's leading role: "**I play a government clerk. He dreams about getting his son to study MBA but his son is interested in sports and has his own dreams. The film deals with the pressure that children undergo these days in school.**"

- The life and times of Imran Khan came to the silver screen in 2012 with the release of a biographical film called *Kaptaan – the Making of a Legend*. The story of the former Pakistan captain follows his life from the winning of the 1992 World Cup, with actor Abdul Mannan taking on the main role.

- A contributor to a British TV series on child rearing was briefly married to a first-class cricketer. Claire Verity – who was condemned for fudging her nursing qualifications – enraged viewers of the 2007 series *Bringing Up Baby* with her strict, and sometimes discredited, views. In 1998, she had married fast bowler Ian Houseman, who appeared in five first-class matches for Yorkshire.

ANDY KIND'S DREAM TEAM

Jack Hobbs (E)
Graeme Smith (SA)
Don Bradman (A)
Sachin Tendulkar (I)
Brian Lara (WI)
Adam Gilchrist † (A)
Ian Botham * (E)
Malcolm Marshall (WI)
Shane Warne (A)
Glenn McGrath (A)
Allan Donald (SA)

British stand-up comedian Andy Kind

NAT COOMBS'S DREAM TEAM

Jack Hobbs (E)
Michael Vaughan * (E)
Viv Richards (WI)
Mark Waugh (A)
Rahul Dravid (I)
Adam Gilchrist † (A)
Ian Botham (E)
Richie Benaud (A)
Waqar Younis (P)
Fred Trueman (E)
Joel Garner (WI)

British comedian and TV and radio presenter Nat Coombs

• During South Africa's tour of England in 1955, Paul Winslow hit a famous Test century at Old Trafford and met his future bride, a British actress. Moira Winslow went on to appear in a number of South African films, including a horror flick called *The Demon* and a 2006 comedy, *Running Riot*.

After career scores of 19, a duck, 11, two and three in his first three Tests, Winslow struck a match-winning 108 against England at Manchester on the 1955 tour. Batting at number eight, he reached his maiden century in first-class cricket with a straight six.

• Len Goodman, a judge on the UK and US panels of the hit shows *Strictly Come Dancing* and *Dancing with the Stars*, played cricket while at school. A professional dancer who won a Life Achievement Award for his work, Goodman was once banned from playing cricket for cheering when he took a wicket in an Under-13s match.

- In 2009, BBC presenter Chris Hollins became the third first-class cricketer to win the channel's *Strictly Come Dancing*. Fast bowler Darren Gough took out the show in 2005, with Mark Ramprakash triumphant the following year. Hollins scored 415 first-class runs for Oxford University in the summer of 1994, with a highest innings of 131 in his final match, against Cambridge at Lord's.

> **"Ramps was unsure about going on *Strictly Come Dancing*. Away from cricket he's really a quiet bloke so I spoke to him and encouraged him to do it. We were two different blokes on the cricket pitch and we were equally different on the dance floor. My dancing was like my cricket. I always believed in entertaining the public, whereas Ramps was all about technique and getting ten off the judges. He is how you expect a dancer to be ... supple, good-looking and with a quite classy technique too."**
>
> 2005 *Strictly Come Dancing* winner Darren Gough

> **"It was an amazing experience overall, but a tough one for me. I tried to put in a lot of hard work and enjoyed it to the fullest. It was nice to learn a bit of salsa and jive."**
>
> Sanath Jayasuriya after appearing on India's *Dancing with the Stars* in 2012

- A British comedian who stars in *Harry Potter and the Prisoner of Azkaban* is related to a former England Test cricketer. Jim Tavaré – best known for his contribution to ITV's *The Sketch Show* – is a first cousin of Chris Tavaré, a batsman who appeared in 31 Tests and one who holds the record for the slowest-ever Test fifty at Lord's. Jim said: **"Whenever I perform my stand-up act at sports benefits I open with 'I'm a cousin of Chris Tavaré but don't worry, I won't be up here all night'."**

- British film-maker and screenwriter Jonathan Lynn, famed for his writing of the hit TV shows *Yes Minister* and *Yes, Prime Minister*, scored a leading role in a cricket telemovie. First broadcast in the UK in 1982, *Outside Edge* – written by Richard Harris – also starred Paul Eddington, who played the part of politician James Hacker in *Yes Minister* and *Yes, Prime Minister*.

JIM TAVARÉ'S DREAM TEAM

Chris Tavaré (E)
Len Hutton (E)
Don Bradman * (A)
Viv Richards (WI)
Sachin Tendulkar (I)
Garry Sobers (WI)
Ian Botham (E)
Alan Knott † (E)
Dennis Lillee (A)
Shane Warne (A)
Muttiah Muralitharan (SL)

British comedian Jim Tavaré

JONATHAN LYNN'S DREAM TEAM

Denis Compton (E)
Peter May (E)
Don Bradman * (A)
Tom Graveney (E)
Viv Richards (WI)
Garry Sobers (WI)
Adam Gilchrist † (E)
Glenn McGrath (A)
Dennis Lillee (A)
Shane Warne (A)
Jim Laker (E)

British actor, film-maker and screenwriter Jonathan Lynn

● One of Gilbert and Sullivan's most famous works was given a new coat of paint in 1995 with a cricket-themed adaptation of *The Mikado* playing to a sell-out audience in Staffordshire. British theatre director Chris Monks first came up with the novel idea while attending a game of cricket: "**With all the padding on they looked like Samurai warriors, and with the bat it was a little like they were carrying a sword.**" In 2010, the production completed a sixth run in England (pictured).

THE Mikado

By W.S. Gilbert and Arthur Sullivan
Adapted and directed by Chris Monks

8 July - 4 September
Box Office 01723 370541
www.sjt.uk.com

- A West Indian umpire has a small role in one of the biggest Walt Disney films ever made. Goland Greaves was an extra in the 2003 blockbuster *Pirates of the Caribbean* starring Johnny Depp.

- A wicketkeeper from the early 1950s made an appearance in one of the top-grossing films of 2010. Frank Parr's cameo in the UK historical drama *The King's Speech* followed an appearance on the TV show *Psychoville* in 2009. Parr achieved 91 dismissals in 49 first-class matches for Lancashire between 1951 and 1954.

- The daughter of an Egyptian-born Test cricketer had a bit part in *Mao's Last Dancer*, a major Australian film of 2009. Chloe Traicos, whose father John Traicos played Test cricket for both South Africa and Zimbabwe, has appeared in other Australian films with a lead role in *Next Door to The Velinsky's*, a 2010 thriller that lists her father as executive producer.

- Cricket has been featured in many children's TV programmes over the years, from *Sesame Street* in the United States to *Teletubbies* in the United Kingdom. The latter once dedicated an episode to the game, with 'Cricket' first going to air on the BBC in 2001.

DAVE THOMPSON'S DREAM TEAM

Jack Hobbs (E)	*British actor and*
Len Hutton (E)	*comedian Dave*
Don Bradman * (A)	*Thompson, a*
Viv Richards (WI)	*former member*
Sachin Tendulkar (I)	*of the* Teletubbies
Garry Sobers (WI)	*children's TV show*
Ian Botham (E)	
Adam Gilchrist † (A)	
Jeff Thomson (A)	
Shane Warne (A)	
Fred Trueman (E)	

- Reg Harris, who played for a theatrical cricket team in his younger days, can lay claim to being one of the oldest persons to have played competitive cricket. Still playing in his nineties for the Northamptonshire village of Bugbrooke in 2003, he also played for the Northampton Repertory Theatre, which included a certain Australian actor named Errol Flynn. "**Not much of a player**," the wicketkeeping Harris later recalled.

- British funnyman Trevor Lock was a handy cricketer in his youth, playing at junior level for Northamptonshire. While appearing in a charity match at Canterbury in 2010, he was good enough to dismiss a former England captain, Chris Cowdrey.

HOW I GOT AN STD PLAYING CRICKET

Trevor Lock

Growing up playing for my school teams, and then Northamptonshire's youth team, cricket gave me many good things; hope for the individual somehow fitting into the whole, the knowledge of the rewards that come from effort and discipline, and how luck and chance are indifferent to both. Playing for my village team also gave me the treasured experience of camaraderie across the generations and, bizarrely, my first STD.

It was the summer of 1991 and after years of Dad's Army-style Sunday friendlies, I was finally beginning to work my way into the first team of Bugbrooke St. Michaels '74 as they challenged the mighty United Social – Northampton's very own West Indies – for the crown of Section One of the Town League. I can't remember who it was I loaned my box to the day we played Northampton Police Force at home but they can't have been out by the time I went in because I remember, as the ninth wicket fell, having no choice but to reluctantly put on a still warm box from the communal club kit bag. At 17, I was the youngest player on the team by some distance, a boy amongst men but nevertheless, despite being hit on the head by a bouncer, I batted out the remaining overs and saved the team a valuable batting point. It was not until two days

61

later when I found myself lying on my back in a hospital gown with a testicle the size of a five-and-a-half ounce match ball that I discovered the true cost of playing in that match.

When I asked the embarrassingly brassy young female doctor how it was that such a terrible thing had happened to one of my most prized belongings, she at first sarcastically, and then incredulously, explained to me what an STD was. To complete my humiliation she even gave me some examples of how I might have contracted it. Now I might have been a precocious cricketer but there was absolutely nothing precocious about my sex life so it was a holy mystery to me, as great as the virgin birth, how I'd managed to get a sexually transmitted disease without actually ever even coming close to having sex (in fact it would be another four years before I'd eventually manage to manoeuvre myself into a situation with any possibility of contracting one via the more traditional method).

At some point once the swelling had gone down and after fielding questions I didn't have answers to from bemused friends, I must have remembered the box. And the men, not boys, on my team that might have worn that box before me and to an extent the mystery of my STD was solved. So when I went back to my A-Level classes I knew that technically I was still a virgin but whilst I might not have been the first in my year to get laid, I had the satisfaction of being the first to get an STD.

- British actor Hugh Grant played cricket while he attended school in London but admits he is "crap" at the game. Grant appeared in a few matches for the first XI at Latymer Upper School in Hammersmith, and says: "**I disgraced the side. I pretended to bat but couldn't. I dropped catches. That was my speciality. I watched my brother lose all his teeth fielding at gully and that made me scared of the ball.**"

"**I've always been crap, but I've always loved it. I've always had nice equipment, if you'll excuse the expression. My aunt used to say it's impossible to dislike a man who likes cricket and I think that's almost true.**"

Hugh Grant

- When former England Test captain and actor C. Aubrey Smith moved to Hollywood to further his movie career, he named his house on Mulholland Drive "The Round Corner" in celebration of his unusual bowling style. The founder of the famous Hollywood Cricket Club in 1932, Smith's home had three stumps and a bat on the roof that acted as a weather vane.

C. Aubrey Smith, the actor

A SELECT FILMOGRAPHY OF C. AUBREY SMITH

Tarzan the Ape Man	Neil Hamilton, Maureen O'Sullivan, Johnny Weissmuller	1932
The Prisoner of Zenda	Ronald Colman, Mary Astor, David Niven	1937
The Four Feathers	John Clements, Ralph Richardson, June Duprez	1939
The Sun Never Sets	Douglas Fairbanks jnr, Basil Rathbone, Barbara O'Neil	1939
Rebecca	Laurence Olivier, Joan Fontaine, George Sanders	1940
Waterloo Bridge	Vivien Leigh, Robert Taylor, Lucile Watson	1940
Dr Jekyll and Mr Hyde	Spencer Tracy, Ingrid Bergman, Lana Turner	1941
Madame Curie	Greer Garson, Walter Pidgeon, Henry Travers	1943
An Ideal Husband	Paulette Goddard, Michael Wilding, Diana Wynyard	1947
Little Women	June Allyson, Peter Lawford, Elizabeth Taylor	1949

- Two England bowlers who each claimed a five-wicket haul in a Test appeared in films that won best picture at the Academy Awards. C. Aubrey Smith, who took 5-19 in his only Test, had a role alongside Laurence Olivier and Joan Fontaine in the 1940 Alfred Hitchcock thriller *Rebecca*. Derek Pringle, who achieved three five-fors in 30 Tests, was an extra in the 1981 British film *Chariots of Fire*.

- The son of an Australian Test cricketer was portrayed in an Academy Award-winning film about US General George S. Patton. All-rounder Arthur Coningham, who appeared in a single Test against England in 1894/95, is the father of Air Marshal Arthur "Mary" Coningham, a senior officer in the Royal Air Force who served with distinction during the Second World War. His part in the 1970 movie *Patton* is played by British actor John Barrie.

- On his way to England for the 2011 India Test series, player-turned-commentator Shane Warne paid a visit to the set of a top-rating TV show in New York. Warne stopped off in the Big Apple to visit his partner Liz Hurley, who was playing a part in the teen drama *Gossip Girl*. When Australian pay-TV station Fox 8 aired Hurley's debut episode in 2011, Warne was being interviewed on *Inside Cricket* in the same time slot on a Foxtel sports channel. According to industry insiders, Warne proved the more popular, pulling 6,000 more viewers.

- One of Britain's former top TV newsreaders was appointed president of the Lady Taverners cricket organisation in 2011, but her first duty was interrupted by a wayward cricket ball. Scheduled to make a speech at the start of a celebrity cricket match at Lord's, Angela Rippon had to leave to get her smashed car windscreen repaired.

- Legendary Australian actor Bill Hunter, star of iconic films such as *Newsfront, Gallipoli, Muriel's Wedding* and *Strictly Ballroom,* had a cricketing trophy named in his honour. The Billy Hunter Cup was contested by a group of Australian actors, including Jeremy Sims and Rhys Muldoon.

- Australian actor Brendan Cowell appeared in two cricketing-themed shows that hit the screens in 2012. Cowell played the part of wicketkeeper Rodney Marsh in *Howzat!,* a TV mini-series that told the story of Australian businessman Kerry Packer and his establishment of the breakaway World Series Cricket competition. The first episode was a ratings winner for Channel Nine, attracting an average audience of 2.097 million, peaking at 2.433 million.

  Cowell was also part of the cricketing film *Save Your Legs!,* a tale about a suburban park cricket team that embarks on a three-match tour around India. The movie, that had its official world premiere at the London Film Festival in 2012, also stars Damon Gameau, who played the part of Greg Chappell in *Howzat!*

  Kiwi actor Ryan O'Kane, who played Jeff Thomson in *Howzat!,* had previously portrayed another Test cricketer on film – New Zealand's Bob Blair in the 2011 TV movie *Tangiwai.*

- Daniel Radcliffe once appeared on the TV show *Inside the Actors Studio* where he raved about cricket to his American audience. During the interview in 2008 with host James Lipton, the *Harry Potter* star compared the drama of Test cricket with drama in theatre and film.

"Cricket is my thing, which I just love with a passion."
Daniel Radcliffe

- Cricket gets a run in the scripts of the US TV drama *Desperate Housewives,* with a mention in a final-year episode. While discussing financial problems concerning a business deal, Mike Delfino reveals a secret about a female friend of the Australian character Ben Faulkner, which leads to talk of cricket players. Cricket is also included in a 2007 episode of *Desperate Housewives*, when long-standing character Susan Delfino talks of going to London to eat crumpets and play cricket.

- Two up-and-coming Indian actresses got their gear off in 2012 to celebrate the IPL final. Poonam Pandey stripped for the Kolkata Knight Riders who won IPL edition-five, while Rozlyn Khan did the same for the losers, M.S. Dhoni's Chennai Super Kings, and said: **"They are the best. My dreams have been shattered with the loss. What I am doing is a small token of appreciation for their efforts."**

Indian model, actress and IPL cricket fan Rozlyn Khan

Royalty and Religion

- The only member of the British royal family to appear in first-class cricket played alongside the great W.G. Grace. Prince Christian Victor, the son of Queen Victoria, scored 35 and a duck in his only first-class match, for I Zingari against a Gentlemen of England XI at Scarborough in 1887.

- Two years after its establishment in 1855, the St Kilda Cricket Club in Melbourne applied unsuccessfully to Queen Victoria for royal patronage. Its wish to become known as "The Royal Cricket Club of Victoria" was also turned down.

- The Duke of Edinburgh once took the wicket of an England Test batsman in a charity match. During a game at Arundel in the 1960s, Prince Philip dismissed Tom Graveney: **"Sheer fluke. Every time I saw Tom afterwards, he always said, 'I'm your rabbit'."**

> **"The saddest thing about professional cricket is that it has completely cut off the progression from club to country. Amateurs play for their club and that's it, and the whole of county cricket, and international cricket, is now professional."**
>
> Prince Philip

- In 2011, Prince Philip gave the royal seal of approval to a new £32m redevelopment of the Edgbaston cricket ground. The only person to be MCC president twice in the 20th century, the Duke unveiled a plaque commemorating his visit.

Prince Philip bowling,
and his son, Prince Charles, batting

- The Australia–New Zealand Test series of 2011/12 was graced by the presence of royalty. The Crown Prince of Denmark was in Hobart with his Tasmanian-born wife Princess Mary, and attended the second day of the second Test, although he confessed to knowing little about the game: **"It's my first cricket match … I have family that's very good at cricket and the rules."**

- Prince Frederick Louis, the eldest son of King George II, was an important early benefactor of the game who started his own cricket team. In 1733, he presented a silver cup to a combined Surrey–Middlesex team following a victory over Kent, believed to be the first example in the game of a cricket trophy.

- When India undertook their first tour of England, a prince led the side as protocol demanded with the Maharaja of Porbandar in charge. According to the Cricinfo website: "A keen cricketer, he was handicapped by being almost useless. Despite that, he was picked to captain the All-India side on their first major tour of England in 1932 when the Maharaja of Patiala had to withdraw through illness. He scored two runs on the whole trip, provoking the quite justified comment that he owned more Rolls-Royces than he had made runs."

  The Maharaja appeared in just six first-class matches in all, with two on either side of four matches in England.

- The Indian batsman Hanumant Singh, who scored a century on his Test debut, was of royal blood, being the son of the ruler of the princedom of Banswara in Rajasthan. Hanumant launched his 14-match Test career with 105 against England at Delhi in 1963/64, the fifth Indian to hit a Test century on debut. A relative, the princely England batsman K.S. Ranjitsinhji (pictured), also began his Test career with a century, scoring 154 not out against Australia at Manchester in 1896. Hanumant's brother Suryaveer Singh – the Maharawal of Banswara – also played first-class cricket, as did a cousin, Prince Indrajitsinhji. Hanumant's uncle was K.S. Duleepsinhji, a nephew of Ranji.

- K.S. Duleepsinhji scored a regal century in his final first-class match overseas sharing a century partnership with another prince, who fell in the nineties. Appearing in a match at Delhi in 1931/32, Duleep scored 173 and the Nawab of Pataudi 91, for the Viceroy's XI against the Roshanara Club. Pataudi – who would later score a century on his Test debut for England – achieved his best bowling figures in first-class cricket, taking 6-111 in the second innings.

  K.S. Ranjitsinhji's nephew K.S. Himmatsinhji kept wicket on his first-class debut for the Viceroy's XI, which also included the Yuvraj of Patiala and his father, the captain, the Maharaja of Patiala. The Maharaja of Porbandar made his first-class debut in the match, captaining Roshanara, scoring 22 – his highest knock at first-class level. After scoring a duck at number three, the Maharajkumar of Vizianagram – a future Indian Test captain – opened the second innings for Roshanara and scored 25.

- The Maharajkumar of Vizianagram, better known as "Vizzy", achieved his highest score in Test match cricket in his maiden innings. Captaining India on his Test debut – against England at Lord's in 1936 – he scored an unbeaten 19 batting down the order at nine. While India lost the three-match series 2-0, Vizzy was knighted by King Edward III in the 1936 King's Birthday Honours list. He became the only cricketer to be knighted while still an active Test player.

- Pakistan import Javed Miandad scored an unbeaten double-century for the Welsh county Glamorgan in 1981 on the day that Prince Charles and Diana Spencer were married at St Paul's Cathedral in London.

Dubbed "the batting Prince of Wales", Javed struck a majestic 200 not out, with 29 fours and a six, on the opening day of the County Championship match against Somerset at Taunton.

When Prince Charles's son William married Kate Middleton in 2011, three batsmen celebrated the event with a first-class century. Opening the batting against Somerset, Hampshire's 21-year-old Liam Dawson finished the Royal Wedding day unconquered on 103, having scored 91 in the first innings of the match at Southampton. Sussex's Naved Arif reached exactly 100 not out – his maiden first-class century – against Lancashire at Hove, while over at Southampton, Ravi Bopara scored a match-winning 136 for Essex against Glamorgan.

ROYAL WEDDING DAY CENTURIES

29 July 1981 (Prince Charles and Diana Spencer)			
Ken McEwan	102	Essex v Kent	Canterbury
Chris Balderstone	100	Leicestershire v Nottinghamshire	Hinckley
John Steele	116	Leicestershire v Nottinghamshire	Hinckley
Javed Miandad	200*	Glamorgan v Somerset	Taunton
Glenn Turner	161	Worcestershire v Northamptonshire	Stourbridge
Phil Neale	125	Worcestershire v Northamptonshire	Stourbridge
Philip Oliver	122	Warwickshire v Yorkshire	Scarborough
29 April 2011 (Prince William and Kate Middleton)			
Ravi Bopara	136*	Essex v Glamorgan	Chelmsford
Liam Dawson	169	Hampshire v Somerset	Southampton
Naved Arif	100*	Sussex v Lancashire	Hove

Liam Dawson went from 0 to 103* on the day before being dismissed the following day for 169. Somerset's Marcus Trescothick brought up a double-century on the 2011 royal wedding day at Southampton progressing from an overnight score of 193* to 227, while Sussex's Ed Joyce went from 63* to 140 against Lancashire at Hove.

- Alex Loudon, who was run out without facing a ball in his only appearance for England, attended the 2011 royal wedding of Prince William and Kate Middleton at Westminster Abbey. The then-partner of the bride's sister Pippa, Loudon made his England debut in a one-day international against Sri Lanka at Chester-le-Street in 2006. A former England Under-19 captain, Loudon's highest score in 76 first-class matches was 172 in 2003.

- Don Bradman was publicly chided in 1948 when he was seen with his hands in his pockets while walking with King George VI in the grounds of Balmoral Castle. In 1977, Dennis Lillee also breached protocol when he asked the Queen for her autograph during the Centenary Test at the MCG. Although she politely refused his request, her office later sent him a signed photograph.

Max Walker, who opened the bowling with Lillee in the Centenary Test, also had a somewhat sticky meeting with her Majesty. To protect his skin, Walker would apply an antiseptic ointment to his fingers and had done so just before his introduction. After shaking her gloved hand, Walker later recalled that he "**... almost dragged the glove when I let go.**"

Cricket and royalty – Don Bradman with King George VI in 1948 and Dennis Lillee with the Queen in 1977

- Coinciding with the Diamond Jubilee celebrations for Queen Elizabeth in 2012, a 77-year-old went public with reminiscences of playing cricket with members of the royal family when he was a child. Derek Chivers is the son of a former head chauffeur for the royals and said: "**I was lucky enough to go everywhere with my father. I used to go up to Balmoral in the school holidays as well as to Sandringham and Windsor Castle. I played cricket with both princesses and it was a happy time. The princesses were both very good.**"

- A Queensland teenager became a right royal hit in the UK in 2011 after scoring an unbeaten triple-century in a 40-over match at Windsor Castle. Opening the batting for the Royal Household Cricket Club, 19-year-old Ashley Gray thumped 358 not out against Tambler Valley Ramblers. He obliterated the previous club record of 177 not out, collected 34 sixes and 26 fours and took part in a record opening stand of 354 with David Skirrow (75).

- The father of Sarah Ferguson, the former wife of Prince Andrew, once set up an indoor cricket centre in the Hampshire town of Dummer. Ronald Ferguson's enterprise became one of the most successful in the county.

- Charles Lennox, the second Duke of Richmond, formed his own cricket team which was involved in a highly controversial incident in 1731. When his Sussex-based team took on a Middlesex XI in Chichester, a pre-arranged time for the match to end upset spectators who rioted resulting in some of the players' shirts being ripped off their backs. A grandson of King Charles II, the Duke's own grandson Charles Lennox appeared in over 40 first-class matches. He made his debut in a match against Kent at Islington in 1786 for the White Conduit Club, a forerunner to the MCC.

- A medium-pace bowler who made his debut for Oman in 2011 is a cousin of the Sultan of Oman and bloodline of the Al Bu Sa'idi dynasty, the world's oldest monarchy. Al Said, referred to as His Highness off the field, learnt his cricket while studying at Oxford University in the UK and said: **"My claim to fame was bowling out Marcus Trescothick for a duck during a junior game with Somerset."**

His Highness Qais Khalid Al Said of Oman during the Asian Cricket Council Twenty20 Cup in Kathmandu in 2011

- Although he only appeared in four Tests, India's Yajurvindra Singh, from the royal house of Bilkha in Gujarat, holds two world records. On his Test debut, he snapped up five catches in the first innings and seven in the match, against England in Bangalore in 1976/77.

- The Middlesex cricket team was invited to Buckingham Palace in 1982 to mark their winning of the County Championship. Prince Philip remarked to slow bowler Dermott Monteith that he was the second Irishman to have been in the palace during the year. The first was Michael Fagan, who had famously broken into the Queen's bedroom.

TIM COSTELLO'S DREAM TEAM

Sunil Gavaskar (I)
Jack Hobbs (E)
Don Bradman * (A)
Sachin Tendulkar (I)
Garry Sobers (WI)
Graeme Pollock (SA)
Adam Gilchrist † (A)
Wasim Akram (P)
Courtney Walsh (WI)
Glenn McGrath (A)
Muttiah Muralitharan (SL)

Prominent Australian Baptist minister, the Reverend Tim Costello

- In 2008, an amateur team from the Netherlands, the Dutch Fellowship of Fairly Odd Places Cricket Club, took on the might of the Vatican. The Dutch XI played against a team of young Indian student priests that made up the Vatican national XI at Rome's Stadio dei Marmi. In the Vatican's first-ever game of cricket, the local boys won the 35-over match, reaching their victory target of 59 in the 21st over with one wicket down.

- A former minister at the St John's Wood synagogue opposite Lord's later set up his own version of the MCC in South Africa. Cyril Harris – chief rabbi of the republic from 1987 to 2004 – established the Ministers Cricket Club, a team for players of all faiths.

- David Sheppard, the only ordained minister to have played Test cricket for England, was captain of Cambridge University in 1952 when his opposite number at Oxford was also a man of the cloth. The Reverend Peter Blake, who played first-class cricket for Sussex, scored 20 in the 1952 university match at Lord's, while Sheppard made 127.

While Sheppard (pictured) was the Bishop of Liverpool, Blake captained Chichester in the final of the *Church Times* Cup in 1983. Sheppard appeared in 22 Tests for England, scoring 1,172 runs, with three centuries, at 37.80.

- The Bishop of Wolverhampton scored a divine century in the *Church Times* Cup in 2009. The Reverend Clive Gregory hit a match-winning 103 not out for the Lichfield diocese against Birmingham.

- During a practice session at a cricket ground in Oxford in 1856, the Reverend Walter Fellows smashed a ball a distance of 175 yards, or 160 metres, from hit to pitch. A record distance for a cricket ball to be hit, he appeared in 24 first-class matches, and died in Melbourne in 1901.

- The Right Reverend Ralph Emmerson was a cricket-loving Yorkshire clergyman who conducted weddings during the summer months in white flannels concealed underneath his cassock. A bishop in the 1970s, he also played the game as an opening batsman and slow bowler in the Yorkshire Council League. In 1956, he was appointed vicar of St Michael's Church at Headingley, the home of Yorkshire cricket.

- In 2010, Kevin Pietersen's brother Tony became the new vicar at the Emmanuel Church in the British town of Workington. The Reverend Pietersen, and his family, moved from South Africa to take up the position.

- In a match against a church team in 1912, a bowler by the name of W. Clarke took three hat-tricks in a single innings. Playing for St Augustine's College against Ashford Church Choir in Kent, Clarke took five hat-tricks in the match.

- His Holiness the 17th Karmapa Trinlay Thaye Dorje, also known as the Black Hat Lama of Tibet, lists his heroes as Buddha and England cricketers Kevin Pietersen and Andrew Flintoff. Holding one of the most senior positions in Buddhism, he plays the occasional game of cricket with monks at his home and said: **"Cricket is a great passion of mine. Cricket can bring people together through sharing time at a match, in a united spirit."**

Cricket at a Buddhist monastery at Darjeeling in India

- China accused the Dalai Lama of faking an interest in cricket in 2010 to curry favour with India. Beijing's ire was raised after the spiritual leader of Tibetan Buddhism was seen at an IPL Twenty20 match in Dharamsala, the Dalai Lama's home in exile. He also attended a match at the same venue in 2011, saying: **"My knowledge of cricket is zero. As a monk when I was growing up, I used to play ping pong. But seeing the enormous response of the Indian fans towards the game, I am quite impressed. So many are enjoying, so I am enjoying."**

- If he hadn't turned out to be a fast bowler for the West Indies, Darren Sammy says he may have become a pastor. The West Indies captain was brought up as a Seventh Day Adventist, admitting: **"I am very religious. I wanted to be a pastor growing up. I was very good at it, actually, but cricket came up and I did not look back."**

  In 1990, West Indies fast-bowling legend Wes Hall paid a visit to a church while in Florida and left a changed man. Inspired by the preacher, Hall attended Bible school and was later ordained a minister in the Christian Pentecostal Church.

- On the same day that he was named in Zimbabwe's squad for the 2012 World Twenty20 tournament, Tatenda Taibu switched from cricket to the Church. The then-29-year-old wicketkeeping batsman pulled the plug on an 11-year international career and said: **"I just feel that my true calling now lies in doing the Lord's work, and although I am fortunate and proud to have played for my country, the time has come for me to put my entire focus on that part of my life."**

"I don't know under what circumstances he made the decision to retire at this young age, but my advice to him would be to keep serving God. Service to God should be the ultimate goal of the life."

former West Indies fast bowler Wes Hall

Twenty20 Tidbits

- When Kenya's Steve Tikolo put on 126 with Alex Obanda at Dubai in 2009/10, he became the first batsman to share in three century stands in Twenty20 internationals. Remarkably, all three winning partnerships came in consecutive matches within the space of just ten days.

Pair	Wkt	Stand	Opp	Venue	Date
David Obuya (60*) and Steve Tikolo (46*)	1st	110*	Scotland	Nairobi	01/02/2010
David Obuya (65*) and Steve Tikolo (56*)	1st	126*	Scotland	Nairobi	04/02/2010
Alex Obanda (79) and Steve Tikolo (50*)	1st	126	Canada	Dubai	10/02/2010

- As many as 30 sixes were struck when Chennai took on Rajasthan at Chepauk in the 2010 IPL, a first in Twenty20 cricket. Chennai opener Murali Vijay helped himself to 11 in his match-winning knock of 127, while Rajasthan opener Naman Ojha swiped six in his unbeaten 94. The match also produced a record number of runs from boundaries, with 336 coming off 39 fours and 30 sixes.

- Opening the batting on his Twenty20 international debut, Canada's 18-year-old Hiral Patel scored a fifty and took part in his country's first-ever hundred-run partnership in the shortest form of the game. Patel struck an unbeaten 88 against Ireland in the Associates Twenty20 Series in Colombo in 2009/10, sharing in a second-wicket stand of 101 with Canada's wicketkeeping captain Ashish Bagai (42). Patel's 88, off 61 balls, became the third-highest score by a debutant in Twenty20 internationals, after Australia's Ricky Ponting (98*) and David Warner (89).

- When Zimbabwe and Bangladesh clashed in their first Twenty20 international, a dozen bowlers were used and each took a wicket.

Zimbabwe created a world first in the match at Khulna in 2006/07 with seven out of seven bowlers used each taking a wicket on debut – Gary Brent (2-40), Anthony Ireland (1-33), Elton Chigumbura (1-22), Prosper Utseya (3-25), Sean Williams (1-28), Keith Dabengwa (1-1) and Chamu Chibhabha (1-14). Bangladesh used five bowlers with each taking a wicket on their debuts. Abdur Razzak claimed 3-17.

- Pakistan's Kamran Akmal and Salman Butt launched the 2010 World Twenty20 tournament in the West Indies in fine style with a hundred-run opening partnership with both scoring 73. Their alliance of 142 against Bangladesh at Gros Islet was then the third-highest partnership for any wicket in a Twenty20 international. On his Twenty20 debut – nine years after his first Test – Pakistan fast bowler Mohammad Sami took 3-29, with two wickets coming in a single over.

- After Sri Lankan spinner Dilruwan Perera took three wickets on his Twenty20 international debut against Australia in 2011, a team-mate took a record six in the following match. In the first game of the series that Sri Lanka won 2-0, Perera claimed 3-26 at Pallekele, while fellow spinner Ajantha Mendis (6-16) made history in game two by becoming the first bowler to claim half-a-dozen wickets in a men's Twenty20 international. In 2007, New Zealand's Amy Satterthwaite had become the first bowler to achieve the feat, taking 6-17 in a women's Twenty20 international against England at Taunton.

- An Irishman and a Kiwi bonded at the crease in 2011 by both scoring centuries while opening the batting in a Twenty20 match in Uxbridge. A 44-ball hundred from Kevin O'Brien (119) and a 53-ball one from former NZ Test batsman Hamish Marshall (102) spurred

Twenty20 big-hitter Hamish Marshall

Gloucestershire to a domestic record-high of 254/3 against Middlesex with a record UK opening stand of 192 and the first example of two centuries in a Twenty20 innings. This was only the second occasion in Twenty20 history of two hundreds in a *match*, after Worcestershire's Graeme Hick (110) and Northamptonshire's Lance Klusener (111*) scored centuries at Kidderminster in 2007.

- A Twenty20 match at Northampton in 2010 went down to the wire with 13 runs off the final ball needed for victory. Yorkshire medium-pacer Richard Pyrah conceded two extras from a no-ball which Nicky Boje hit for six, then Boje struck the extra delivery to the boundary for four to tie the match. Earlier, Yorkshire's South African import Herschelle Gibbs struck a maiden Twenty20 century, reaching 101 not out off 53 balls.

- In 2004, Queensland all-rounder Andrew Symonds hit the highest score for Kent in 20-over cricket, with 146 against Lancashire at Tunbridge Wells. In 2010, and now playing for Surrey, Symonds took 5-18 against his old team, at Beckenham, the best bowling figures in Twenty20 cricket versus Kent. In the same match, teenager Jason Roy, a batsman yet to engage in first-class cricket, became the first player to score a Twenty20 century for Surrey. Appearing in just his third match, 19-year-old Roy struck an unbeaten 101, from 57 deliveries, adding 63 runs from 27 with Symonds, who made 31.

- After Keith Barker took a Twenty20 hat-trick against Yorkshire in 2010, he took a wicket first up in his next match to make it four in four. The Warwickshire left-arm quick took 4-19 – and a hat-trick – in the Friends Provident match at Birmingham and then 2-23 two days later against Worcestershire on the same ground.

  The Warwickshire–Worcestershire match featured just one 50 off the bat, an unbeaten 53 from Jonathan Trott. He was the only opening batsman in the match not to fall for a first-ball duck.

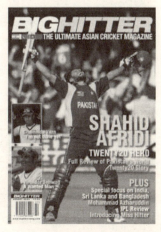

- Shahid Afridi celebrated his 50th Twenty20 international with a fifty. The first player to appear in as many matches, Afridi hit an unbeaten 52 against Sri Lanka at Hambantota in 2012.

- Pakistan import Abdul Razzaq was mauled during a Twenty20 match at Taunton in 2010, conceding a record 16 runs per over. Representing Hampshire, Razzaq failed to take a wicket against Somerset on his way to figures of 4-0-64-0, which, at the time, were the eighth most expensive bowling stats in Twenty20 history. The week before, his Hampshire team-mate Danny Briggs returned figures of 4-0-5-3 against Kent at Canterbury, which represented the fourth most economical return in Twenty20 cricket.

- Despite his burgeoning reputation as a Twenty20 specialist, Australia's David Warner failed to reach 50 in 13 innings for Middlesex in 2010. His best of 43 came in his penultimate match, against Hampshire at Southampton. He finished his contract for the summer in a match at Chelmsford, smashing 37 off 20 balls, his second-best knock of the season. He pummelled five consecutive boundaries off Maurice Chambers, an attack that prompted an exchange of words between the two before intervention from one of the umpires and the Essex captain James Foster.

- Due to a depleted squad during its tour of England in 2011, India's elder statesman Rahul Dravid appeared in his first game of Twenty20 international cricket, becoming the first player to make his debut and retire in the same match. Aged 38 years and 232 days, Dravid became the oldest player from a Test nation to appear in a Twenty20 international. Batting at number three in the match against England at Manchester, Dravid impressed with 31, which included three consecutive sixes off the bowling of Samit Patel.

- A Champions League match in 2009/10 was delayed by more than 90 minutes at Bangalore's Chinnaswamy Stadium due to a bomb scare. Police discovered traces of explosives in a bag owned by a young cricketer who had been staying at the ground's academy. He was arrested, and later released without charge, with the Cape Cobras defeating the Victoria Bushrangers in a match reduced to 17 overs per side. Monde Zondeki accounted for the Victorian openers Rob Quiney (0) and Brad Hodge (0) with the first and third balls of the match. Bizarrely, the pair was dismissed for ducks in their next match, just four days later, both batsmen falling to Australian slow bowler Nathan Hauritz in a semi-final in Delhi.

- Two Australian-born cricketers took a hat-trick on the same day during England's Twenty20 Cup in 2008. On 15 June, the West Australian-born Leicestershire all-rounder Jim Allenby became the first bowler to take four wickets in four balls in Twenty20 cricket, with 5-21 against Lancashire at Manchester. The eighth bowler to take a Twenty20 hat-trick in England, Victorian left-armer Dirk Nannes (4-28), had become the seventh, for Middlesex against Essex at Chelmsford, on the same afternoon.

Allenby, who was born in Perth in 1982, made a single appearance for his state, given a go in the Australian Twenty20 Big Bash tournament in 2006/07. Opening the batting with Luke Ronchi against South Australia at Perth, Allenby scored four – a boundary – and was not required to bowl. In 2009, Allenby hit three fifties in a row opening for Leicestershire, including a maiden Twenty20 century (110), against Nottinghamshire.

- Former Zimbabwe Test batsman Mark Vermeulen struck a half-century in his first three Twenty20 matches, doing so in two days in 2009. On 13 May, Vermeulen hit 74 on his Twenty20 debut for Westerns against Easterns, and then smacked 108 against Centrals at Bulawayo. The next day, he made it three fifties in three innings with 53 against Northerns on the same ground. He missed out by just three runs in making it four in four, dismissed for 47 against Westerns on the same day he made his 53.

- Batting for the first time in a Twenty20 international since 2008, a recalled Justin Ontong smashed four consecutive sixes against New Zealand at Wellington in 2011/12. The South African all-rounder hit a quickfire 32, punishing Kane Williamson, who went for 26 runs in his second over. With four sixes, but no other boundaries, James Franklin (28) matched Ontong's feat in the following match at Hamilton, while Richard Levi (117*) exploded with the fastest Twenty20 international century to date. Appearing in just his second match for South Africa, Levi became the first batsman to hit more than ten sixes in a Twenty20 international, getting 13, and reaching his hundred off a record-low 45 balls.

- A 12th man took out the man-of-the-match award during the Friends Provident Twenty20 tournament in the UK in 2010. Leicestershire's Matt Boyce lifted the prize after running out three Warwickshire batsmen in the match at Birmingham.

- Rana Kalangutkar only appeared in two matches in the shortest form of the game, becoming the first 14-year-old to play domestic Twenty20 cricket. Aged 14 years and 168 days, he debuted for Goa against Karnataka in India's Inter State Twenty20 Tournament in 2006/07. He batted at number 11, scoring an unbeaten five, and was not called on to bowl.

- When Carlton Saunders made his debut for Turks and Caicos in 2007/08, he became the first 50-year-old to play top-class Twenty20 cricket. Saunders failed to take a wicket and was not required to bat in the game, against Montserrat in Coolidge during the Stanford 20/20 series.

Aged 50 years and 92 days, he was joined in the team by his 41-year-old debutant brother, Henry. Another 14 over-40s made their debuts in the tournament, with 49-year-old Mario Ford, an all-rounder, representing the Bahamas. His brother, 44-year-old Andrew, also made his Twenty20 debut in the tournament, playing together in a match against Jamaica.

A number of youngsters, including two 16-year-olds, also played in the tournament. Montserrat's Shernyl Burns – at 16 years and 110 days – was the youngest, debuting in the same match as the oldest, 50-year-old Charlton Saunders from Turks and Caicos.

- Three old-timers dusted off the cobwebs in the Australian summer of 2011/12 to play in the Twenty20 Big Bash League. Appearing in his first professional match since 2008, 40-year-old Stuart MacGill (4-0-21-2) starred on debut for the Sydney Sixers, dismissing the Brisbane Heat opening pair Matthew Hayden and Brendon McCullum in the opening game at the SCG. It was his first domestic Twenty20 match since 2003, with a record eight years and 175 days between appearances.

Match number two featured Shane Warne (2-0-19-0), aged 42, playing for the Melbourne Stars, while 40-year-old Brad Hogg (3-0-27-1) made his big-time comeback for the Perth Scorchers. A leading light in the BBL, Hogg was recalled for the national team for a Twenty20 series against India following his retirement in 2008 and said: "**It's unbelievable. I feel like I'm 21 again and to be honest it's just a dream come**

WHAT IS STANFORD 20/20 CRICKET?

OK, IMAGINE BASEBALL, BUT WITH PARTIES, WAY MORE COLOR, BLACK BATS, CHICKEN ROTIS, HORNS, SINGING FROGS, A WHOLE DIFFERENT SET OF RULES, NO STRIKES, HUNDREDS OF RUNS, MORE ACTION, MORE WAYS TO SCORE, MORE WAYS TO GET HURT, THE BATTER PLAYS OFFENSE AND DEFENSE, THE BATTER IS CALLED A "BATSMAN," COOLER UNIFORMS, RUM, LOTS OF RUM, THE OCCASIONAL GOAT, MORE WARRIORS, LESS WHINING, MORE HEAT, MORE HUMIDITY, THE FIELDERS CATCH BARE-HANDED, NO EMPTY SEATS, STANDING ROOM ONLY, NO PRIMADONNAS, PLAYERS THAT CARE AND HAVE PASSION, FANS THAT CARE AND HAVE PASSION, 2/3 OF THE WORLD IS WATCHING, SINGERS, FIRE EATERS, DANCING, LOTS OF DANCING, MORE MUSIC, ON AN ISLAND, PLAYERS THAT EARN THEIR MONEY, MORE SPECTACULAR PLAYS, AND FT. COLLINS, YOU GOTTA SEE THIS.

LEARN CRICKET AT YOUGOTTASEETHIS2020.COM THEN WATCH! JANUARY 26 - FEBRUARY 24

true." On his return to the Australian side in Sydney, Hogg had missed a record number of Twenty20 internationals (40) over a five-year period since his last game, against England at the SCG in 2007/08.

- The West Indies launched the 2007 ICC World Twenty20 in spectacular fashion by hoisting a 200-run total and the first international century in the shortest form of the game. Chris Gayle scored 117, hit ten sixes and took part in a 145-run opening stand with Devon Smith (35) in the match against South Africa in Johannesburg. Herschelle Gibbs (90*) and Justin Kemp (46*) then combined for a match-winning second-wicket stand of 120, the first time both teams had achieved a century partnership in the same Twenty20 international.

- England opened their account against the Netherlands at the 2009 World Twenty20 in style by recording their first-ever century stand for the first wicket. Ravi Bopara, with 46, and Luke Wright (71), took the opening partnership to 102, but it was the Netherlands who stole the show, successfully chasing down a total of 163 thanks to a man-of-the-match 49 from Tom de Grooth. Victorian debutant Dirk Nannes was also a part of the winning team, having opened the bowling with figures of 4-0-30-0. After two matches with the men in orange, he became the first player to appear for two countries in Twenty20 internationals, making his debut for Australia a few weeks later against England at Old Trafford.

- Tamil Nadu all-rounder Chandrasekharan Ganapathy had a horror trot with the bat in 2006/07, copping three ducks in four days during an Indian domestic Twenty20 tournament. In his next Twenty20 innings, a whole 29 months later, he made it four ducks in a row.

- Two debutants opened the bowling for the West Indies in a Twenty20 international in 2011, sharing four wickets between them and an unexpected win. Left-arm medium-pacer Krishmar Santokie – who had yet to play first-class cricket – took 1-17 against England (88) at The Oval, while fellow debutant Garey Mathurin, a left-arm spinner, took a match-winning 3-9.

- A few days after scoring his first Test century, David Warner brought up his maiden ton in domestic Twenty20 cricket. In his first match as captain of the Sydney Thunder franchise in the just-launched Big Bash League in 2011/12, Warner scored a match-winning 102 not out against the Melbourne Stars at the MCG. With a strike rate of exactly 200.00, the dynamic opener thrashed six fours and six sixes.

  Warne's opening partner, Chris Gayle, went to town in the Thunder's next match, becoming the first batsman to score ten sixes in a domestic Twenty20 match in Australia. Playing against the Adelaide

Strikers in Sydney, Gayle smashed 11 sixes on his way to a match-winning 100 not out, scored off 54 balls.

- Scotland opened the bowling with two debutants in a T20 international against Afghanistan at Sharjah in 2012/13 and both claimed a wicket in their first over. Iain Wardlaw took 2-30, while Neil Carter took 2-27. Matt Machan, also on his debut, took the most wickets (3-23) and scored the most runs (42*) for Scotland in a match won by Afghanistan by 27 runs.

- A few days after scoring 116 in a 50-over match against Scotland in 2011, Namibia's Craig Williams repeated the dose in a Twenty20 match against the same opposition and at the same venue. Opening the batting at Windhoek, Williams hit 116 – off 48 balls – with two fours and 14 sixes, a record number for his country.

    Williams hit a second Twenty20 ton a month later, again at Windhoek, scoring 125 against Kenya, a match that featured two 150-run partnerships. The first, of 160 between Kenya's Collins Obuya (100*) and Rakep Patel (73*) for the third wicket, was followed by a 154-run stand – also for the third wicket – between Williams and Raymond van Schoor (33*). Williams's match-winning knock included ten fours and eight sixes. The following day, in another game against Kenya at Windhoek, his team-mate Louis van der Westhuizen hit a match-winner, reaching 145 off 50 balls with 14 fours and 12 sixes. He got to the 100 mark off just 35 deliveries, one ball shy of Andrew Symonds's world-record 34-ball century for Kent versus Middlesex at Maidstone in 2004.

- New Zealand's domestic Twenty20 tournament in 2011/12 threw up a slew of records, with four centuries and a world record double-hundred partnership in three consecutive matches in three days. In an HRV Cup match at Auckland, both sides made 200-run totals with two unbeaten centuries from openers. Batting first, Auckland made 202/4 with 100 not out from Pakistan import Azhar Mahmood. In reply, Canterbury finished with 205/3, punctuated by an unbeaten 101 from Rob Nicol, both batsmen reaching the 50-run mark off 31 balls.

    The following day, at New Plymouth, Central Districts openers Jamie How and Peter Ingram both smashed eight sixes while putting on 201 against Wellington at New Plymouth, the first-ever double-century partnership for the first wicket in Twenty20 cricket. While How, with 102, brought up a maiden Twenty20 ton, his partner missed out, dismissed for 97. An oddity occurred in the next day's match at Hamilton with Kane Williamson and Tim Southee opening both the batting and bowling for Northern Districts against Otago. Brendon

McCullum – who was playing in two different domestic Twenty20 tournaments at the same time – scored an unbeaten 103, with seven fours and eight sixes. McCullum racked up a few frequent flyer points over the summer, criss-crossing the Tasman and playing for both Otago in the HRV Cup and for Brisbane Heat in the Australian Big Bash League.

Score	Batsman	4s	6s	Match	Date
100*	Azhar Mahmood	10	3	Auckland v Canterbury	17/01/2012
101*	Rob Nicol	3	9	Canterbury v Auckland	17/01/2012
102	Jamie How	8	8	Central Districts v Wellington	18/01/2012
103*	Brendon McCullum	7	8	Otago v Northern Districts	19/01/2012

- En route to an easy win over Northamptonshire in 2010, Pakistan's Shahid Afridi retired out, the first such instance in Twenty20 cricket. Afridi left the field with his score on 42, whipped up off just 14 balls with six fours and two sixes.

- A Malaysian-born spinner rewrote the record books in 2011 by becoming the first bowler to take six wickets for less than ten runs in a Twenty20 match. Playing for Somerset against Glamorgan at Cardiff, Arul Suppiah took a match-winning 6-5, a world record performance that beat Sohail Tanvir's 6-14 for Rajasthan in the 2008 IPL.

- After picking up 3-21 with the ball in a Twenty20 international against New Zealand at Wellington in 2006/07, a rampaging Sanath Jayasuriya scored a record 80 per cent of Sri Lanka's reply with the bat. Opening up with Upul Tharanga, Jayasuriya thrashed an unbeaten 51 in the rain, collecting ten fours and a six off 23 balls in 23 minutes. In a match decided by the Duckworth-Lewis system, the visitors reached 62/1 to secure an 18-run victory.

- In a Twenty20 international at Bridgetown in 2010, Ravindra Jadeja was called upon twice to bowl and was carted for six consecutive sixes. In his first over, Shane Watson hit his last three deliveries for six, while David Warner hit the first three balls of his next over for six. Jadeja's two overs cost him 38 runs, while Watson hit 54 with six sixes and Warner 72 with seven sixes, the two sharing an opening stand of 104.

- Although Afghanistan lost the final of the 2011/12 World Twenty20 Qualifier tournament, the up-and-comers began the match at Dubai with a six and took a wicket with the first ball of Ireland's innings. Chasing a victory target of 153, Ireland's Paul Stirling smashed 79 off 38 balls, reaching his fifty off 17, which, at the time, was the second-fastest Twenty20 international half-century of all time, behind Yuvraj Singh's 12-ball effort against England at Durban in 2007/08.

- Playing for his third Twenty20 side in three different countries in three months, Chris Gayle scored a century on his debut on the opening day of the 2011/12 Bangladesh Premier League. Batting with Pakistan's Ahmed Shehzad (56*), Gayle unleashed a brutal unbeaten 101 off 44 balls, taking part in a world record partnership of 167 for the Barisal Burners against the Sylhet Royals at Mirpur. It was the highest opening stand batting second in Twenty20 cricket, with Gayle helping himself to seven fours and ten sixes.

  Three months previously, Gayle had struck an unbeaten 109 for the Zimbabwe side Matabeleland Tuskers in the Stanbic Bank Twenty20 and three weeks later an unbeaten 102 on his debut for the Sydney Thunders in the Australian Twenty20 Big Bash.

- A 17-year-old powered his side to victory in 2011/12 with a five-wicket haul on his Twenty20 debut. Zia-ul-Haq, a Pakistan Under-19s player, picked up a man-of-the-match 5-23 for the Lahore Lions against the Faisalabad Wolves in Rawalpindi. In the same competition the day before, the Lahore Eagles lost four wickets – with three run-outs – off the final three balls of their innings against Rawalpindi Rams.

- A 20-over match played at Nairobi in 2009/10 was tied after Uganda's Arthur Kyobe carried his bat for his maiden Twenty20 fifty. Chasing Scotland's 109 in the second match of the Kenya Twenty20 Tri-Series, Kyobe got to 51 with the scores level and was only the third batsman to carry his bat in Twenty20 cricket. Scotland then triumphed in a one-over eliminator to decide the match.

- As a 16-year-old, England batsman Alex Hales once hit 55 runs off a single over in a Twenty20 game at Lord's. Picked for his fast bowling, Hales took advantage of three no-balls, clubbing eight sixes and a four in a 25-ball innings of 69. He said: **"That is as well as I've ever hit the ball. My natural instinct is to attack and I've always been a big hitter, so Twenty20 suits me."**

  On his England debut in 2011 – a Twenty20 international against India at Old Trafford – Hales was out for a duck, but came back powerfully in his second match with an unbeaten half-century in a record-breaking win. Opening the batting against the West Indies at The Oval, Hales belted his way to 62 not out, and in partnership with Craig Kieswetter (58*) guided England to their first ten-wicket win in a Twenty20 international. Their 128-run opening stanza became England's best in the game, and their first century partnership in a Twenty20 international against Test-playing opponents. Ravi Bopara – who coincidentally was part of England's only other century opening stand at the time, against the Netherlands in 2009 – starred with the ball, taking 4-10, creating new best figures by an England bowler in Twenty20 internationals.

- South Africa hosted a one-off Twenty20 international against India in 2011/12, in which the winners prevailed without taking a single wicket. Chasing a target of 83 from 7.5 overs in a match marred by rain, India's openers Robin Uthappa and Gautam Gambhir made it unscathed to 71. All six South Africans who made it to the crease left with a strike rate in excess of 145.00, with the highest of 533.33 from Albie Morkel (16*), who hit a four and two sixes off the only three balls he faced.

  Two weeks later in the IPL, Morkel, playing for the Chennai Super Kings, stunned the Royal Challengers by smashing 28 off seven balls with two fours and three sixes for a strike rate of 400.00. Earlier in the game, Vinay Kumar posted a 600.00 strike rate, hitting a six off the only ball he faced.

- When Titans' number three batsman Faf du Plessis picked up 5-28 at Johannesburg in 2011/12, he became the first bowler to take five wickets in an innings in two consecutive Twenty20 matches. The seventh bowler used against the Lions, he came into the match having taken 5-19 in his previous Twenty20 appearance, five months before, against Easterns at Pretoria.

- In his final Twenty20 international, Australia's Brett Lee bowled the West Indies' Fidel Edwards for a first-ball duck, and then went the same way himself when batting, courtesy of the same player. Lee got Edwards with what turned out to be his final ball in Twenty20 internationals, and, curiously, both fast bowlers took career-best figures of 3-23 in the match at Bridgetown in 2011/12.

- Bangladesh spinner Elias Sunny followed a five-wicket haul in his first Test innings with another on his debut in Twenty20 internationals. With match-winning figures of 5-13, and a maiden over, against Ireland at Belfast in 2012, Sunny became the first bowler to take a five-for on his Twenty20 international debut. In the same match, fellow debutant Ziaur Rahman also made the record books, hitting an unbeaten 40, an innings that contained five sixes but not a single four.

  Chasing 191 for victory, Ireland fell short by 71, after posting a record ninth-wicket stand in all Twenty20 internationals. Gary Wilson (41*) and the number ten batsman Max Sorensen (12*) put on 47 runs in partnership.

- After making his first-class debut for New South Wales in 2011/12, Timm van der Gugten starred on his debut for the Netherlands with a five-wicket haul against Sussex in the 2012 Caribbean Twenty20 tournament. In a match won by the English county side, the 20-year-old paceman took 5-21, with the Netherlands bowling opened by another debutant from Australia, former WA batsman Michael Swart.

- Batting at number seven in a 2007 World Twenty20 match at Johannesburg, Dwayne Smith smashed four sixes and a four off just seven balls. The West Indies batsman went ballistic against Bangladesh, hitting 29 in seven minutes at the crease, finishing with a record strike rate of 414.28.

  Opening the batting for the Windies against New Zealand at Lauderhill in Florida in 2012, Smith hit the first ball of the match for six, and repeated the dose off the fourth ball. In the second of the two-game series, Smith got a six off the second and third balls of the match.

- When the Rawalpindi Rams beat the Sialkot Stallions at Lahore in 2010/11, it brought to an end the longest winning streak in Twenty20 history. Chasing 198 for their 26th win in a row, the Stallions pulled up 13 runs short, after Hammad Azam took 4-50. Between February 2006 and October 2010, the Stallions had won a world-record 25 consecutive Twenty20 matches.

  During the same competition – the Faysal Bank T-20 Cup – in 2011/12, the Quetta Bears established another world record, but this time in the negative. By losing to the Falcons at Karachi, the Bears incurred their 20th consecutive defeat in Twenty20 cricket, becoming the first team to do so.

- In a warm-up match against New Zealand in the 2012 World Twenty20 tournament, the South African pair Richard Levi and Faf du Plessis were dismissed for the same score by the same fielding and bowling combination having both faced the same number of balls. Both were caught by the wicketkeeper B.J. Watling off Adam Milne for 24 off 20 balls, after both had scored two fours and a six.

- One ball into the 17th over of a Twenty20 match against Gloucestershire at Hove in 2012, Sussex's Murray Goodwin brought up a 50, while his partner, Scott Styris, was on 27. After 19.4 overs, Goodwin had progressed by just one, whereas Styris had raced to 100. The 37-year-old New Zealand all-rounder reached his hundred off 37 balls in 37 minutes, hitting five fours and nine sixes. James Fuller was harshly treated, conceding 19 runs per over with figures of 1-57 off three. Styris collected a record 38 runs, including three sixes, off his final over, and said: "**I'm just pleased I got a few in the middle. I'm just a slogger these days. They all seem to go, even when I don't want them to.**"

- During their record low total of 80 in a Twenty20 international, England secured a first in the shortest form of the game with players batting at number one and at number 11 making the two highest scores of the innings. Opener Craig Kieswetter hit 35, while the last man Jade Dernbach contributed 13 in the match, against India in Colombo during the 2012 World Twenty20. In his first match for India in a year, Harbhajan Singh starred with 4-12, a record bowling performance by an Indian bowler in Twenty20 internationals.

- When Virender Sehwag struck 73 against Rajasthan Royals in the 2012 IPL, he became the first batsman to string together five consecutive half-centuries in Twenty20 cricket. With previous innings of 57, 87 not out, 73 and 63, the Delhi Daredevils' captain beat the previous best of four consecutive Twenty20 fifties, a record shared by Kent's Joe Denly, Queensland's Lee Carseldine and Somerset's Marcus Trescothick.

- Chris Gayle became the first batsman to top 1,500 runs in Twenty20 cricket in a calendar year when he passed the historic milestone during his stint with the Sydney Thunder in the 2012/13 Big Bash League. The West Indian struck 1,532 runs in 38 innings with three centuries, 13 fifties and a strike rate of 151.68. The previous best had been 1,497 by Gayle himself in 31 innings the previous year.

- Australia annihilated India in a 2012 World Twenty20 match, with Shane Watson and David Warner becoming the first pair to score 1,000 runs for the first wicket. Chasing 141 for victory in Colombo, the Australians made it to 100 off exactly ten overs, winning the match in 14.5, then the fewest number of overs to chase down a Twenty20 international target of 140-plus.

  Watson dominated by scoring 72 off 42 balls with seven sixes, while Warner hit an unbeaten 63 off 41. Their opening stand of 133 represented a new high for Australia for any wicket in a Twenty20 international, with Warner and Watson becoming the first opening pair to produce three century partnerships for the first wicket. Earlier, Watson had taken 3-34 – it was the 12th consecutive Twenty20 international in which he bowled that he had taken a wicket, a new world record, and he made it 13 in a row in his next match with 2-29 against South Africa. With another score of 70, Watson won his fourth consecutive man-of-the match award in the tournament, his eighth overall, overtaking Pakistan's Shahid Afridi.

- A local derby between the Big Bash League Melbourne teams lived up to its name in the 2012/13 edition with an ugly mid-pitch altercation between Shane Warne and Marlon Samuels. When the West Indies import was batting for the Renegades, Warne, the captain of the

Melbourne Stars, all of a sudden lost his cool, man-handling Samuels and screaming **"f**k you Marlon"**. A few minutes later, tensions reached boiling point when he threw the ball-hitting Samuels, who then hurled his bat down the pitch in the direction of Warne.

The spat was a follow-on from an earlier incident in which Samuels had grabbed the shirt of David Hussey to stop him taking a run. Hussey said: **"I think he** [Samuels] **tried to block me to prevent me from taking a two, but in hindsight it probably prevented me from running myself out, so it was probably a good thing."**

Two overs later, Samuels's night was over when he top-edged a ball from Lasith Malinga into his helmet and had to leave the field with a bloodied face. The fiery clash – won by the Renegades – was played in front of an MCG crowd in excess of 46,000, a record for an Australian domestic Twenty20 match.

- Pakistan gobbled up South Africa at Centurion in 2012/13 with Umar Gul taking 5-6 for the second time in his T20 career. Pakistan began the match with a hefty 195/7, and Mohammad Hafeez (86) becoming the first Pakistani to pass the 1,000-run milestone in T20 internationals and later the first to achieve the all-round double of 80 runs and three wickets in a match. Gul's 5-6 included the first instance of three batsmen being dismissed first ball by the same bowler in a T20 international.

Family History

- Identical twins Hamish and James Marshall both topped 170 in the same innings of a first-class match in New Zealand's Plunket Shield in 2009/10. During Northern Districts' record-busting 726 against Canterbury at Rangiora, all 11 batsmen reached double figures, with Hamish out for 170 and James unbeaten on 178.

- A special cricket match took place in England in 2011 that celebrated an event 18 years previously when three members of a cricket club became fathers within 13 hours of each other. All three sons went to follow in their fathers' footsteps to play cricket together. A 20-over 'Dads and Lads' match was played to note the 18th birthdays of Michael Bodo, John Wigfield and Jack Fuller, whose fathers had all played for the Flitwick cricket club.

- When Zimbabwe re-entered the Test arena in 2011, two of the debutants in its first match in almost six years – against Bangladesh in Harare – were the sons of former first-class cricketers. Craig Ervine's father, Rory, played three matches for Rhodesia in 1977/78, while Kyle Jarvis's dad, Malcolm, played in five Tests for Zimbabwe in the early 1990s, including the country's first.

- Appearing in his first first-class match in his native Zimbabwe in six years, Sean Ervine posted two 150-plus centuries and a 150-run stand with his brother Craig. Playing for Southern Rocks against Mid West Rhinos at Masvingo in 2009/10, Sean scored 208 – his maiden first-class double-century – in the first innings, adding 178 for the fifth wicket with Craig, who hit 81. In the second innings, Sean scored 160 and 368 for the match.

- During a tour of England by the New Zealand women's team in 1954, an aunt of Kiwi all-rounder James Franklin batted for over five hours to save a Test match at Worcester. Appearing in just her second Test, Joyce Clothier scored an unbeaten 37 at the top of the order off 134 overs faced by the New Zealanders (174/6), who had been set a target of 338 for victory.

- Dan Rixon, the son of former Australian Test wicketkeeper Steve Rixon, took all ten innings wickets in a club match in Scotland in 2011. A wicketkeeper himself, Dan took his record-breaking haul of 10-21 when asked to bowl for the Edinburgh Academicals XI against Gala in the Scottish Cup. In 2008, Rixon had topped the run-scoring charts for Surrey county league side Morrow, hitting 881 runs, with three centuries, at 62.93.

- Following a three-year hiatus, Mali Richards was back in the first-class game in 2009/10, making his debut for his father Viv's former team, the Leeward Islands. Opening the batting against Trinidad and Tobago in Barbados, Mali made scores of two and six. Prior to his Caribbean first-class debut, Mali had appeared in a dozen matches for Oxford and MCC, the last in 2007.

- When identical twins Mark and Maurits Jonkman represented the Netherlands in the British CB40 competition in 2010, the tournament's programme mistakenly featured the same photograph for each player. Both are medium-pace bowlers, with Mark making his one-day international debut in 2006 and Maurits playing in his first match the following year.

The Netherlands' pace-bowling identical twins
Mark and Maurits Jonkman

- When Kenya took on the Netherlands in Nairobi in 2009/10, their two debutants were related to other Kenyan one-day international cricketers. Shem Ngoche joined his brother Nehemiah Odhiambo in the team, while fellow newcomer, the unrelated Nelson Odhiambo, is the nephew of Thomas Odoyo, who made his ODI debut in 1995/96.

- South African-born Wellington batsman Craig Cachopa made his first-class debut in 2011/12, losing his wicket in the match against Auckland to his brother Bradley. He became the third brother in the Cachopa family to play first-class cricket after Carl, who made his debut for Auckland in 2004/05.

- A nephew of former England opener Chris Tavaré made his debut in first-class cricket in 2010, opening the batting against his uncle's former county. Playing for Loughborough MCC University against Kent at Canterbury, Will Tavaré was dismissed for a duck in his first innings. Another of Chris's nephews played cricket, with Matthew Tavaré appearing for the Gloucestershire Under-14s in 2008.

- At the end of the 1993 Ashes series, both Steve and Mark Waugh commanded a Test career average of 39. After his first 27 Tests, Mark had an average of 39.34, alongside a 39-run bowling average and 39 catches. His highest score with the bat had been 139 not out against the West Indies at St John's in 1990/91. Steve had played in 58 Tests by that time, averaging 39.44.

- In a first-class career of 648 matches, Ernest Tyldesley achieved 102 centuries. His older brother Johnny made 86 hundreds in 608 matches. Both played for Lancashire and England, both scored in excess of 35,000 runs, and both had a career average in the 40s. Johnny, who made his Test debut in 1898/99, had a top score of 295 not out, while Ernest, who first played for England in 1921, had a best score of 256 not out. Their combined total of 188 centuries and 76,771 runs are both records for a pair of brothers in first-class cricket.

THE FIRST-CLASS CAREER RECORDS OF THE TYLDESLEY BROTHERS

Johnny Tyldesley (1898/99 to 1909)

M	Inns	NO	Runs	HS	Avge	100s	50s
608	994	62	37897	295*	40.66	86	193

Ernest Tyldesley (1921 to 1928/29)

M	Inns	NO	Runs	HS	Avge	100s	50s
648	961	106	38874	256*	45.56	102	191

- Test wicketkeeper David Bairstow fathered two wicketkeeping sons, one of whom also played for England. In 2011, Jonny Bairstow scored an eye-catching unbeaten 41 on his one-day international debut against India at Cardiff, becoming just the 13th son to follow in the footsteps of his father. David appeared in 21 ODIs, and four Tests, with his other son, Andy, also playing first-class cricket, appearing in three matches for Derbyshire in 1995.

- The one-day international between India and New Zealand at Delhi in 1999/2000 marked a special family moment with the Indian pair of Vinit Gupte and Surinder Sharma standing in the middle. Their fathers – M.Y. Gupte and Har Sharma – had both umpired Test matches, although not together.

- When Ann Browne played at the 1993 World Cup, she became the third member of her family to represent the West Indies. A wicketkeeper, she appeared in 11 one-day internationals, the final one as West Indies captain in 1997/98. Her older sister Louise played in nine Tests and eight ODIs, making her debut as captain in the first Test against Australia at Montego Bay in 1975/76. Their younger sister Beverly also made her Test debut in the same match as Louise, going on to appear in a total of 11 Tests and eight one-dayers.

- Anil Lashkari and his son Neil both played cricket and batted alongside each other in a major ICC tournament. Anil appeared in a dozen first-class matches, mostly for the Indian side Gujarat, in the 1950s, and batted with his son in three matches for the United States, against Israel, Sri Lanka and Wales, in the 1979 ICC Trophy in England.

- When Yorkshire won the County Championship in 2001, two of their squad were brothers-in-law. Darren Lehmann, who married Craig White's sister Andrea, scored close to 1,500 first-class runs for the county, while his brother-in-law topped 500. Yorkshire-born White – who represented Australia in Under-19 Tests – opposed his brother-in-law during the 2002/03 Ashes, dismissing him in consecutive innings, for five at Adelaide and 42 at Perth. In one-day international cricket, White began and ended his career with matches against Australia, nabbing Lehmann (37) for a third time during his farewell appearance for England in the 2003 World Cup at Port Elizabeth.

- Within his first dozen matches at Test level, the West Indies' Darren Bravo had scored double the number of centuries as his famous cousin Brian Lara had achieved at the same time. Batting against India at Kolkata in 2011/12, Bravo's 136 was the West Indies' 100th Test hundred against India bringing them level with England, which, at the time, also had exactly 100 Test tons against the Indians.

Bravo's Test numbers after 12 matches – 941 runs at 47.05 – were identical to those of Lara after his first 12. He said: "**I am quite** honoured by the fact I am compared with Brian Lara. He is definitely my role model. I play my natural game and look something like Lara, but nevertheless I know that emulating him will be difficult."

	Inns	Runs	Avge	Balls	SR	100s	50s	4s	6s	Boundary runs
Lara	20	941	47.05	1517	62.03	1	7	119	3	494
Bravo	20	941	47.05	1996	47.14	2	6	97	17	490

"My mother and Brian are first cousins. My grandfather [mother's father] is Brian Lara's mother's brother."

Darren Bravo

"He will bat and bat and bat. He does not bowl, all he likes to do is bat. He has patterned himself on the great Brian Lara and we all know how Lara liked big hundreds."

Darren Bravo's half-brother, the Test-playing Dwayne Bravo

The batting style of Savion Lara, Brian Lara's 17-year-old cousin in 2011

● During the Sydney grade competition in 1935/36, three brothers from the Central Cumberland club combined to take all ten wickets in an innings. In a first-grade match against Paddington, Arthur Howell took 4-31, while Norman took 4-43 and Bill 2-17. Identical twins

David and Dennis Hourn shared all ten wickets in two matches for Waverley, a unique performance in Sydney grade cricket.

BROTHERS TAKING ALL TEN WICKETS IN AN INNINGS IN SYDNEY FIRST-GRADE CRICKET

Frank (6-24) and Stanley (4-33) Ridge	Manly v Canterbury	1894/95
William (6-47) and Ernest (4-49) Hume	Redfern v Sydney	1900/01
Arthur (4-31), Norman (4-43) and Bill (2-17) Howell	Central Cumberland v Paddington	1935/36
Norman (8-32) and Alan (2-27) McGilvray	Paddington v Glebe	1936/37
Vince (5-35) and Vic (5-58) Emery	North Sydney v St George	1955/56
Dennis (9-72) and David (1-25) Hourn	Waverley v Central Cumberland	1974/75
Dennis (5-43) and David (5-32) Hourn	Waverley v Sydney	1981/82
John (8-99) and Paul (2-101) Grimble	Sydney University v Penrith	1992/93

- A pair of brothers joined forces in a match in South Africa in 2011/12, with each picking up a five-wicket haul in the same innings. Representing Namibia in a first-class match against KwaZulu-Natal in Pietermaritzburg, Nicholass Scholtz took 5-103 while his younger brother Bernard Scholtz took 5-112.

- A family of cricketers celebrated a day of unbridled success during the Cornwall League in England in 2007 with one member taking a hat-trick. Martin Strick struck 41, along with his hat-trick, for the Redruth XI in the first division while his brother Adrian hit a half-century for the second XI. In another grade, their father Tony scored an unbeaten 60, with his teenage nephew Nathan hitting an unbeaten 32 after Nathan's dad Roger had taken 5-24.

- When Zimbabwe hosted New Zealand in a Twenty20 international at Harare in 2011/12, one debutant from each side was the son of a former Test player. The 21-year-old Doug Bracewell became the third member of his family to have represented New Zealand, with his father, Brendon, appearing in six Tests and one one-day international. Doug's uncle John Bracewell played in 41 Tests and 53 ODIs, while two other uncles – Douglas and Mark – played first-class cricket, as did a cousin, Michael. For Zimbabwe, Malcolm Waller – the son of Andy Waller, who played in two Tests in 1996 – also made his Twenty20 international debut.

  In the second Twenty20 – also in Harare – the New Zealand bowling attack was opened by the sons of two former first-class cricketers. Bracewell, with 3-25, was joined by debutant Graeme Aldridge, whose father Charles had appeared in four first-class matches for Canterbury in the 1970s.

  Bracewell and Waller then both made their Test debuts in the same match, at Bulawayo, with the latter scoring an unbeaten 72, matching his dad who made a half-century on his debut, at the same venue, against England in 1996/97. Bracewell also rose to the occasion, becoming just the seventh New Zealand debutant to take five wickets in an innings, picking up 5-85. His father had an equally impressive start to his Test cricket career, dismissing England openers Mike Brearley (2) and Graham Gooch (0) during his first eight deliveries on his debut at The Oval in 1978. Brendon and Doug Bracewell became the eighth father and son to have played Test cricket for New Zealand.

- England fast bowler Stanley Christopherson, who appeared in a single Test match in 1884, had nine brothers who also played cricket. The Kent brothers often fielded a family XI – The Christophersons – which was boosted by the inclusion of their father, Derman. A president of the MCC, Stanley's brother Percy also played first-class cricket, appearing in one match together, for Kent against Sussex in 1887.

- When Sarah Coyte made her Test debut for Australia, she played under the captaincy of Alex Blackwell, both of whom have cricket-playing twins. Coyte's twin brother Adam has played youth cricket for Australia, while Blackwell and her twin Kate have both played Test cricket. Ian Healy's wicketkeeping niece Alyssa Healy also made her debut in the same match as Sarah, a one-off Test against England at Bankstown Oval in Sydney in 2010/11.

- Batting for the first time in a competitive game of cricket in eight years, Steve Waugh had the joy of doing so with his young son Austin. The two batted together in a charity Twenty20 match at a suburban cricket ground in Sydney in 2011.

The rare sight of a father and son batting together – Austin Waugh and his dad Steve in a Twenty20 fundraiser in Sydney in 2011

- Of the 52 Test centuries scored by Steve and Mark Waugh, both made two scores of exactly 100. Steve's first such dismissal came against the West Indies at Sydney in 1992/93, with his second also against the Windies, at Kingston in 1998/99. Mark's first innings of 100 also came at Sydney, during the second Test against South Africa in 1997/98, with his second at Brisbane in 1999/2000 in the first Test against Pakistan. The Australian Test record for being dismissed the most times on exactly 100 is three, by Graeme Wood.

- In the first Test of the Sri Lanka–Zimbabwe series in 1996, Muttiah Muralitharan dismissed a pair of brothers with consecutive deliveries. Murali bowled Grant Flower for 27 in the second innings in Colombo then got his incoming older brother Andy for a duck with his next ball. The Waugh twins also suffered a similar misfortune in a Test match, when Pakistan's Saqlain Mushtaq dismissed Mark then Steve with consecutive balls during the second Test at Sharjah in 2002/03.

- While the West Indies were doing battle in the 2012 World Twenty20 tournament, Shivnarine Chanderpaul and his teenage son slaughtered a local club side with a double-century partnership. Representing Gandhi Youth against Transport Sports, Shivnarine scored an unbeaten 143, while his young son Tagenarine hit 112 not out. Their unbroken 256-run third-wicket stand was the backbone of a massive 125-run win for their team in the 40-over match.

Shiv Chanderpaul's son Tagenarine with West Indies superstar Chris Gayle

  In 2012/13, Tagenarine made his first-class debut for Guyana. Shivnarine (aged 18) and Tagenarine (16) both made their first-class debuts as teenagers and both made their debuts in the same fixture – Guyana versus Leeward Islands – with the elder Chanderpaul doing so in 1991/92. A little later, they played together for the first time in a first-class match, against Trinidad and Tobago at Port-of-Spain. Shivnarine (108) celebrated the occasion with his 65th first-class century, while his son made 42 and 29 opening the batting.

- In the same month that his oldest son made his Test debut, Geoff Marsh's other boy was named in Australia's Twenty20 squad. Mitchell Marsh – who captained Australia to victory in the 2010 Under-19s World Cup – joined his brother Shaun for a two-match series against South Africa in 2011/12. In their first match together – at Johannesburg – Mitchell out-scored his brother, 36 to 26, striking four sixes in 21 balls.

  Back home, Shaun was then dropped from Australia's one-day international squad, while Mitchell was included. It came just a few days after Geoff Marsh had been sacked as coach of Sri Lanka following a disappointing series in South Africa.

- During the Big Bash League in 2011/12, Mitchell Starc dismissed brothers Shaun and Mitchell Marsh with consecutive deliveries in a match at the SCG. On the same day, the younger brother of Australian Test all-rounder Andrew McDonald made his debut for the Melbourne Renegades playing under his captaincy. The leg-spinning Brenton McDonald took one wicket in his first BBL match, while Andrew scored one run, in a loss against the Hobart Hurricanes at the Blundstone Arena in Hobart.

- One shot away from a Test century against India at Bridgetown in 1952/53, Clyde Walcott was sent packing on 98, dismissed lbw. The umpire who raised his finger to terminate the innings was Walcott's uncle, Harold Walcott.

- In 2011, the younger brother of a record-breaking batsman also made the record books by becoming the youngest-ever cricketer to take part in inter-school competition in India. Six-year-old Musheer Khan – whose brother Sarfaraz had scored a record-breaking quadruple-century in the Harris Shield at the age of 12 in 2009 – made his debut in the Giles Shield Under-14s, taking 6-11.

- The younger brother of Doug Walters, Terry, was once 12th man in a Sheffield Shield match for New South Wales. In the same season – 1971/72 – he played in a three-day match for Northern New South Wales against a World XI, a side that included the likes of Sunil Gavaskar, Graeme Pollock and Tony Greig.

- During celebrations that marked the SCG's 100th Test match, a descendant of Australia's first Test captain was on hand as a flag-bearer. Siobhan Gregory – the great-great-granddaughter of Dave Gregory – had applied for the honour through a junior cricket club that chose the 11-year-old unaware of her famous link with the game and the SCG. She said: "**It was a big surprise when they picked me.**" Siobhan was selected to lead the Australian and Indian teams on to the field on day four of the second Test of the 2011/12 series between the two countries.

    Dave Gregory led Australia in their first three Tests, playing his first-class cricket for New South Wales, as did three brothers and three nephews. Four members of the clan went on to play Test cricket, with Ned Gregory making the first Test duck, against England at Melbourne in 1876/77, a match captained by his brother Dave. Ned's son Syd – who was born on the site of the SCG – appeared in 58 Tests, scoring four centuries, with a highest of 201. Another of Dave's nephews, Jack, was a fast bowler of some note, who appeared in 24 Tests after World War One.

- On his way to his second five-wicket haul of the season in 2011/12, the son of a former Test cricketer took the wicket of the son of another former Test player. Fremantle's captain Chris Wood – son of Graeme Wood – was dismissed lbw by Subiaco-Floreat's Matthew Thomson – son of Jeff – in the Perth first-grade competition. The game also featured Mitchell Marsh, son of Geoff.

- On his Test debut, Shingi Masakadza joined his brother Hamilton in the Zimbabwe XI and both claimed a wicket. The debutant took 1-102 against New Zealand at Napier in 2011/12, while Hamilton, in his 19th Test, took 1-45. They provided just the 11th occasion of brothers taking at least one wicket each in the same Test, and the second for Zimbabwe after Paul and Bryan Strang. The West Indies' Pedro Collins and his half-brother Fidel Edwards performed the feat five times in six consecutive Tests in the calendar year of 2004.

- In a two-day match at Clifton in 1859 an 11-year-old W.G. Grace batted at number 11 while his brother Alfred opened the innings. Playing against the South Wales Cricket Club, the Clifton team also included W.G.'s father Henry, brother Edward and an uncle, Alfred Pocock.

- During the England–Australia Test match at The Oval in 1880, the Grace family made history with three brothers gracing the field. W.G. was joined in the team by E.M. and G.F., both of whom appeared in their only Test. All three opened the batting during the match – E.M. and W.G. opened the first innings, while G.F. opened the second with Alfred Lyttelton.

- In 2011/12, the son of Australia's current bowling coach achieved career-best figures in a nail-biter at the Gabba taking 7-24. Set 68 to win the Sheffield Shield match against Queensland, they got there by the skin of their teeth at 68/9. By taking the first seven wickets to fall, Alister McDermott matched his father Craig, who had also taken the first seven wickets in a first-class innings, in the fifth Test against England at Perth in 1990/91.

- Of the record 37 players who made their one-day international debuts under the captaincy of Sri Lanka's Arjuna Ranatunga, three were his brothers. Dammika Ranatunga debuted alongside his brother against India at Pune in 1990/91; Nishantha against Zimbabwe at Sharjah in 1992/93 and Sanjeeva against Pakistan at Colombo in 1994.

- When Arthur Cotterill made his debut in 1865/66, he became the first of eight members of his family to play first-class cricket. Arthur appeared in ten matches for the New Zealand side Canterbury, while four brothers – Charles, Edward, Henry and William – and three sons – Keith, Basil and George – also played first-class cricket.

- Pakistan's Shahid Afridi has an older and a younger brother who also played first-class cricket. Neither got anywhere near the lofty heights of the flamboyant all-rounder, with Tariq Afridi appearing in two first-class matches in 1999/2000 and Ashfaq Afridi playing in one match, in 2008/09.

- In a Twenty20 match in Dubai in 2011/12, Kenyan brothers Shem and James Ngoche were run out off consecutive deliveries by the same fielder. Scotland's Richie Berrington pulled off a hat-trick of run-outs, including nabbing the Ngoche brothers with the penultimate and final balls of the match.

- In a three-day match at Oxford in 1969, the opposing wicketkeepers each had a twin brother who also played first-class cricket. Stuart Westley – whose twin Roger played in the same XI – kept wicket for Oxford University, while Derek Taylor did the job for Surrey. Derek's twin Mike played first-class cricket for Nottinghamshire and Hampshire.

  On two occasions, Derek Taylor caught his identical twin brother for a duck. The first occasion came in a County Championship match at Nottingham in 1970 when Derek was playing for Somerset; the second instance was in a Benson and Hedges Cup match at Taunton in 1974.

- Jemma Barsby and her brother Corey both made their state debuts for Queensland in 2010/11 following in the footsteps of their father Trevor who appeared in 111 first-class matches. Jemma made the news in 2012 with her unusual bowling style, which saw the then-17-year-old medium-pacer changing between right-arm and left-arm during matches. She said: **"I was getting sick of my brother smashing me around the backyard everywhere, so I tried bowling with a different arm. I started landing them pretty well bowling with my other arm and so I just kept mixing it up."**

- In a comeback match for Australia in 1979/80, Ian Chappell scored a half-century under the captaincy of his brother Greg. Ian scored an unbeaten 63 against the West Indies in the World Series Cup on 21 December 1979, having scored 63 in his previous appearance, against the same opposition and under the same captain on 20 December 1975.

  The interval of four years and a day is the longest break for a pair of brothers appearing alongside each other in one-day internationals. In 2011/12, Yusuf Pathan rejoined his brother Irfan in the line-up for the India–Pakistan ODI at Mirpur, after an interval of three years and 38 days between appearances together.

- Batting against Pakistan in 1994/95, Andy and Grant Flower produced a double-century partnership in which both brothers passed 150. Their 269-run stand for the fourth wicket against Pakistan in Harare was the biggest of the Test and the highest-ever partnership between a left-handed batsman who bowls right-handed and a right-handed batsman who bowls left-handed. Andy, Zimbabwe's wicket-keeping captain, scored 156, while his younger brother scored a Test-best 201 not out. Overtaking the previous best fraternal Test stand of 264 between Greg and Ian Chappell, the Flowers shared the man-of-the-match award that celebrated Zimbabwe's first-ever Test victory.

MOST CENTURY PARTNERSHIPS
IN TESTS BY BROTHERS

#	Brothers	Stands	Wkt	Matches		
9	Mark and Steve Waugh (A)	231	4th	4th Test v West Indies	Kingston	1994/95
		197	3rd	5th Test v England	The Oval	2001
		190	4th	5th Test v England	Sydney	1998/99
		153	5th	5th Test v England	Birmingham	1993
		153	4th	2nd Test v New Zealand	Perth	1997/98
		133	4th	1st Test v England	Birmingham	2001
		116	4th	2nd Test v South Africa	Sydney	1997/98
		112	4th	2nd Test v West Indies	Kingston	1998/99
		107	4th	2nd Test v England	Lord's	2001
6	Ian and Greg Chappell (A)	264	3rd	1st Test v New Zealand	Wellington	1973/74
		201	3rd	5th Test v England	The Oval	1972
		159*	3rd	1st Test v West Indies	Brisbane	1975/76
		129	3rd	2nd Test v West Indies	Bridgetown	1972/73
		121	3rd	4th Test v West Indies	Georgetown	1972/73
		100	3rd	1st Test v England	Brisbane	1974/75

When the Flowers made their debuts for Zimbabwe in 1992/93, both took part in a century-run partnership, a first for brothers in Test match cricket. Grant (82) opened the batting in their country's first Test – against India at Harare – with Kevin Arnott (40) and put on exactly 100, while Andy (59) shared a 165-run stand for the sixth wicket in the same innings with Dave Houghton (121). Prior to their fraternal feat, only six other pairs had previously shared in a century partnership on their Test debuts.

- During the month of March in 2012, Ken Rutherford's son Hamish scored his maiden century in first-class cricket and two hundreds in the match followed by a maiden double. Opening the batting for Otago against Northern Districts at Hamilton, he hit 107 – his maiden first-class ton – and 118, and then struck 239, three matches later, against

Wellington in Dunedin. Hamish's dad had also scored a first-class double-century, with a triple, while his uncle Ian also scored a 200.

Hamish got to his pair of tons at Hamilton in double-quick time, reaching his two centuries on consecutive days. His first on the third came off 91 balls, while his second came off 109. Exactly a year later, he marked his Test debut with 171 against England in Dunedin. In 1984/85, his dad had made a pair on his Test debut, against the West Indies at Port-of-Spain.

- Charles Coventry, who scored a Zimbabwe-record 194 not out in a one-day international, is the son of a ODI umpire. His father – also named Charles Coventry – umpired five one-day internationals, making his debut at Bulawayo in 2000/01. His son, who became Zimbabwe's youngest-ever first-class player at the age of 15, made his Test debut at the same ground in 2005/06.

- A decade after his last first-class match, Denis Streak made a comeback in 1995/96 playing alongside his son. Making up the numbers for Matabeleland in the final of the Logan Cup against Mashonaland, a 46-year-old Denis and his son Heath played in a winning side captained by Wayne James, who scored 99 and 99 not out and claimed 13 dismissals behind the stumps.

- Carlisle Best famously scored a six off the first ball he hit in Test cricket, on his debut for the West Indies in 1985/86. Twenty-six years later, his nephew Tino Best (95) struck a six on his way to the highest score by a number 11 batsman in Test match cricket, against the same opposition – England – at Birmingham, in 2012. Tino said: **"My uncle Carlisle Best always wanted me to be a Test batsman. To fall five runs short, I know he's disappointed."**

- Play was called off after the second day of a first-class match in South Africa in 1937/38 following the death of the brother of one of the players. North Eastern Transvaal's Dudley Helfrich scored 62 in the match against Griqualand West, but proceedings were soured with the passing of his 18-year-old brother Basil, who had played in 13 first-class matches. Two other brothers also played first-class cricket – Ken, who appeared in eight matches, and Cyril, who appeared in 47.

- In a first-class match at Calcutta in 1952/53, three brothers named A.K. Das Gupta represented Bengal in a semi-final against Mysore. Ajit made a duck and eight opening the batting, Benu made 13 and four at number three, while Anil hit 17 and seven at six.

Ajit and Benu both scored a single century each in first-class cricket – 117 and 104 respectively – while Anil had a highest score of 34.

- A nephew of the legendary Inzamam-ul-Haq etched his name in the record books in 2012 when he took part in the first-ever double-century partnership for Pakistan in an Under-19 one-day international. On his debut, 16-year-old Imam-ul-Haq scored 88 against India at Kuala Lumpur, sharing a second-wicket stand of 212 with Sami Aslam.

- New Zealand's Doug Bracewell marked his first Test in Australia with a duck, just as his father had done three decades before. Playing in the first Test at Brisbane in 2011/12, Doug made an 18-ball duck, while his dad Brendon made a duck in his first Test at Brisbane in 1980/81, a match that also featured his brother John.

  Later in the season, Doug made two ducks against South Africa in Hamilton, signalling just the second instance of a father and son bagging a pair in Test match cricket. Brendon had made two ducks on his Test debut – against England at The Oval in 1978 – while John Bracewell also made a pair – in Test cricket's 1,000th match, at Hyderabad in 1984/85 – making it three from the Bracewell family. The first father and son to make Test pairs were the West Indies' Everton Weekes and David Murray. Weekes fell in such fashion at The Oval in 1957, while the wicketkeeping Murray copped a pair against Pakistan at Multan in 1980/81.

- When Sachin Tendulkar was bowled for the 50th time in his Test career, he became part of a family feat by losing his wicket to an uncle and his nephew. John Bracewell got him at Christchurch in 1989/90, with his nephew Doug Bracewell taking his wicket for a first time, at Bangalore in 2012. Doug became the 150th bowler to dismiss Tendulkar in Test match cricket.

- Ian Chappell denied his brother Greg the chance to score a century during the 1975/76 Sheffield Shield when he caught him on 99 off the bowling of Terry Jenner at the Adelaide Oval. Greg was also out in the 90s in a 1980/81 match when he was dismissed by younger brother Trevor, who took his wicket for 94 at Brisbane.

FAMILY FEUDS: ONE CHAPPELL INVOLVED IN THE DISMISSAL OF ANOTHER IN FIRST-CLASS CRICKET

G.S. Chappell c I.M. Chappell b Prior 2	Queensland v South Australia, Brisbane	1974/75
G.S. Chappell c I.M. Chappell b Jenner 99	South Australia v Queensland, Adelaide	1975/76
G.S. Chappell c Whitney b T.M. Chappell 94	Queensland v NSW, Brisbane	1980/81
T.M. Chappell c G.S. Chappell b Thomson 111	NSW v Queensland, Sydney	1980/81
T.M. Chappell lbw b G.S. Chappell 58	NSW v Queensland, Newcastle	1981/82

- In the same match in which India's Lala Amarnath made his final first-class appearance, his son Surinder made his first-class debut. Lala appeared for the Maharashtra Governor's XI, while his son played for the Chief Minister's XI in the three-day match at Poona in 1963/64.

- Graeme and Peter Pollock made their limited-overs debuts together in a side selected by a poll of South African radio listeners. Representing a South African XI against an Australian XI at Johannesburg in 1966/67, Graeme marked his List A debut with a match-winning unbeaten 132, while his brother took 2-63.

- A 21-year-old Canterbury all-rounder who made his debut for the Netherlands in 2012 is the grandson of the only player to appear in Tests for both the West Indies and New Zealand. The great-grandfather of Logan van Beek – a former New Zealand youth international – also played first-class cricket. Victor Guillen appeared in a single match for Trinidad in 1921/22, while Sam Guillen played in five Tests for the West Indies and in three for New Zealand during the 1950s.

- During his Test career for Pakistan, Hanif Mohammad played in matches against India's Lala Amarnath, Datta Gaekwad and Vijay Manjrekar. Hanif's son, Shoaib Mohammad, played against their sons in Tests – Mohinder Amarnath, Anshuman Gaekwad and Sanjay Manjrekar.

- Appearing in his first first-class match at The Oval, Luke Wells scored a century on the ground where his father had made a duck in his only Test for England. In 1995, Surrey stalwart Alan Wells received a long-overdue Test invitation for the sixth match of the series against the West Indies at The Oval, but was consigned to a first-ball duck and an unbeaten three off 39 balls. Playing against his dad's old team, Luke avenged his father's disappointment by scoring 108 for Sussex in the 2012 County Championship, a match that also contained an unbeaten 72 from Mike Gatting's nephew Joe.

    Luke's uncle Colin Wells also played for England, appearing in two one-day internationals as a batsman in the 1985 Four-Nations Cup.

- The glorious career of New Zealand's Richard Hadlee began in 1972/73 when he claimed the first of his 431 wickets, a caught-and-bowled that replicated the feat of his brother Dayle who did so at Lord's in 1969. The first Test wickets of both Ian and Greg Chappell were also caught-and-bowled.

- When the Pakistan Cricket Board began to retire some of its senior staff in 2010, questions were raised about the birth dates of brothers and former first-class cricketers Sultan and Azmat Rana. An inquiry was launched after viewing the birth certificates of Azmat – a regional PCB coach – and Sultan, the then-head of domestic cricket, which indicated the same date of birth. It was a case that stumped human resources staff at the board. The PCB said: "**It is strange because while their date of births are the same, which means they are twins, they have never been known as twins and, in cricket circles, the general impression has been that Azmat is older than Sultan. According to their current date of birth they will turn 60 years in less than a year's time and will have to retire under the new regulations.**"

Two of their brothers – Shafqat Rana and Test umpire Shakoor Rana – and two nephews, Maqsood Rana and Mansoor Rana, also played first-class cricket. Maqsood and Mansoor both appeared in one-day internationals for Pakistan in 1990, while Azmat and Shafqat played Test cricket.

- When Jamie Overton made his first-class debut in 2012, he batted at number 11 behind his twin brother Craig who came in at ten. Both remained unbeaten in Somerset's first-innings total of 512 for 9 declared against Surrey at The Oval. With a score of 34 not out, the fast-bowling Jamie opened the attack with South Africa's Vernon Philander and took 2-62 and 0-18, while his brother, a right-arm medium-pacer, went wicketless.

TWINS TO HAVE PLAYED FIRST-CLASS CRICKET

	DOB	First-class debut	Major teams
Alfred Payne	07/12/1831	1852	Oxford University, MCC
Arthur Payne		1854	Oxford University, MCC
Edward Ede	22/02/1834	1861	Hampshire
George Ede		1864	Hampshire
Joshua Spencer-Smith	17/12/1843	1864	Hampshire
Orlando Spencer-Smith		1866	Oxford University, Hampshire
Herbert Phipps	08/08/1845	1865	MCC
Walter Phipps		1867	Southgate
Charles Pigg	04/09/1856	1876	Cambridge University, MCC
Herbert Pigg		1877	Cambridge University, MCC
Frank Stephens	26/04/1889	1907	Warwickshire
George Stephens		1907	Warwickshire
Jack Denton	11/11/1890	1909	Northamptonshire
Billy Denton		1909	Northamptonshire
Dudley Rippon	29/04/1892	1914	Somerset
Sydney Rippon		1914	Somerset
Norman Walsh	08/02/1902	1923/24	South Australia
Laurence Walsh		1930/31	South Australia
Lisle Nagel	06/03/1905	1927/28	Victoria, Australia
Vernon Nagel		1932/33	Victoria
Peter Garthwaite	22/10/1909	1929	Oxford University
Clive Garthwaite		1930	Army
Alec Bedser	04/07/1918	1939	Surrey, England
Eric Bedser		1939	Surrey

Cecil Harris	10/06/1924	1946/47	Rhodesia
Mervyn Harris		1949/50	Rhodesia
Mike Taylor	12/11/1942	1964	Nottinghamshire, Hampshire
Derek Taylor		1966	Surrey, Somerset
Stuart Westley	21/03/1947	1968	Oxford, Gloucestershire
Roger Westley		1969	Oxford University
David Howell	20/05/1958	1976/77	Eastern Province, Transvaal
Ian Howell		1981/82	Eastern Province, Border
George Reifer	21/03/1961	1979/80	Barbados
Elvis Reifer		1984	Hampshire, Barbados
David Varey	15/10/1961	1981	Cambridge, Lancashire
Jonathan Varey		1982	Oxford University
Steve Waugh	02/06/1965	1984/85	New South Wales, Australia
Mark Waugh		1985/86	New South Wales, Australia
Junior McBrine	16/09/1963	1985	Ireland
James McBrine		1986	Ireland
Darlington Matambanadzo	13/04/1976	1993/94	Mashonaland
Everton Matambanadzo		1993/94	Mashonaland, Zimbabwe
James Marshall	15/02/1979	1997/98	Northern Districts, NZ
Hamish Marshall		1998/99	Northern Districts, NZ
Mark Jonkman	20/03/1986	2006/07	Netherlands
Maurits Jonkman		2007	Netherlands
Craig Overton	10/04/1994	2012	Somerset
Jamie Overton		2012	Somerset

- Fifty-five years after his grandfather last played for England, Nick Compton made his Test debut, signalling the first set of grandfather-grandson batsmen to play for England. Denis Compton made his Test debut, aged 19, in 1937 and played in 78 matches, scoring 5,807 runs at 50.06. Nick made his Test debut at the age of 29 against India at Ahmedabad in 2012/13 and said: "**I am not as good as my grandfather. But who was and who is? Nobody in this country.**"

Nick's father, Richard, appeared in seven first-class matches for Natal, while an uncle, Patrick, and a great-uncle, Leslie, also played the first-class game.

GRANDFATHERS AND GRANDSONS
TO PLAY TEST CRICKET

Vic Richardson (A)	Ian, Greg and Trevor Chappell (A)
George Headley (WI)	Dean Headley (E)
Jahinger Khan (I)	Bazid Khan (P)
Maurice Tremlett (E)	Chris Tremlett (E)
Denis Compton (E)	Nick Compton (E)

Appearing in his fifth Test match - at Dunedin in 2012/13 - Compton (117) brought up his maiden Test century, a day after Ken Rutherford's son Hamish had done so for New Zealand. When Compton reached his three figures, it marked only the second instance of a grandfather-grandson combination scoring centuries in Tests after Australia's Vic Richardson and Ian and Greg Chappell. With a score of 100 in his next innings, at Wellington, Compton matched his grandad who also scored his second Test century – at Lord's in 1939 – in his sixth Test.

- Percy Herbert got his one and only chance to play first-class cricket when his nephew Percy Fender invited him to appear in a benefit match in 1920. Herbert arrived at the ground a day late after the Players of the South had scored 551/9. It then rained for the next two days, thus ending his first-class career without ever seeing a ball bowled.

- On the same day that Sachin Tendulkar celebrated 22 years of international cricket, his son Arjun made his debut in the Harris Shield Under-16s school tournament. Opening the bowling for Dhirubhai Ambani School in 2011, Arjun took a match-winning 8-22 against Jamnabai Narsee.

- Ben Hilfenhaus achieved something with the bat that his second cousin and Tasmanian team-mate Ricky Ponting never did, and that was to score a half-century in a Test match at Lord's. Batting at number ten against Pakistan in 2010, Hilfenhaus scored an unbeaten 56, his maiden half-century in Test match cricket. In eight innings at the home of cricket, Ponting never reached 50, with a best of 42 in the 2005 Ashes.

A Team Effort

- After conceding a first-innings lead at Nottingham in 2011, England edged closer to dethroning the world's number one team of the day with a record-breaking victory. With a first-innings total of 221 against India, England became the first country to win a Test by a runs margin of 300 or more after trailing. Down by 67, England came up with a huge 544 and then bowled out India for 158.

  A rarity in Test cricket, Tim Bresnan (5-48 and 90) and Stuart Broad (6-46 and 64) both achieved the match double of a five-wicket haul and a fifty. It was only the second time that team-mates had achieved the feat in the same Test, after Australia's George Giffen (5-76 and 58) and Albert Trott (8-43 and 72*) against England at Adelaide in 1894/95.

- On a day when riots engulfed the UK city of Birmingham in 2011, Edgbaston went ahead and staged the third England–India Test with Virender Sehwag copping a king pair on his return to the national side. Playing in his first match in seven months, it was his first pair in Test cricket and the fourth by an Indian opener, and only the second king pair at Test level after Bangladesh's Javed Omar in 2006/07, who, uniquely, was out to the first ball of both innings.

  England opener Andrew Strauss was back in the runs scoring 87, his first half-century in nine Test innings, and said: **"Let's divorce the cricket match from what is going on in the country, which is clearly not our proudest hour as a country. You can divorce the two. I think this is an opportunity for cricket to, maybe, put a feel-good factor into the newspapers and show that not everything is bad."**

  Strauss and his opening partner Alastair Cook put on a first-wicket stand of 186, with the latter going on to bust a number of Test records.

One shot away from a triple-century, Cook made 294 in 803 minutes from 545 balls and with 33 boundaries. It was the highest score at Edgbaston, overtaking Peter May's 285 against the West Indies in 1957 and the second-longest in terms of balls faced in a Test against India, after Geoff Boycott's 555-ball 246 at Leeds in 1967.

Cook's 294 formed part of England's 710/7 declared, their third-highest total of all time and highest against India. Three of India's bowlers conceded 150 in the carnage – pacemen Shanthakumaran Sreesanth with 0-158 and Ishant Sharma 1-159, and spinner Amit Mishra 3-150. While India lost the match and their number one Test ranking, Rahul Dravid became the first batsman to reach the 10,000-run mark in Tests from the number three position. India went down by an innings and 242 runs, their heaviest defeat in Test match cricket since losing by an innings and 285 to England at Lord's in 1974.

- When South Africa beat England by 80 runs in a one-day international at Southampton in 2012, the Proteas became the first country to hold the number one ranking in all three forms of international cricket. At the same time, Australia had dropped down to number nine in Twenty20 internationals, just ahead of Ireland and Zimbabwe, but with a loss to Pakistan at Dubai a short time later, slipped below the Irish.

- During the ICC Intercontinental Shield in 2010, Namibia scored a monumental 600-run total against Uganda at Windhoek. Their first-innings 609 became the highest total in first-class cricket not to include a century. All 11 players reached double figures, with six progressing to 50. For Uganda, two of their batsmen – Lawrence Sematimba (106) and Roger Mukasa (121) – scored their maiden first-class centuries.

- The 2010 Varsity match played at Oxford witnessed a record opening stand while the first three batsmen to make it to the crease all scored centuries. Oxford University's wicketkeeping opener Dan King (189) and his partner Sam Argawal (117) struck a record 259-run first-wicket stand in just 56 overs, putting to rest a record that had stood for 125 years. At Lord's in 1886, Oxford openers Kingsmill Key and William Rashleigh had put on 243 against Cambridge. Oxford's number three Avinash Sharma then piled on the agony for the visitors with an unbeaten 185 on his first-class debut, sharing a 149-run stand with King as the hosts made it to 611/5 before declaring.

Dan Pascoe, a university student from Canberra, took 5-38 in Cambridge's first innings while Argawal took 5-78 in the second with Oxford victorious by an innings and 28 runs.

- During the 2010 County Championship, Glamorgan achieved back-to-back innings victories for the first time since 1948. The two wins – by an identical margin of an innings and four runs – came in home matches at Cardiff against Northamptonshire and Gloucestershire. In the second match, eight Gloucestershire batsmen fell leg before wicket in the first innings, a record-equalling number in first-class cricket.

A few weeks previously, the match between Gloucestershire and Sussex at Bristol featured a record 18 lbws; Gloucestershire's meeting with Glamorgan at Cheltenham three months later also contained 18 lbw dismissals.

MOST LBWs IN A FIRST-CLASS MATCH IN THE UK

18	Gloucestershire (6/2) v Sussex (5/5)	Bristol	2010
18	Sussex (3/6) v Middlesex (6/3)	Hove	2010
18	Gloucestershire (5/4) v Glamorgan (4/5)	Cheltenham	2010

The world record is 19 in the match between Patiala and Delhi at Patiala in 1953/54

- A first-class match in South Africa in 2010/11 that was scheduled for three days was all over in one. With the first innings of the match at Kimberley restricted to 85 overs, Easterns were bundled out for 85 in 30. Griqualand West responded with 123, before disposing of their opposition for another two-figure total of 76 and reaching 39/2 for an eight-wicket win. As many as 24 batsmen failed to reach double figures, with 11 falling for ducks. Completed in 95.1 overs, it was the first time since Kent beat Worcestershire in 1960 that a first-class match had been done and dusted in a single day.

- In New Zealand's second innings of 199 at Wellington in 1967/68, all ten batsmen fell to fielders other than the wicketkeeper, a unique occurrence in Test match cricket. Although India's Farokh Engineer held on to a couple of catches in the first innings, he was not required in the second. His opposite number in the match, Roy Harford, was playing in the last of his three Tests for New Zealand and took seven catches behind the stumps, including five in the first innings.

- Between the end of 1989 and the beginning of 1992, Australia played 40 consecutive one-day internationals without a debutant. It represented a record run in the 50-over game, only broken by the introduction of Victorian paceman Paul Reiffel at the SCG in 1991/92. Next on the list is 38 matches, also by Australia in a 12-month period between January 2003 and January 2004.

- After Ryan ten Doeschate had scored a century at the 2011 World Cup, the Netherlands innings ended in bizarre fashion with four consecutive run-outs. The Dutch made it to 306 in the game against Ireland at Kolkata, but not before they lost four wickets in three balls, with the first – Atse Buurman – run out following a wide. In the previous over, Buurman's stumps were shattered twice in three deliveries by Boyd Rankin but he survived both times, thanks to no-balls.

- When Kent made 225 against Essex at Chelmsford in 2012, only two of their batsmen reached double figures. After slumping to 9/5, Darren Stevens and Geraint Jones saved the show with a 194-run stand. With the first five in the order failing to reach ten, Stevens hit 119 at number six and Jones added 88 at number seven, with the final four in the order then also falling for less than ten. Their partnership of 194 represented 86.20 per cent of Kent's total while their 207 runs made up 92 per cent. The other nine batsmen scored a total of 11 runs combined.

- Despite heavy rain ruining the first two days of the Rawalpindi versus Quetta match at Islamabad in 2008/09, a result was attained in what turned out to be the shortest first-class match on record. After both teams had forfeited their first innings in the quest for an outright result, Quetta was bundled out for 41 with Rawalpindi reaching the victory target in 40 balls. The match lasted just 20.1 overs.

- After winning the toss at Cape Town in 2011/12, Sri Lanka's Tillakaratne Dilshan put South Africa in to bat, a move that backfired big time. The home side rattled up a significant 580/4 declared, their highest total against Sri Lanka to date, and the highest total in all Test cricket that contained four, or fewer, extras. Three batsmen hit centuries, with Jacques Kallis scoring 224 off 325 balls. In his first match in a year, Alviro Petersen made a majestic return to Test cricket, scoring 109 and sharing a 205-run stand with Kallis, a partnership made up entirely of runs off their collective bats, i.e. no extras.

   In the previous Test at Durban, Sri Lanka (338) had made their highest score in a Test in South Africa, while South Africa (168) made their lowest against Sri Lanka. The tourists went on to a historic win over the Proteas, their first in South Africa.

- Sri Lanka slumped to their biggest defeat in 50-over cricket in 2011/12, posting the lowest-ever total by any country batting second in a one-day international. Chasing South Africa's 301 at Paarl, Sri Lanka fell for 43 in 20.1 overs to lose by 258 runs, with both openers posting a duck for just the second time in their history. At one point Sri Lanka was five wickets down for nine, and then six for 13, with their innings producing just one double-figure contribution, a 19 from number seven Kosala Kulasekara.

  For only the second time in ODI history, three batsmen from the side batting first each scored more runs than the total realised by the team batting second. Hashim Amla hit 112, Jacques Kallis 72 and A.B. de Villiers got 52. The first instance also occurred in South Africa during the 2003 World Cup, when Australia (301/6) dismissed Namibia for 45 at Potchefstroom. Matthew Hayden led the charge with 88, while Andrew Symonds scored 59 and Darren Lehmann an unbeaten 50.

- After putting on 13 runs against Colts in Sri Lanka's domestic 50-over tournament in Colombo in 2012/13, Saracens then suffered the biggest-known collapse in a major cricket match. Saracens lost all ten wickets for just six runs to be all out for 19, with Chathuranga Kumara taking 5/7 and Kanishka Alvitigala 4/11.

- In the wake of a 4-0 flogging at the hands of England in 1962, as many as ten members of Pakistan's 17-man squad never played Test cricket again. The record number for a post-war Test series belongs to South Africa, which defeated Australia by the same margin of 4-0 in 1969/70. With South Africa rubbed out of Test cricket due to the government's apartheid policies, none of the 15 players represented their country again. However, one did go on to play more Tests – 22 years later – with spinner John Traicos lining up for Zimbabwe, making his debut in 1992/93.

- During Tasmania's Sheffield Shield total of 399 against South Australia at Adelaide in 2011/12, five of their batsmen were dismissed consecutively leg before wicket. Three bowlers shared the spoils, with each taking three wickets in the innings – Joe Mennie (3-88), Peter George (3-91) and Nathan Lyon (3-111).

- Despite being dismissed for 190 during the 2011/12 Sheffield Shield, Victoria's innings in the match at Hobart contained a 150-run partnership. David Hussey and Matthew Wade scored 74 and 80 respectively, while all their team-mates, bar one, failed to reach double figures.

- Just two months on from the humiliation of failing to reach 50, Australia went past 500 in the SCG's 100th Test match staged in 2011/12. After the carnage at Cape Town which saw the Australians all out for 47, they marked a most prestigious event in Sydney with a 600-run total, albeit after a shaky start of 37/3. For the first time in Australia – and just the second time overall – more than 600 runs were added to a Test total after the loss of the first three wickets for less than 50.

  Australia charged to 659/4 declared, with a triple-century from Michael Clarke and the first-ever instance of two 250-run partnerships in a single Test innings. Australia's effort of 622 runs beat the West Indies (631), who added 604 runs after being 27/3 against India at Delhi in 1948/49.

  Australia's run glut against the Indians continued in the following Test at Perth, reaching 214 at the fall of the first wicket which meant Australia had scored a record 836 runs for the loss of just one batsman since being 37/3 in Sydney. Australia also became the first country to put together three consecutive double-century partnerships, with stands of 288, 334 and 214.

Stand	Wkt	Batsmen	Match		
288	4th	Ricky Ponting and Michael Clarke	2nd Test v India	Sydney	2011/12
334*	5th	Michael Clarke and Mike Hussey	2nd Test v India	Sydney	2011/12
214	1st	Ed Cowan and David Warner	3rd Test v India	Perth	2011/12

MOST TEST RUNS SCORED WHILE LOSING ONE WICKET

836	Australia	37/3 to 659/4d	2nd Test v India	Sydney	2011/12
		0/0 to 214/1	3rd Test v India	Perth	2011/12
737	Sri Lanka	14/2 to 751/4	1st Test v South Africa	Colombo	2006
617	Sri Lanka	231/8 to 233/8	2nd Test v West Indies	Kingstown	1997
		0/0 to 615/2	1st Test v India	Colombo	1997/98

- South Africa piled on a record number of runs in 1999, passing the 1,600-mark for the loss of ten wickets. After the dismissal of Hansie Cronje in the second innings of the Centurion Test of 1998/99 against the West Indies, the Proteas scored another 143 for one to finish at 399/5 declared. In their next Test, at Auckland, the South Africans made 621/5 declared against New Zealand and then 442/1 declared at Christchurch. Prior to the dismissal of Daryll Cullinan for 152 in the third Test at Wellington, South Africa was 403/3, which meant a grand total of 1,609 runs had been scored for the loss of ten wickets.

  Between the Sydney and Perth Tests in 2011/12, Australia accumulated 962 runs for the loss of ten wickets – from 659/4 at the SCG to the loss of the sixth wicket at 303 at the WACA.

- During the Cape Town Test in 2011/12 which saw 23 wickets taken on the second day, Australia posted the worst-ever numbers by middle-order batsmen in a Test match. Occupying spots three to six in the batting order, Ricky Ponting (0), Michael Clarke (2), Mike Hussey (0) and Brad Haddin (0) contributed just two runs, which overtook the previous low of three runs by the West Indies' Ramnaresh Sarwan (0), Shivnarine Chanderpaul (0), Brian Lara (0) and Ryan Hinds (3) against Australia in at Kingston in 2003/04. Coincidentally, both teams were dismissed for the same total of 47.

  In South Africa's innings of 96 on the same day, Jacques Rudolph (18) and Graeme Smith (37) provided just the fourth instance in Test history of openers both reaching double figures in an innings, and the remaining nine failing to do so.

LOWEST TEST TOTALS AT THE FALL OF THE NINTH WICKET

9th wkt	Total	Inns	Match		
21	47	3rd	Australia v South Africa	Cape Town	2011/12
25	44	4th	Australia v England	The Oval	1896
26	26	3rd	New Zealand v England	Auckland	1954/55
30	30	4th	South Africa v England	Port Elizabeth	1895/96
30	30	2nd	South Africa v England	Birmingham	1924

Chasing 111 to beat England at The Oval in 1896, Australia lost their seventh wicket at 14 and their ninth at 25 – Tom McKibbin helped the tourists to 44 by hitting 16 at number 11, the only double-figure score of the innings

- On its way to a total of over 500 in Colombo in 2012/13, a member of the Moors Sports Club missed out on a first-class double-century by one run while a team-mate failed by one to get a century. In its 519 against the Sri Lanka Air Force Sports Club, Janaka Gunaratne was left on 199 not out, while Rajitha Wickramarachchi was out for 99. The two shared a 224-run partnership for the seventh wicket.

- When Canada collapsed to an all-out total of 45 during the 1979 World Cup, their number ten collected the 100th duck in one-day international cricket. Out for nought on his debut – against England at Manchester – Robert Callender made another in his next, and final, match, against Australia at Birmingham. By a strange coincidence, the 100th duck in a Test match also came in a total of 45. During the first Test at Sydney in 1886/87, England's Billy Barnes went for Test cricket's 100th nought as the visitors fell for a first-innings 45, the lowest score for a team that went on to claim victory.

- South Africa established a new high in one-day internationals during the 2007 World Cup, when four of their batsmen combined for a record number of sixes in an innings. In a rain-reduced 40-over match against the Netherlands at St Kitts, Herschelle Gibbs (72) led the way with seven, including a world-first six in an over. Mark Boucher (75*) hit four, Graeme Smith (67) two and Jacques Kallis five, in his unbeaten 128, whacking sixes off the final three balls of the innings. Three days later, India equalled South Africa's record of 18 sixes – off their full 50 overs – against Bermuda at Port-of-Spain.

- In a one-day international at the SCG in 1992/93, the West Indies sent down a record 19 maiden overs against Pakistan which spluttered to an all-out total of 81. Medium-pacer Phil Simmons, opening the bowling with Curtly Ambrose, was the star of the day with figures of 4/3 with eight maidens off his ten overs. Each of the six West Indies bowlers used achieved at least one maiden over each, matching 19 by India against East Africa in a 60-over World Cup match at Leeds in 1975.

- On his Test debut in 2009/10, New Zealand's Peter Ingram was one of three batsmen run out against Bangladesh at Hamilton. He fell in such fashion after both of the openers – B.J. Watling and Tim McIntosh – had also been run out, the first, and to date only, example of the first three batsmen in a Test innings all being run out.

- When Tasmania faced Victoria at the MCG in 2000/01, their first three batsmen retreated to the pavilion after scoring a duck. Dene Hills, Jamie Cox and Scott Mason all failed to score, with the openers both making a pair in each innings, a first in Australian first-class cricket. Tasmania's David Saker reached the 200-wicket milestone when he dismissed Victorian opener Jason Arnberger for a first-ball duck; Mathew Innes reached 100 wickets when he got Hills for nought in the first innings, while Ian Harvey passed the 200-wicket milestone after dismissing Damien Wright for a duck in Tasmania's second innings.

- Backing up a rare Test win in Australia in 2011/12, New Zealand blew away Zimbabwe at home for its biggest victory of all time. After a first-innings total of 495/7 declared at Napier, they decimated the Zimbabweans twice on the same day. All out for 51 in their first innings – in which only one batsman reached double figures – Zimbabwe then folded for 143, with the Black Caps triumphant by an innings and 301. The previous instance of a Test side falling twice in a day was also by Zimbabwe against the New Zealanders, at Harare in 2005. Three Zimbabweans featured in both debacles – Tatenda Taibu, Hamilton Masakadza and Graeme Cremer – while three New Zealanders – Brendon McCullum, Daniel Vettori and Chris Martin – also played in both Tests.

  The first five wickets in Zimbabwe's first innings at Napier fell for 19 and for 12 in their second. Both of their openers made identical scores in both innings – Tino Mawoyo with two and two, while Masakadza made a pair within just a few hours.

TEST SIDES DISMISSED TWICE IN A DAY

India	58 and 82	3rd Test v England	Manchester	1952
Zimbabwe	59 and 99	1st Test v New Zealand	Harare	2005
Zimbabwe	51 and 143	Only Test v New Zealand	Napier	2011/12

- On the same day that Zimbabwe were shot out for a record-low 51 by New Zealand at Napier in 2011/12, England was dismissed for their lowest total in a Test against Pakistan. Chasing 145 for victory at Abu Dhabi, the number one-rated England fell for 72 and lost by 72, for their second defeat in a row at the hands of a resurgent Pakistan.

  For only the fifth time in their history, England was defeated chasing a fourth-innings target of less than 150 and it was their second such defeat in 110 years after the Wellington Test of 1977/78 in which they were bowled out for 64 chasing 137. Coincidentally, the margin of defeat in both Tests was exactly the same – 72 runs.

  On the 125th anniversary of their worst-ever Test total of 45 – against Australia at Sydney in 1886/87 – England lost their last five wickets in just 11 balls, while seven batsmen scored less than two, the second-most in Test history. For only the sixth time in Tests, the number 11 batsmen made 0 or 0 not out in all four innings. Spinner Abdur Rehman (6-25) claimed a maiden five-wicket haul, and eight for the match, while Saeed Ajmal assisted with 3/22, reaching the 100-wicket milestone in his 19th Test, the quickest for Pakistan. The match featured 29 bowled and lbw dismissals, a new world record.

  Three Tests came to an end on the day – 28 January – with Australia wrapping up the fourth Test at Adelaide to hand India their second consecutive 4-0 whitewash in an overseas series. With Australia taking the required four wickets on the final day for a 298-run win, 22 wickets tumbled at Napier and 16 at Abu Dhabi resulting in a record number of Test wickets – 42 – to fall in a single day.

MOST TEST WICKETS IN A DAY

Date	M	Wkts	Runs	
28/01/2012	3	42	493	Australia v India 4-35, New Zealand v Zimbabwe 22-297, Pakistan v England 16-161
28/12/1996	3	40	531	Australia v West Indies 15-231, South Africa v India 16-161, Zimbabwe v England 9-139
24/11/1990	3	38	568	Australia v England 13-192, India v Sri Lanka 12-143, Pakistan v West Indies 13-233

- After finishing day one on 99 and day two on 222/2, Pakistan masterminded a miraculous history-making win over England at Dubai in 2011/12. The opening day featured 16 wickets to fall and ten single-figure dismissals, with Pakistan skittled out for just 99, the ninth instance of a country falling one run short of triple figures in a Test innings. Stuart Broad (4-36) wrecked the Pakistani top order, with only Asad Shafiq able to hold his head high – he scored 45 or 45.45 per cent of the total, the best performance by a batsman where Pakistan had been dismissed for less than 100.

> **"Not seen that many wickets fall in a day's play since 1996 in my back garden."**
>
> England fast bowler Stuart Broad

Six Pakistanis fell leg before in the first innings, with nine on the opening day, in a series that produced a world-record number of lbws – 43 – in a three-match contest. With a second-innings fight back of 365 – and a century from Younis Khan (127) and Azhar Ali (157) – Pakistan became the first country to fall for 99 in a Test and go on to win.

No England batsman scored a century in the series they lost 3-0, with England's batting average of 19.06 their lowest since the 1888 Ashes against Australia. Jonathan Trott's aggregate of 161 runs was England's best, and their lowest in a three-Test series since Billy Barnes topped the batting charts with 90 runs in four innings in 1888. Ian Bell was the worst of the bunch in the 2011/12 series, scoring just 51 runs in six innings at an average of 8.50. But there was some solace for the losers, with Alastair Cook passing the milestone of 6,000 Test runs at the age of 27 years and 43 days, becoming the youngest England batsman to do so.

For the first time in their history, England was dismissed for a total below 200 (192, 160, 72 and 141) four times in a three-match Test series. It was the second time in six months that the number one-ranked side had been whitewashed in a Test series, after India's 4-0 loss to England in 2011.

- The opening day of a first-class match between Kenya and Ireland at Mombasa in 2011/12 featured 22 catches. Of the 22 wickets that fell, 21 went to spinners – and of the 22 catches only one was taken by a wicketkeeper. All over in two days, Ireland (75 and 152) prevailed, beating Kenya (109 and 108) by ten wickets, with one bowler from each side achieving a ten-wicket haul. Hiren Varaiya took 6/22 and 6/51, while two of Ireland's bowlers shared all 20 wickets that fell across both innings – South African-born Albert van der Merwe taking 5/41 and 6/27 and George Dockrell 5/37 and 4/50.

- In a County Championship match at Folkestone in 1932, four bowlers shared all the wickets that fell in a contest won by Kent in two days. Opening pair Danny Mayer (5-25 and 4-48) and Derek Foster (5-81 and 6-82) took all 20 wickets for Warwickshire, while Kent's Tich Freeman took 17 (8-31 and 9-61) and Alan Watt two, with the other wicket falling via a run-out.

In a first-class match at Cape Town in 1902/03, South African Test players George Rowe (5-86 and 4-135) and Bonnor Middleton (5-50 and 5-72) combined to take 19 wickets, with the other a run-out, while Bill Howell took 17 (8-31 and 9-23) and Bert Hopkins three for the touring Australians. Howell picked up a hat-trick in the second innings and five wickets in five balls.

- On the same day that a UK cricket club remembered the death of a past player, their first XI was bowled out for six. Chasing Huish and Langport's 195 in the 2012 Somerset Cricket League, Barrington lasted just 12 overs. According to one of their players, Steve Redwood, it represented a dark day in the club's history: **"I have never known anything like it and I have certainly seen some poor performances having played for the club for around 20 years. To make it worse, Monday was seven years to the day that our captain died during a game."**

- A junior Chinese cricket team went down in a heap in a competition in Thailand in 2012, losing a match by 349 runs. In the Asian Cricket Council Under-16 Challenge Cup, Afghanistan reached a sizeable

358 for the loss of four wickets after the Chinese had turfed at least 17 catches in the field.

China's reply began painfully with both of their openers retiring hurt on nought and the team disintegrating to an all-out total of nine, which included just three runs off the bat.

SCOREBOARD

AFGHANISTAN v CHINA – CHIANG MAI 2011/12

AFGHANISTAN

		R	B
Javed Ahmadzai *	b Minjian Han	36	39
Abdul Sabor Akhundzada	c Jinfeng Chen b Jiajie Shen	68	63
Parviz Khan	c Gaofeng Hu b Jiajie Shen	79	54
Tariq Khan	not out	83	42
Sayed Hakim Karimi	c Jiajie Shen b Minjian Han	13	8
Imran Khan	not out	51	36
Extras	(2 nb, 20 w, 3 lb, 3 b)	28	
Total	(4 wkts – 40 overs)	**358**	

CHINA

		R	B
Minjian Han	retired hurt	0	9
Suqing Tian	retired hurt	0	7
Gaofeng Hu*	c Abdul Saboor Akhundzada b Shafiullah Mohammad	2	9
Huanhui Wang	b Shafiullah Mohammad	0	2
Jiajie Shen	b Naveen ul-Haq Tarakhil	1	3
Haonan Xu	b Naveen ul-Haq Tarakhil	0	3
Lisheng Zhang †	b Naveen ul-Haq Tarakhil	0	2
Fuqiang Liu	run out	0	8
Jinfeng Chen	b Naveen ul-Haq Tarakhil	0	6
Bo Li	b Naveen ul-Haq Tarakhil	0	3
Gaofeng Hong	not out	0	0
Extras	(2 w, 4 b)	6	
Total	(all out – 8.4 overs)	**9**	

- When Essex hosted Nottinghamshire at Chelmsford in 2007, both sides topped 700 with each securing three individual centuries. Nineteen bowlers were used in a game that produced just 20 wickets and 1,554 runs in two-and-a-bit innings. Essex declared their first innings at 700/9 with hundreds from the wicketkeeper James Foster (204), Queensland all-rounder Andy Bichel (148) and number nine Graham Napier (125). The visitors replied with a record 791 and centuries from Mark Wagh (107), Samit Patel (117) and wicketkeeper Chris Read (240), the first time opposing keepers had scored a double-century in the same first-class match.

- Chasing a target of 392 to beat Durham at Chester-le-Street in 2012, the Durham University side fell for 18, the equal tenth-lowest total in first-class cricket since 1900. The nine wickets that fell – one batsman was absent injured – were shared by three bowlers, with Western

Australia's Callum Thorpe taking 3/4 and the New Zealand-born Ben Stokes 4/3. In a total mismatch, Durham MCCU had been 18/6 in their first innings before making it to 117. The students ended up losing the game by 373 runs.

The debacle brought back memories of another recent collapse when Surrey was blasted away for a wafer-thin 14 in 14.3 overs by Essex in the 1983 County Championship. Seven batsmen failed to score, with a best of six from opening batsman Grahame Clinton. Bowling unchanged, former West Indies medium-pacer Norbert Phillip took 6/4 off 7.3 overs, while Neil Foster took 4/10 off seven.

• The third Test of the Pakistan–New Zealand series in 1976/77 was a high-scoring affair with three batsmen from the same side uniquely scoring a century and a half-century. The Karachi match saw over 1,500 runs with Majid Khan scoring 112 and 50, Javed Miandad 206 and 85 and Mushtaq Mohammad 107 and an unbeaten 67. Majid scored a hundred runs before lunch on the first day – emulating Victor Trumper, Charles Macartney and Don Bradman – while Javed, at the age of 19 years and 141 days, became the youngest batsman to score a Test match double-century. Warren Lees (152) hit his first century in first-class cricket and the first by a New Zealand wicketkeeper in a Test, sharing a 186-run seventh-wicket partnership with Richard Hadlee (87). Imran Khan (3-107 and 2-104) conceded a hundred runs in each innings before being banned for bowling for an abundance of short-pitched deliveries.

THREE BATSMEN WITH A CENTURY
AND HALF-CENTURY IN SAME TEST

Herbie Collins (114 and 60), Jacks Hobbs (115 and 57), Herbert Sutcliffe (59 and 115)
Australia v England, Sydney, 1924/25

Clyde Walcott (54 and 108), Everton Weekes (162 and 102), Mushtaq Ali (54 and 106)
West Indies v India, Calcutta, 1948/49

Basil Butcher (52 and 118), Garry Sobers (110 and 52), Doug Walters (110 and 50)
Australia v West Indies, Adelaide, 1968/69

Majid Khan (112 and 50), Javed Miandad (206 and 85), Mushtaq Mohammad (107 and 67*)
Pakistan v New Zealand, Karachi, 1976/77

Mike Atherton (131 and 74), Robin Smith (121* and 61*), Sachin Tendulkar (68 and 119*)
England v India, Manchester, 1990

• New Zealand made history in the first Test at Dunedin in 2011/12 when they gained a first-innings lead over South Africa without an individual half-century. The home team scored 273 with a highest knock of 48 from Brendon McCullum, while South Africa's 238 contained three fifties, from Graeme Smith (53), Hashim Amla (62) and Jacques Rudolph (52). It was the first such example in Test history, overtaking an instance of two fifties by England at Cape Town in 1909/10. Batting first in the fourth Test against South Africa, the tourists scored 203, with half-centuries from Frank Woolley (69) and Morice Bird (57), but were overtaken by South Africa with 207 that was scored without the benefit of an individual fifty.

- New Zealand was all over Zimbabwe in the land of the long white cloud in 2011/12 with victories in all formats of the game. After a record innings victory in the Test match at Napier, New Zealand then gained significant wins in the one-day and Twenty20 internationals that followed. Following an easy 90-run win in the first ODI at Dunedin, they stepped up a gear in the next two, with 372/6 at Whangarei, going one run better at Napier and posting 373/8, the first time a country had passed 370 in consecutive ODIs. The New Zealanders blasted a record 32 sixes over the two games – 16 in each – while Zimbabwe fast bowler Brian Vitori went for 105 runs, conceding a world-record 11.66 off his nine overs at Napier.

  After taking the first Twenty20 match by seven wickets at Auckland, New Zealand made it back-to-back wins in the second at Hamilton, the 220th Twenty20 international. In a match in which both teams passed 200, New Zealand openers Rob Nicol (56) and James Franklin (60) posted 103, the 20th hundred-run stand in Twenty20 internationals. Kane Williamson scored an unbeaten 20, hitting two fours and a six off consecutive deliveries in the final over, becoming the first batsman to hit 20 runs off five balls in a Twenty20 international.

- New Zealand came close to topping the 1,000-run mark in their 2011/12 one-day international series against Zimbabwe, scoring 993 in the three-match series, with a record difference of 443 runs between the two sides. In 2010/11, South Africa scored 1,023 runs in three games against the same opposition – 351/6 at Bloemfontein, 273/2 at Potchefstroom and 399/6 at Benoni.

- In 2011, Australia suffered one of the biggest collapses in international cricket as Sri Lanka's Lasith Malinga took a record-breaking hat-trick. Batting first at Colombo, Australia went from 210/5 to 211 all out, losing their last five wickets for one run, a record collapse. Malinga became the first bowler to take a hat-trick three times in one-day internationals and said: **"I realised that I had become the first bowler to take three hat-tricks in ODI cricket only after the match. I am extremely happy that I emulated the feat of two other fast bowlers whom I had seen and admired, Wasim Akram and Chaminda Vaas."**

- South Africa pulled off a ten-wicket win over Sri Lanka in 2011/12 and became the first country to knock off of a victory target without facing a legal delivery. Set two to win, Sri Lanka's Dhammika Prasad overstepped and was hit for one by Alviro Petersen, giving Graeme Smith his 41st Test win as captain.

- After granting first-class debuts to their two opening batsmen for a County Championship match at Chester-le-Street in 2011, Nottinghamshire lost their first four wickets on the same score. After a 21-run start from debutants Sam Kelsall and Karl Turner, Notts lost their first four wickets on 21, with Durham's opening bowlers – Callum Thorp and Graham Onions – both on a hat-trick at the same time.

- The West Indies opened their account against Australia at Port-of-Spain in 2011/12 with the top five in the batting order all dismissed lbw. A first in Test match cricket, each of the wickets was claimed by a different bowler – Michael Beer, Ben Hilfenhaus, James Pattinson, Mike Hussey and Nathan Lyon.

  As many as 18 bowlers were used throughout the series and each took at least one wicket. A record number for a three-match Test series, the number equalled the 18 successful bowlers employed by England and Australia in the five-match 1905 Ashes.

- In South Africa's first innings at Johannesburg in 2011/12, nine different Australians took a catch. It was a Test record, matching nine taken by the West Indies against England in 1997/98, and nine by New Zealand against the West Indies in 2002, both instances occurring at Kensington Oval in Bridgetown.

- During the 2011 World Cup, Ireland became the first team to successfully chase a 300-run total twice in the showcase limited-overs tournament. The only other countries prior to Ireland to achieve the feat in the World Cup were Sri Lanka in the 1992 edition and England in 2007.

Sri Lanka 313/7 (49.2 overs)	Zimbabwe 312/4 (50)	New Plymouth	23/03/1992
England 301/9 (49.5)	West Indies 300 (49.5)	Bridgetown	21/04/2007
Ireland 329/7 (49.1)	England 327/8 (50)	Bangalore	02/03/2011
Ireland 307/4 (47.4)	Netherlands 306 (50)	Kolkata	18/03/2011

- Chasing 244 to beat Sri Lanka in a ODI in Colombo in 2012, Pakistan went belly-up and lost six wickets for ten runs. In the space of four balls, Thisara Perera (4-42) changed the course of the game by claiming a hat-trick and a run-out. Six Pakistanis fell for a duck, with the partnership aggregate of 13 runs between the fourth and ninth wickets being Pakistan's worst-ever effort in a one-day international.

With opener Azhar Ali remaining unbeaten on 81 in Pakistan's all-out total of 199, the match provided the first example of a batsman carrying his bat and a bowler taking a hat-trick in the same ODI.

Thirty-four-year-old spinner Sajeewa Weerakoon claimed his first wicket in a one-day international in his second match having taken 895 domestic wickets before making his Sri Lanka debut.

- When England took to the field for the fourth Test at Johannesburg in 1964/65, all 11 of their players had uniquely taken a Test wicket. In the previous Test at Cape Town, Geoff Boycott picked up 3-47 in South Africa's second innings, his first wickets at Test level. Twenty players bowled in the match, a first in Test cricket, with Boycott and Ken Barrington (3-4) recording their best analyses for England.

- Sri Lanka beat England at Galle in 2011/12, despite losing their first three wickets for fewer than 15 runs in each innings. With totals of 318 and 214, they handed the number one Test side a fourth consecutive defeat. It was only the fifth instance in Test history of a side losing its first three wickets for 15 or under in both innings of a match, with Sri Lanka the first one to claim victory.

- Within the space of a few days in 2011/12, the Adelaide Oval hosted two tied 50-over matches, a one-day international and the final of the domestic Ryobi Cup. South Australia and Tasmania both scored 285, with the top-of-the-table hosts lifting their first one-day trophy in 25 years. After his dumping from the Australian side, Ricky Ponting made a rare one-day appearance for his state, his first since 2007/08. After man-of-the-match George Bailey scored 101, Ponting chucked away his pads to free himself up with two runs needed off the final ball. In a mad scramble, James Faulkner (2*) and Ponting (75*) ran through for a bye, enough only to level the scores.

    The ground also produced the first tie between India and Sri Lanka with both teams scoring 236/9 off 50 overs. Each team picked up eight extras, the top scorers for each side were run out, the two captains made the second-highest scores and there was an identical number of fours (15) and sixes (2) from both teams. The fifth and sixth wickets fell at the same score for both sides, while both teams lost their ninth wicket on the penultimate ball of their innings. Numbers two to four in India's line-up – Sachin Tendulkar, Virat Kohli and Rohit Sharma – were each dismissed for the same score of 15.

- In a 2003 World Cup match at Durban, Kenya used up all 50 overs against Australia, scoring 174/8. No team was able to match the feat against Australia in the World Cup again until Kenya did so during the 2011 tournament, with 264/6 off 50 at Bangalore.

- A Currie Cup match at Bloemfontein in 1925/26 made the record books with Orange Free State posting a century stand for the last wicket in each innings. Len Tuckett and Lancelot Fuller added 115 for the tenth wicket in their first-innings 303 in the match against Western Province, while Tuckett and Frank Caufield put on 129 in their second-innings 250, a total which contained four ducks and three half-centuries.

- With a first-innings lead over Baroda in the 2010/11 Ranji Trophy final, Rajasthan won their first-ever first-class title then defended it successfully the following year. Ashok Menaria (101) scored his third century in consecutive matches – in his only Ranji Trophy appearances of the season – while Bhargav Bhatt took 5-103 in the first innings.

  In the 2011/12 final against Tamil Nadu at Chennai, Rajasthan opener Vineet Saxena played one of the longest innings in first-class history, occupying the crease for 15 hours. With 26 fours and two sixes, his 257 out of a first-innings 621 took 907 minutes and came off 665 balls. It was only the second double-century by a Rajasthan batsman in a Ranji Trophy final, after Hanumant Singh's 213 not out against Bombay in 1966/67. Saxena shared a 236-run opening partnership with Aakosh Chopra (94), with century stands for the first three wickets of the innings, a first in a Ranji final.

LONGEST INNINGS IN FIRST-CLASS CRICKET

Hrs	Mins	Score	Batsman	Match	
16	55	271	Rajeev Nayyar	Himachal Pradesh v Jammu at Chamba	1999/00
16	10	337	Hanif Mohammad	Pakistan v West Indies at Bridgetown	1957/58
15	7	257	Vineet Saxena	Rajasthan v Tamil Nadu at Chennai	2011/12

- The third Sri Lanka–Pakistan Test at Pallekele in 2012 produced an oddity with the highest score in the first innings from both sides made by *three* batsmen. Asad Shafiq made 75 for the tourists in the first innings, a score then matched by Sri Lanka's Tharanga Paranavitana and Thisara Perera. For Paranavitana, it was his fifth score between 72 and 76 in Tests against Pakistan, the first batsman to do so against a particular opposition.

  The only previous example of the highest score in the first innings of a Test which was shared by three players came at Karachi in 1972/73. In Pakistan's 445/6 declared, Majid Khan and Mushtaq Mohammad both made 99. In England's first-innings 386, the top score was also 99, by Dennis Amiss, the only Test to contain three individual scores of 99.

- In the third Test at Auckland in 1972/73, both New Zealand and Pakistan made first-innings totals of 402 in which the highest individual score from each side was the same. Majid Khan made 110 for the visitors, a score matched by Brian Hastings. At Adelaide in 1968/69, the top first-innings score from both sides in the fourth Australia versus West Indies Test was also 110, from Garry Sobers and Doug Walters.

- In consecutive Tests played in 2012, a first-innings total of 350 or more was overtaken by the side batting second with the loss of just two wickets. South Africa did so in a big win over England at The Oval, followed a week later by the West Indies against New Zealand in Antigua. After the Kiwis made 351 in the first Test, the home side passed the total surrendering its second wicket at 355. Such an effort had only been achieved three times previously in Test cricket.

- Despite the worst possible of starts in both innings of a Test at Faisalabad in 2004/05, Sri Lanka managed to go on and win. With a pair for their captain Marvan Atapattu and two zero-run opening partnerships, Sri Lanka (243 and 438) beat Pakistan (264 and 216) by 201 runs. Atapattu's opening partner Sanath Jayasuriya scored 253 in the second innings, after producing their ninth opening stand worth nought, and did it a tenth and final time, against New Zealand at Wellington later in the same season.

MOST ZERO-RUN OPENING PARTNERSHIPS IN TEST CRICKET

#	Pair	Country	Period
11	Alastair Cook and Andrew Strauss	England	2006-2012
10	Marvan Atapattu and Sanath Jayasuriya	Sri Lanka	1998-2005
8	Matthew Hayden and Justin Langer	Australia	2003-2006

- Despite a record-low total of 54 in the Bangladesh National Cricket League in 2008/09, Khulna were good enough to go on and beat Chittagong. Following a total of 69 in their previous first-class match, Khulna's 54 represented a new low in Bangladeshi first-class cricket.

- During the 2007 South Pacific Games, New Caledonia twice conceded totals of 400 in the 50-over cricket tournament played in Somoa. Fiji reached 403/8 and then blew way the New Caledonians for 20 in 16 overs, with numbers two to six dismissed for a duck. Their loss by 383 runs preceded an even bigger flogging three days later when Papua New Guinea compiled 572/7 off 49 overs. Three batsmen hit centuries – Arua Uda (123), Kila Pala (146) and Mahuru Dai (105) – on their way to a record victory margin of 510 runs.

- When Zimbabwe hosted New Zealand in a one-day international at Bulawayo in 2011/12, a record number of runs was scored after four batsmen had registered a duck. The match aggregate of 657 included three noughts from the winners Zimbabwe, and two centuries from the losers. Kane Williamson scored 100 not out, his second hundred in one-day internationals, both of which were in a losing cause.

- The Ashes series of 2010/11 opened in record-busting style with England becoming the first country to reach 500/1 in a Test match and not lose another wicket. Following a duck in the opening over of the first Test at the Gabba, England captain Andrew Strauss set up the run-fest with a second-innings century (110) and England's first 150-run opening stand in a Brisbane Test.

Strauss and Alastair Cook became England's most prolific opening pair in Test cricket during their partnership of 188, bettering the aggregate of Jack Hobbs and Herbert Sutcliffe. The first set of England openers to both score a century in the same innings of an Ashes Test since 1938, Cook scored 235 not out, his maiden first-class double-century and the 300th double-century in the annals of Test cricket. With 67 in the first innings, Cook's match aggregate of 302 runs broke Matthew Hayden's ground record of 300 (197 and 103), against the Ashes tourists of 2002/03.

Cook also took part in a century stand for the second wicket with Jonathan Trott, who scored an unbeaten 135, providing the first occasion in England's history of the top three in the batting order all scoring a century in an Ashes Test. Their unconquered stand of 329 was a record for England in Australia in a monstrous second-innings total of 517/1 declared. The first time a team had reached 500/1 in Ashes history, it was England's highest score at the Gabba and biggest second-innings total in Australia, surpassing their 475 at Melbourne in 1894/95.

With a 307-run stand earlier in the match by Australia's Mike Hussey (195) and Brad Haddin (136), the match provided just the

second occasion in Test history of two triple-century stands in the same match. Their sixth-wicket partnership in Australia's first-innings total of 481 was the first triple-century stand by the home side in a Test at the Gabba, eclipsing the previous highest of 276 between Don Bradman and Lindsay Hassett against England in 1946/47. It was the third-highest partnership for the sixth wicket in Australian Test history, just 39 runs shy of the 346 stand by Bradman and Jack Fingleton versus England at the MCG in 1936/37.

TESTS IN WHICH TEAMS REACHED 500/1

Score	Total	Inns			
615/1	952/6d	1st	Sri Lanka v India	Colombo	1997
538/1	713/3d	1st	Sri Lanka v Zimbabwe	Bulawayo	2004
533/1	790/3d	1st	West Indies v Pakistan	Kingston	1957/58
522/1	650/6d	1st	Australia v West Indies	Bridgetown	1964/65
517/1	517/1d	2nd	England v Australia	Brisbane	2010/11
514/1	583/7d	1st	South Africa v Bangladesh	Chittagong	2007/08

• In their only one-day international on home soil in 2012, India became the first country to lose their top four batsmen in the order bowled for single figures. In the match – which was lost to Pakistan at Chennai on the penultimate day of the year – India lost Virender Sehwag for four, Gautam Gambhir for eight, Virat Kohli for a duck and Yuvraj Singh for two. Their number five, Rohit Sharma, was also out for a single-figure score of four.

India went on to add 198 runs after being 29/5, the second-best recovery for a side five down for less than 30. Mahendra Singh Dhoni was the saviour, scoring an unbeaten 113, the first captain to score a one-day international century at number seven. Debutant Bhuvneshwar Kumar became the 17th player, and the second Indian, to take a wicket with his first delivery in a one-day international.

• The Bangladesh Under-19s gave Qatar a hiding in a 50-over match in Malaysia in 2012, with one of their number scoring a double-century and another taking a nine-wicket haul. After scoring a pair in his previous match – a first-class game in Dhaka – Soumya Sarkar struck 209 in his side's 363/7 in the Under-19s Asia Cup.

Abu Haider, a 16-year-old left-arm medium-pacer, then cut through Qatar with 9-10 off 5.4 overs. He was denied a shot at all ten, with one batsman absent injured. Out for 35 in 11.4 overs for a 328-run loss, no batsman reached double figures with a best of nine from their number eight.

• When Auckland copped a hiding at the hands of Canterbury in 1877/78, their miniscule second-innings total of 13 was bloated by eight extras. Seven batsmen failed to get off the mark in the first-class game at Auckland Domain, with the highest score of two outweighed by eight byes, which represented 61.54 per cent of the total.

In the 2012/13 Twenty20 Asia Cup at Guangzhou in China, the Hong Kong women's team fell for 15 chasing Pakistan's 157, with extras the biggest contributor to their total. As in the Auckland–Canterbury game, seven batters failed to get off nought, with six ducks, and nine extras, all of which were wides. Nida Dar took 3/0 off 1.1 overs, while Qanita Jalil took 3/7.

- The final of the 2010 Hong Kong Sixes finished in a blaze of glory with Australia hitting an unlikely 48 runs off the final over to beat Pakistan. Chasing 133 for victory, David Warner (35*) and Ryan Carters (31*) combined to blight Imran Nazir's eight-ball over, and with the assistance of a number of extras, took Australia to a remarkable two-wicket win.

- To mark the 700th domestic one-day game in Australia, Victoria pulled off a whopper of a win over Queensland on the back of a record double-century opening partnership. Batting first against the Bulls at the Gabba in 2012/13, Rob Quiney, with 119, and Aaron Finch, with 154, added a state-record first-wicket stand of 226 on their way to a state-record total of 379/2. Captaining Victoria for the first time, Finch scored his first century in List A cricket, becoming the first Victorian to score a 150, and also claimed his first wicket (1-0-2-1) in his 44th match.

  Later in the same season, Finch played another blinder in the same competition, scoring 140 off 124 balls against New South Wales at North Sydney. David Hussey also scored 140, unbeaten, with the pair setting up the biggest successful run chase in Australian domestic one-day history. Hunting a target of 351, Victoria got across the line with four wickets down after 46.4 overs.

- After losing their first wicket for a duck at The Oval in 2012, South Africa established the highest-ever Test innings with the loss of just two wickets. Following Alviro Petersen's nought, Graeme Smith celebrated his 100th Test with a century (131), sharing a second-wicket stand of 259 with Hashim Amla, who then collaborated with Jacques Kallis in a record-breaking splurge worth 377. South Africa declared at 637, after Amla (311*) had become the first South African to score a Test match triple-century. Kallis finished with 182 not out, a PB in Tests against England.

  It was only the second instance in Test history of an innings containing two 250-run partnerships, after Michael Clarke added 288 with Ricky Ponting and an unbroken 334 with Mike Hussey against

India at the SCG earlier in the year. It was also just the second time that a team had provided double-century stands for the second and third wickets, after England against the West Indies at Nottingham in 1957. Their match-winning 637 represented the first time a country had passed 600 in a Test innings in which just two wickets fell and where no batsman was dismissed in double figures.

England also began The Oval match with a duck, with Andrew Strauss falling to the fourth ball. Jonathan Trott (71) then joined Alastair Cook (115) in a major revival, signalling just the third time England had scored 150-plus runs for the second wicket following a first-wicket stand of nought. They got to 170, with the previous occasion, at Perth in 2006/07, also involving a Strauss duck, a Cook century (116) and a stand of 170.

Strauss's duck was his 15th at Test level, and saw for the fifth time his opening partner scoring a century. Marcus Trescothick (180) was the first to do so, at Johannesburg in 2004/05, with Cook supplying the next four instances – 116 at the WACA in 2006/07, 106 against the West Indies at Manchester in 2007, another innings of 106, against Sri Lanka at Lord's in 2011, and 115 in 2012.

Three of the openers scored ducks in the match – Petersen, Strauss and Cook – with England losing by an innings. It was the seventh time that a team batting first had lost by such a margin after scoring 350 or more in its first innings, with South Africa's win one of the most comprehensive in the history of Test match cricket. The difference in runs per wicket between the winners (318.50) and the losers (31.25) at 287.25 was the biggest to date.

- Australia took the world's number one-rated team to the cleaners in 2012/13 with consecutive 500-run totals and consecutive double-centuries from their captain. After 565/5 declared in the first Test against South Africa at Brisbane, Australia then made 550 in the first innings of the second Test at Adelaide. The opening day saw a mind-boggling 482 runs scored with the first-ever example of two centuries and a double-century from the same side on the first day of a Test. After an unbeaten 265 at the Gabba, Michael Clarke (230) led the charge with 224, the most runs in a day in a Test in Australia, bettering Don Bradman's 223 on day one against the West Indies at Brisbane in 1930/31. David Warner chipped in with a 112-ball 119, while Mike Hussey scored 103 after making 100 in Brisbane.

Faf du Plessis was hit for a six by Warner off his first delivery on his Test debut, while fellow spinner Imran Tahir copped a hiding, going for 159 off 21 overs on the opening day's play. He ended the innings with figures of 0-180, with no maidens off 23 overs, and the Test with 0-260 off 37 and an economy rate of 7.02. He became the first bowler to concede 260 runs in a Test without taking a wicket, overtaking Pakistan's Khan Mohammad (0-259) against the West Indies at Kingston in 1957/58.

Du Plessis starred with the bat and was named man of the match after innings of 78 and 110 not out, becoming the first South African batsman to score a fourth-innings century on Test debut. Over 464 minutes, du Plessis faced 376 balls, the most deliveries for a debutant in the fourth innings of a Test. Despite Australia's two 500-run totals, both Tests were drawn, signalling the first time since 1921 that two consecutive Tests between the two countries had resulted in a draw.

MOST RUNS ON THE OPENING DAY OF A TEST IN AUSTRALIA

494/6	Australia v South Africa	Sydney	1910/11
482/5	Australia v South Africa	Adelaide	2012/13
428/3	Australia v West Indies	Brisbane	1930/31

MOST CENTURIES FROM ONE SIDE ON OPENING DAY OF A TEST

#	Batsmen	Test		
3	Percy McDonnell 103 Billy Murdoch 145* (211) Tup Scott 101* (102)	Australia v England	The Oval	1884
3	David Warner 119 Michael Clarke 224* (230) Mike Hussey 103	Australia v South Africa	Adelaide	2012/13

In the following Test at Perth – a match that determined which of the two countries would be number one in the world – du Plessis became the first batsman in Test history to pass 70 in his first three innings. After his 78 and unbeaten 110 at Adelaide, du Plessis hit 78 not out at the WACA, the only half-century in the Proteas' first-innings total of 225. In the second innings, A.B. de Villiers (169) scored his first Test century as a wicketkeeper reaching his ton with three consecutive reverse sweeps, Hashim Amla hit a match-winning 196, while South Africa's number six Dean Elgar missed out, bagging a pair.

- After winning the toss and batting at Cape Town in 2012/13, New Zealand imploded for 45 in just 116 balls, their shortest-ever completed innings in a Test. With the Kiwis down and out before lunch on the opening day of the first Test at Newlands, it represented the first occasion that a team had been dismissed for under 50 in a Test innings that took place in the first week of a calendar year.

Vernon Philander – who took 5-15 on debut against Australia (47) at the same venue 14 months previously – was in red-hot form with 5-7, while Dale Steyn completed 300 Test wickets in his 61st match.

He became the third-fastest to reach the milestone after Dennis Lillee (56) and Muttiah Muralitharan (58), while Richard Hadlee and Malcolm Marshall also got there in 61.

South Africa became the first side to have three batsmen scoring more runs than the opposition did on the opening day of a Test, with Alviro Petersen finishing on 103 not out, Hashim Amla 66 and Jacques Kallis 60. Daniel Flynn (8) took part in seven partnerships without reaching double figures, matching the record of Mick Commaille (1*) during South Africa's total of 30 against England at Birmingham in 1924.

A month on from its demolition of the Kiwis, the South Africans again dismissed a Test side for under 50. In reply to South Africa's first-innings total of 253 at Johannesburg, the Pakistanis made just 49, their lowest Test total to date, with Steyn picking up 6-8.

• When Sri Lanka hosted Bangladesh at Galle in 2012/13, seven batsman hit centuries with a record-equalling eight scored over the five days. Just 15 days after taking a hat-trick in a first-class match, Mohammad Ashraful became the first Bangladesh batsman to pass 150 twice in Test cricket while a team-mate went on to score their country's first double-century. With a total of 638, Bangladesh passed 600 for the first time with three batsmen scoring centuries, another first for Bangladesh. Sri Lanka's first-innings total of 570/4 declared also contained three individual centuries, with 142 to Kumar Sangakkara and maiden Test hundreds from Lahiru Thirimanne (155*) and wicketkeeper Dinesh Chandimal (116*).

Ashraful hit 190 and, in partnership with Mushfiqur Rahim, put on 267 for the fifth wicket, the biggest partnership to date for Bangladesh in Tests. With a neat 200, Rahim became the first Bangladesh captain and the first Bangladesh wicketkeeper to pass 150 in a Test, while Nasir Hossain scored a maiden ton of 100. It was the first time a score of exactly 200 and one of 100 had been scored in the same Test innings.

Rahim's 200 came in Bangladesh's 76th Test, the longest wait for a country's maiden double-century. England is next on the list with 75 Tests, followed by India (45), South Africa (26), Sri Lanka (25), New Zealand (18), Pakistan (16), Australia (16), Zimbabwe (9) and the West Indies (6).

Sangakkara scored a pair of centuries, a first in his Test career, while Kithuruwan Vithanage hit 59, the highest score by a debutant in the second innings of a Test having not batted in the first.

Cricket and Other Sports

- The grandfather of an England batsman who made his debut in 2011 was a tennis player of some note who appeared at Wimbledon. Alex Hales made a duck on his England debut, in a Twenty20 international at Old Trafford: **"My grandfather Denis played Rod Laver at Wimbledon – he took him to five sets – and I was probably more likely to be a tennis player than a cricketer when I was 15."**

- International athlete Sidney Kiel, who held the South African record for the 120 yards hurdles, also played first-class cricket. Kiel scored as many as three centuries in just 14 appearances for Western Province, including an unbeaten 139 in his second match, against North East Transvaal at Cape Town in 1938/39. He finished fifth in the final of the hurdles event at the 1938 Empire Games in Sydney.

- International footballer Don Clarke, regarded as one of the legends of New Zealand rugby union, also played first-class cricket. He appeared in 31 rugby Tests for New Zealand and in 27 first-class matches for Auckland and Northern Districts, taking 4-31 in the first innings of his first-class debut in 1950/51. In his final season of cricket, Clarke achieved his best with both bat and ball in the same match, scoring 47 and taking 8-37 – and a maiden ten-wicket haul (10-78) – for ND against Central Districts at Wanganui in 1962/63. On the footy field, Clarke hit the headlines in 1959 with a then-world record six penalty goals that enabled the All Blacks to squeak home against the British Isles 18-17 in Dunedin.

- New Zealand All Black Conrad Smith played cricket as a youngster, bowling fast for various representative sides in Taranaki. Smith played cricket throughout his schooldays, making his New Zealand football debut in 2004. He said: "**I was reasonably quick and opened up the throttle off a long run. I loved it and I guess that was the closest you got in cricket to getting the same sort of physical rush you do in rugby. It was a bit of a buzz trying to unsettle the batsmen down the other end.**

"**I know enough about cricket to understand it is a cruel sport. I would never judge anyone who plays it. The mind games in that sport are cruel. It is a very tough individual sport within a team game and I love watching it.**"

● Rob Andrew celebrated 1985 by making his England debut in rugby union and becoming captain of the Cambridge University first-class cricket team. In 17 first-class matches, Andrew scored 658 runs with a highest score of 101 not out against Nottinghamshire at Trent Bridge in 1984, and had a best of 82 not out in domestic limited-overs cricket. He made the first of his 71 rugby appearances for England in 1985, the same year that he captained a combined universities cricket team against the touring Australians.

THE FIRST-CLASS CAREER RECORD OF ROB ANDREW

M	Inns	NO	Runs	HS	Avge	100s	50s	Cts	Wkts	BBI	Avge
17	33	2	658	101*	21.22	1	3	6	12	3-77	70.58

RUGBY UNION TEST CAREER RECORD

M	Starts	Sub	Pts	Tries	Conv	Pens	Drop	Won	Lost	Drew
76	74	2	407	2	34	87	23	53	21	2

"**I was born more a cricketer that rugby player. I was brought up on a farm in Yorkshire so I played a lot of Test matches in the yard and scored a lot of hundreds off my younger brother.**"

former England rugby captain and Cambridge University captain
Rob Andrew

● A former Pakistani first-class cricketer swapped his bat for a golf club in the 1990s after an accident had rendered him disabled. Saleem Raza, who appeared in two first-class matches in 1986/87, made his debut in the Disabled British Open golf tournament in 2010, in which he finished 10th. He said: "**I started my career as a golfer in 1997 and right from the beginning I proved my worth in the game and earned a lot of respect by winning different national** level events. My first achievement was second position in the Punjab Open Golf Championship in 1998. Then I continued performing well in every tournament and was declared the best disabled golfer in 2008."

- A first-class cricketer who famously claimed a hat-trick on his debut later played golf for India. Joginder Rao's budding first-class career – which featured a record three hat-tricks in his first two matches – was cut short by a parachuting accident. After five first-class matches for Services in 1963/64, Rao took up golf as both a player and course designer.

- Matt King, who played in the Melbourne Storm's 2007 NRL grand final win, was behind a cricket product called 'Crackit', a cross between a cricket bat and a tennis racket. According to the State of Origin and Australian international, it was designed to encourage children to **"… pick up a cricket bat and send the ball flying a lot easier. I dreamt this up with good times in mind."**

MATT KING'S DREAM TEAM

Sachin Tendulkar (I)
Matthew Hayden (A)
David Boon (A)
Brian Lara (WI)
Steve Waugh * (A)
Jonty Rhodes (SA)
Adam Gilchrist † (A)
Andrew Flintoff (E)
Chris Cairns (NZ)
Curtly Ambrose (WI)
Glenn McGrath (A)

Australian rugby league player Matt King

- New South Wales batsman Bobby Madden, who had a highest score of exactly 100 in first-class cricket, also played soccer. After four matches in the early 1950s, Madden was dropped for a period of nine years and stamped his comeback with an innings of 99 against Queensland at the SCG in 1959/60. He also played at centre-half for Australia in a football international against China in 1953.

- Bill Haughton represented Ireland at both cricket and hockey. In his only first-class match, Haughton, a middle-order batsman, was dismissed for a pair, against Glamorgan in 1953.

- Philip Snow, who captained Fiji in five first-class matches on a tour of New Zealand in 1947/48, was a top-class table-tennis player. He captained the Leicestershire second-XI before the war and played table tennis in Fiji, becoming a singles and doubles champion.

- Indian tennis star Sania Mirza won her first Grand Slam trophy as the wife of a Pakistan Test captain in 2012 by winning the mixed doubles at the French Open. Before her marriage to Shoaib Malik, she had won the mixed doubles with the same partner, Mahesh Bhupati, at the Australian Open in 2009.

- Rugby league's Aaron Woods cut down the great Steve Waugh in a charity match in 2011 when the former Australian captain was close to scoring a century. The 46-year-old Waugh was dismissed for 91 – scored off 48 balls – at Drummoyne Oval in suburban Sydney, a match in which former Australian rugby league star Hazem El Masri also scored a fifty. Former Socceroos goalkeeper Mark Bosnich also starred, taking the wicket of South Sydney's Mick Crocker in his first over.

- On the eve of the 2012 Australian Grand Prix, Australia's Mark Webber and world champion driver Sebastian Vettel enjoyed a friendly game of cricket. Assisted by Victorian batsman Brad Hodge, Webber – a cricket fan of some note who shares his birthday with Don Bradman – gave some tips to his Red Bull German team-mate at St Kilda Beach, a stone's throw from the Formula One race track in Melbourne.

> **"A trip to India is incomplete without the delicious food and a game of cricket. Cricket as a sport requires a lot of concentration and hand-eye co-ordination, especially under extreme conditions, and so does Formula One."**
> Mark Webber prior to the 2012 Indian Grand Prix

- Tony Harris, who scored exactly 100 runs in Test match cricket in the late 1940s, appeared in five rugby internationals. Harris, an attacking right-hand batsman, and Springbok fly-half, was part of a historic South African rugby Test series win in New Zealand in 1937.

- Wallabies footballer Berrick Barnes played junior cricket for Australia in the early 2000s, sharing the stage with promising up-and-comers such as Callum Ferguson and Tim Paine. A wicketkeeper, Barnes appeared in five matches in the 2001/02 Australian Under-17 Championships, achieving two stumpings. He made his football debut during the 2007 Rugby World Cup, and was man-of-the-match in the Wallabies' win over Wales in the third-place play-off in the 2011 World Cup.

- During the Varsity Match at Lord's in 1949, the top four batsmen in the Oxford University line-up were all England rugby internationals. Transvaal-born Murray Hofmeyr – who scored a pair of fifties in the match – appeared in 44 first-class games and in three rugby Tests, while his opening partner Brian Boobbyer appeared in 40 first-class matches and nine union internationals.

  Number three batsman Christopher Winn played in 59 first-class matches, for Sussex and Oxford, winning eight rugby caps while the Cape Town-born Clive van Ryneveld played at the highest level in both sports, cricket for South Africa and rugby union for England.

- All-rounder Dan Christian, who made his debut for Australia in a Twenty20 international in 2009/10, is related to a former boxing champion. His uncle Trevor Christian was an Australian light middleweight champion of the 1960s and later a world championship referee.

- The Australian-born England Test batsman Adam Hollioake entered a different sporting arena in 2012 when he made his debut in the world of martial arts. Aged 40, Hollioake, who appeared in four Tests and 35 one-day internationals, had his first bout as a cage fighter at an event on Queensland's Gold Coast. His three-round martial arts debut ended in a draw and he said: **"In hindsight I would have taken a bit longer to prepare for this. I made a silly mistake in the first round and that cost me. I won the second round and the third round was a non-event really."**

- In the same year that he reached the milestone of 5,000 runs in first-class cricket, New South Wales batsman Les Poidevin won the 1906 Swiss Open tennis title and represented Australasia in the Davis Cup. Poidevin also excelled at rowing and won a number of golfing tournaments.

- West Indies batting legend Gordon Greenidge won the inaugural World Aids Day Golf Tournament in Trinidad in 2011. The long-time partner of Desmond Haynes, Greenidge played the event with Carlos Baynes, with the pair shooting a 13-under-par round of 58 to win the event by two shots.

- The football-playing medium-pace bowler Jim Standen is the only person to win the County Championship and the FA Cup in the same year. He played alongside the cricket-playing Geoff Hurst for the 1964 West Ham cup-winning side and took 64 wickets at 13.00 for Worcestershire when they won the championship for the first time.

- Graham Henry, who coached the New Zealand All Blacks to victory in the 2011 World Cup, is a former first-class cricketer. Henry appeared in six first-class matches – as a wicketkeeper five times for Canterbury in 1965/66 and as an opening batsman in a single appearance for Otago, against his former team, in 1967/68.

- New Zealand batsman Noel McGregor appeared in 25 Tests and later took up lawn bowls. A member of the NZ side that made a Test-record low 26, he became both a player and an administrator. He said: **"I like bowls because if I make a mistake with my first bowl of the day I get another 41 chances. If I made a mistake at cricket I spent the rest of the day in the grandstand watching."**

- The parents of South African batsman Paul Winslow, who hit a Test century at Manchester in 1955, are both champion tennis players. Winslow's mother Olive won a number of championships in South Africa, and was reportedly the first female tennis player to show her ankle at Wimbledon. His father Charles won two gold medals – in singles and doubles – at the 1912 Stockholm Olympic Games.

- South Africa's Mike Procter married a tennis player who once took on Billie-Jean King at the US Open. Maryna Godwin, who represented South Africa in the Federation Cup, appeared at the French Open, Wimbledon and the US Open in 1968.

- During the 1965 Wimbledon tennis championship, two of Europe's top players combined to dismiss an Australian Test batsman in a friendly game of cricket. In a Players v Press match, Bob Cowper – who later became the first batsman to score a Test match triple-century in Australia – was caught by the Netherlands' Tom Okker off the bowling of Italy's Nicola Pietrangeli. Okker – who reached a career-high ranking of three in the world in 1969 – and Pietrangeli – who won the French Open in 1959 and 1960 – had never played cricket before.

Cowper was also a gifted tennis and rugby player, following in the footsteps of his father Dave Cowper, who captained the Australian rugby union team in 1933. Regarded as one of the country's best non-professional tennis players, Bob Cowper was crowned the Australian amateur singles and doubles champion in 1979.

Dave Cowper, father of Test batsman Bob Cowper, the first Victorian to captain Australia's rugby union team; he also competed at sprinting, finishing third in national trials for the 100m staged to select a team for the 1932 Olympic Games

- The first player to score a goal in the FA Cup also played first-class cricket. Jarvis Kenrick struck twice in Clapham Rovers' 3-0 win over Upton in 1871, and also scored two goals in the FA Cup final of 1878. In his only first-class cricket match, Kenrick scored 11 at number ten and took one wicket for Surrey against Sussex at The Oval in 1876.

- On the same day that Alastair Cook scored his 20th Test match century, one of his former team-mates finished the opening day of the 2012 British golf Open at two under par. James Morrison appeared in England youth teams alongside players such as Cook, Tim Bresnan and Ravi Bopara before turning to golf.

- Indian fast bowler Tinu Yohannan was a star athlete in his younger days, winning gold and silver in the high jump at junior state level. The son of a former Asian Games record-holder in the long jump, Yohannan appeared in three Tests and three one-day internationals in the early 2000s.

- The brother of a first-class cricketer went on to coach the first Chinese tennis player to win a singles final at a Grand Slam championship. Former Danish tennis player Michael Mortensen – whose brother Ole appeared in 157 first-class matches for Derbyshire – became coach to Li Na, who won the women's crown at the French Open in 2011.

- Down by two games to love in the 2012 one-day international series against England, Australia's coach urged his players to follow the fighting spirit of tennis champion Roger Federer. Micky Arthur used the example of the Swiss legend who had lost the first two sets against Frenchman Julien Benneteau at the 2012 Wimbledon championships, before recovering to win 4-6, 6-7 (3), 6-2, 7-6 (6), 6-1. Australia's batting coach Justin Langer also invoked Federer's fighting comeback and said: **"Great comebacks, like surprise defeats, often become folklore in sport and while this short ODI series isn't the same magnitude of the Ashes we are going to have to draw on every inch of inspiration and skill if we are to recover this series. Federer's courageous comeback is something we can draw from but it is the way he went about the contest that may provide the most valuable feedback."**

  The pep talk didn't work with Australia losing the next one-day international a day after Federer had beaten Novak Djokovic to seal a place in the Wimbledon final against Britain's Andy Murray. Present in the Royal Box at Wimbledon to witness the marquee semi-final showdown was Federer fan Sachin Tendulkar.

- Champion Indian badminton player Saina Nehwal dedicated her winning of the 2012 Swiss Open to Sachin Tendulkar. She revealed that Tendulkar's scoring of his 100th international century had inspired her to overcome a form slump, saying: **"When he scored that 100 it was semi-finals day. I got a lot of inspiration from him. I told myself I also have to do well. I can win that title, and that happened."**

- A spinner who twice claimed figures of 4-9 against international opponents in a two-year period was a member of Ireland's rugby union squad for the 2003 World Cup. Neil Doak appeared in a number of cricket matches for Ireland – with two first-class appearances – and played rugby for a number of teams, including Ulster. In the 1996 European Championship, Doak took 4-9 against Gibraltar in Denmark, repeating the feat in the 1996/97 ICC Trophy in Malaysia, taking 4-9 against Israel.

- For a fund-raiser in 2007, a former Somerset batsman played a round of golf at every course in New Zealand. Ricky Bartlett, who appeared in 51 first-class matches, reportedly played 31,594 shots over 7,542 holes in 363 days.

- After finishing equal runner-up in the Victorian Seniors Golf Open in 2011, Dean Jones turned professional. The former Australian batsman completed three years as an amateur golfer around the country before turning pro in 2012, playing the Australian Seniors Tour. He said: **"If you have a dream and you want to do something, have a dip, don't be ten years later having a beer saying 'I wish I'd had a go.' My major problem was 'Am I good enough?' But I played the Victorian Senior Open last year and I finished third. It gave me the belief that I can cut the mustard, that I can compete with these guys."**

- Leonard Crawley, a double-centurion at first-class level and a doubles tennis champion, was a leading golf correspondent for the *Daily Telegraph*. A top-class golfer himself – and a gold medal-winning ice skater – Crawley struck over 5,000 runs in first-class cricket, mostly for Essex and Worcestershire in the 1920s and 1930s.

- During a golf tournament in the United Arab Emirates in 2012, former world number one Tiger Woods revealed an interest in cricket. The Abu Dhabi Golf Championship was run at the same time as the Pakistan–England Test match at the Sheik Zayed Stadium: **"Have**

CHURCHMAN'S CIGARETTES

L. G. CRAWLEY

I followed cricket? I have, a little bit. I have met some of the guys ... that certainly helps ... because now you have personal interest in it, so that's what makes it a little bit more exciting."

- Zimbabwe fast bowler Henry Olonga has a brother who captained his country at rugby union. Victor Olonga appeared in 14 rugby internationals for Zimbabwe during the 1990s.

- Three West Australians who played Test cricket in the 1980s also played football in Perth. Geoff Marsh played a season of Aussie Rules football for the South Fremantle club in the West Australian Football League in 1978, while Graeme Wood played for East Fremantle between 1975 and 1977. Wicketkeeper Tim Zoehrer also played for Wood's club, in 1982.

Marsh's son Mitchell, who made his first-class debut for WA in 2009/10, also dabbled in Aussie Rules football before turning full-time to cricket. In 2008, Mitchell represented his state in the AFL National Under-18 Championships and also played cricket in the Australian Under-17 and Under-19 Championships. His best with the bat came in the Under-17s, with an unbeaten 79 against the ACT in Melbourne in 2007/08.

Mitchell's sister excelled in the sporting world as well, becoming a leading basketball player. Melissa Marsh stood tall in the Women's National Basketball League, making her debut for Perth in 2001/02, later captaining the West Coast Waves.

MELISSA MARSH'S DREAM TEAM

Shane Watson (A)	*Australian*
Geoff Marsh (A)	*basketball*
Shaun Marsh (A)	*player*
Steve Waugh (A)	*Melissa*
Allan Border * (A)	*Marsh*
Mitchell Marsh (A)	
Adam Gilchrist † (A)	
Shane Warne (A)	
Glenn McGrath (A)	
Dennis Lillee (A)	
Bob Massie (A)	

- While Duncan Fletcher captained Zimbabwe at the 1983 World Cup, his sister Ann Grant had captained Zimbabwe's hockey team at the 1980 Olympics. Due to a boycott of the Moscow Games by a number of countries, a request was sent to Zimbabwe, which put together a team in a matter of weeks before competition began. They came out on top, securing Zimbabwe's only gold medal at the Games. She said: **"During a vital match when a short corner penalty was flicked high into the goal and as post player, I reached up with my left hand, caught the ball and rolled it along the back line which would have made my brother Duncan very proud. Except that all these actions were highly illegal and resulted in a penalty stroke which won that particular match. I was devastated."**

The sister of another Zimbabwean cricketer captained a women's hockey team at the Olympics, with Lindsey Carlisle leading South Africa at Sydney and Athens. The older sister of Zimbabwe Test captain Stuart Carlisle, she was also South Africa's team leader at the 2006 Commonwealth Games in Melbourne.

- Jamie Siddons, who appeared in a one-day international in 1988/89, was the last sportsman to play at the highest level of Australian Rules football and for Australia at cricket. In 1984, Siddons played in two VFL matches for the Sydney Swans, kicking a goal against North Melbourne at the SCG.

- While captain of Australia, Michael Clarke swapped his cricket bat for a gear shift making his debut as a rally driver. He got behind the wheel of a Mitsubishi Lancer for two stages of the 2012 Rally of Queensland. Clarke said: **"I've always had a lot of respect for any driver – Formula One, V8s, rally – but I've always thought rally driving would be the hardest. Having experienced it, I have the utmost respect for it and the successful rally drivers, because it is so hard to get on the gravel and control the car, at pace as well."**

- Before turning to cricket, India's Rahul Dravid had impressed at hockey. He was good enough to be chosen to represent the junior Karnataka state team.

> **"Rahul had a rock-like presence. He is a credit to our school, state and country."**
>
> Indian Olympic hockey player and former schoolmate of Rahul Dravid, Anil Aldrin

- Despite not having been an Olympic sport since 1900, cricket was included in the opening ceremony at the 2012 Games in London. Put together by award-winning film director Danny Boyle – famed for *Slumdog Millionaire* and *Trainspotting* – a game of village cricket featured in the opening moments of the extravaganza that highlighted things quintessentially British.

The 1900 Olympics at Paris is the only Games to include cricket which saw Great Britain win a gold medal against the host nation in a 12-a-side two-day match at the Vélodrome de Vincennes. The Netherlands and Belgium were touted as possible participants in the event, but pulled out leaving the Devon and Somerset Wanderers club, representing Britain, and the French Athletic Club, mostly British expatriates living in Paris, representing France. The England side included two players with first-class experience – Somerset's Alfred Bowerman and Montagu Toller.

Another first-class cricketer appeared at the Paris Olympics. Claude Buckenham, a fast bowler who played for Essex from 1899 to 1914, was a member of the Upton Park football team that won the inaugural Olympic football tournament at the 1900 Games. He then played in four Tests against South Africa in 1909/10, taking 21 wickets at 28.23.

- Just before the London Olympics in 2012, the fast-running, fast-bowling Yohan Blake had taken 4-10 in a Twenty20 match for the Kingston club in Jamaica. Hot on the heels of winning gold in London, the world-champion sprinter was back in action on the cricket field, scoring 20 in another Twenty20 game. Representing Bartley XI against a Correctional Services team in Jamaica, Blake struck a six which shattered the window of a nearby parked car. He said: **"I was a bit nervous as I haven't batted in a while but I just had to play myself in and with 20 off 21 balls that's what I did. The owner of the car said 'that's just cricket'. It was a wonderful six but I know the owner of the car, he's a good guy."**

- Ward Prentice, a wicketkeeper, played first-class cricket for New South Wales, rugby league for the Western Suburbs club and union for Australia. He made his rugby debut for the Wallabies against Wales in 1908, appearing in 32 games in all, including six Tests. He appeared in two first-class cricket matches, eight years apart. His first game came in 1912/13, his second in 1920/21. He took two catches, but failed to score a run in either match.

The Australian rugby union squad of 1908, with cricketer Ward Prentice in the middle row, second from right

- The New York-born George Wright is the only sportsman to have played first-class cricket and Major League baseball. He made his debut for the USA in 1883, scoring 12 and returning first-innings figures of 6-6-0-0 against the Gentlemen of Philadelphia. Inducted into the Baseball Hall of Fame in 1937, the Boston Red Stockings shortstop is the father of Beals Wright, who won a gold medal at tennis at the 1904 Olympic Games.

- After appearing in six first-class cricket matches for Queensland in the 1960s, Johnny Brown played rugby league for Australia. In ten first-class innings, he scored 163 runs with a best of 36 on his debut, against the touring Pakistanis at the Gabba in 1964/65. A champion football player in his home state, Brown pulled on the Australian jersey for a match in the 1970 World Cup tournament played in Great Britain.

- New Zealand medium-fast bowler Don Cleverley, who appeared in a Test against Australia in 1945/46, was a national amateur boxing champion. His brother Alf represented New Zealand at boxing at the 1928 Olympic Games in Amsterdam.

- Former New Zealand batsman Craig McMillan dodged an offer to take on Jesse Ryder in the boxing ring in 2012. The invitation came after McMillan had criticised Ryder's batting in a Twenty20 match. McMillan said: **"I have no desire to box. It is being billed to settle a grudge and I don't want to be a part of it."**

Ryder then found a willing partner in Mark Watson, a New Zealand sports-radio presenter. In a bout staged in Auckland, the Wellington batsman knocked his opponent to the floor in the 20th second and won the event by technical knockout after one minute and 54 seconds. He said: **"What a rush. I've never felt anything like that before. I've trained pretty well and I stuck to what I knew. Now I can get on with my life."**

Later in the same year, Andrew Flintoff donned the gloves for a debut fight at Manchester Arena. In front of a 6,000-strong crowd, Flintoff took on a 23-year-old American, Richard Dawson, and after the prescribed four rounds, was declared the winner. Flintoff said: **"On a global scale, it's obviously nowhere near [cricket] … I've had a novice heavyweight fight and it was brilliant."**

DANNY GREEN'S DREAM TEAM	
David Boon (A)	*World*
Justin Langer (A)	*champion*
Viv Richards (WI)	*Australian*
Sachin Tendulkar (I)	*boxer*
Allan Border * (A)	*Danny*
Adam Gilchrist † (A)	*Green*
Ian Botham (E)	
Shane Warne (A)	
Joel Garner (WI)	
Dennis Lillee (A)	
Jeff Thomson (A)	

- A South African rugby Test player once hit Ian Botham for three consecutive sixes in a first-class match in England. In the second of his 11 first-class matches for Oxford University, Nick Mallett hit a second-innings 27 against Somerset in 1980 before losing his wicket to Botham, lbw. Later a coach of the Springbok and Italy rugby teams, Mallett achieved his best batting and bowling figures in the same match – 52 and 5-52 – against Glamorgan at The Parks in 1981.

- After completing seven first-class cricket matches for Cambridge University in 1951, John Cockett represented Great Britain at hockey at the 1952 Stockholm Olympics. He made a first-class cricket comeback the following year, but completed a pair in the match, for Minor Counties against the 1953 Australians, at Stoke-on-Trent.

  Cockett also took part in the 1956 Olympics at Melbourne, which featured four other first-class cricketers in the hockey tournament, three from Australia and one from New Zealand. Ian Dick, who played for Western Australia, was Australia's captain, with Brian Booth, who scored five centuries in 29 Tests, and Maurice Foley, who appeared in three matches for WA in 1953/54, also in the squad. Dick was Australia's first Olympic hockey captain, scored Australia's first Olympic hockey goal and was a member of every Australian team between 1948 and 1958. He also managed to squeeze in a first-class cricket debut in 1950/51.

Bruce Turner, who appeared in 15 first-class matches for Central Districts, also played hockey at the Melbourne Games, and led his country in the sport at the Rome Olympics in 1960.

FIRST-CLASS CRICKETERS WHO APPEARED AT THE OLYMPIC GAMES

Player	Games	Team	Event	Medal
Alfred Bowerman (Somerset)	Paris 1900	GB	Cricket	Gold
Montagu Toller (Somerset)	Paris 1900	GB	Cricket	Gold
Claude Buckenham (Essex, England)	Paris 1900	GB	Football	Gold
Johnny Douglas (Essex, England)	London 1908	GB	Boxing	Gold
Reginald Pridmore (Warwickshire)	London 1908	GB	Hockey	Gold
Arthur Page (Oxford University)	London 1908	GB	Real Tennis	-
Henry Brougham (Oxford University)	London 1908	GB	Rackets	Bronze
Arthur Knight (Hampshire)	Stockholm 1912	GB	Football	Gold
	Antwerp 1920	GB	Football	-
Cyril Wilkinson (Surrey)	Antwerp 1920	GB	Hockey	Gold
Jack MacBryan (Cambridge University, Somerset, England)	Antwerp 1920	GB	Hockey	Gold
Alastair MacCorquodale (Middlesex, MCC)	London 1948	GB	Athletics	Silver
Michael Walford (Oxford University, Somerset)	London 1948	GB	Hockey	Silver
John Cockett (Cambridge University)	Helsinki 1952	GB	Hockey	Bronze
	Melbourne 1956	GB	Hockey	-
Brian Booth (New South Wales, Australia)	Melbourne 1956	Aus	Hockey	-
Ian Dick (Western Australia)	Melbourne 1956	Aus	Hockey	-
Maurice Foley (Western Australia)	Melbourne 1956	Aus	Hockey	-
Chuni Goswami (Bengal)	Melbourne 1956	India	Football	-
Bruce Turner (Central Districts)	Melbourne 1956	NZ	Hockey	-
	Rome 1960	NZ	Hockey	-
David Acfield (Cambridge University, Essex)	Mexico City 1968	GB	Archery	-
	Munich 1972	GB	Archery	-
Ric Charlesworth (Western Australia)	Munich 1972	Aus	Hockey	-
	Montreal 1976	Aus	Hockey	Silver
	Los Angeles 1984	Aus	Hockey	-
	Seoul 1984	Aus	Hockey	-

- While taking part in the 2010 Commonwealth Games in Delhi, Australian hockey great Jamie Dwyer kept a close eye on the progress of the India–Australia Test series. Dwyer, who once met Sachin Tendulkar at a hockey competition in Chennai in 2005, lavished praise on the Indian maestro who scored a series-winning double-hundred and a fifty in the second Test at Bangalore: **"I am a big fan of Sachin Tendulkar. I just love his batting. He is a role model not only for India but for the entire sporting world."**

JAMIE DWYER'S DREAM TEAM

Sachin Tendulkar (I)
Jack Hobbs (E)
Don Bradman * (A)
Brian Lara (WI)
Garry Sobers (WI)
Jacques Kallis (SA)
Adam Gilchrist † (A)
Shane Warne (A)
Imran Khan (P)
Dennis Lillee (A)
Muttiah Muralitharan (SL)

Australian hockey star Jamie Dwyer

- England rugby league legend Martin Offiah also played rugby union and cricket. A winger, he appeared in 33 Tests for Great Britain in the 1980s and 1990s, and opened the bowling for the Essex second XI in 1985.

MARTIN OFFIAH'S DREAM TEAM

Sachin Tendulkar (I)
Geoff Boycott * (E)
Viv Richards (WI)
Don Bradman (A)
Brian Lara (WI)
Alan Knott † (E)
Ian Botham (E)
Shane Warne (A)
Dennis Lillee (A)
Michael Holding (WI)
Joel Garner (WI)

Former England rugby league star Martin Offiah

The Name Game

- For the first three matches against Bangladesh A in 2011/12, the top six in the England Lions' batting order were players whose first name began with the letter J. The openers were Jason Roy and Joe Root, followed by James Vince, James Taylor, Jonny Bairstow and Jos Buttler. Batting at either number ten or 11 was Jack Brooks.

- When the Sri Lankans took to the field for their opening match of the 2007 England tour, the MCC side contained two players named Matthew J. Wood. One of them was making his first-class debut, becoming the third Matthew J. Wood to appear in first-class cricket.

- During a first-class match at Lahore in 2009/10, both teams fielded a player named Sarfraz Ahmed. In the Quaid-e-Azam Trophy fixture at Gaddafi Stadium, the PIA captain and wicketkeeper took ten catches over the two innings, without nabbing his namesake who dismissed him twice for the Water and Power Development Authority XI.

- Doug Bracewell, the New Zealand fast bowler, was named after a famous Australian Test cricketer. Bracewell's father was a big fan of Australian batsman Doug Walters.

- After dismissing the great West Indies batsman Frank Worrell in a match in India in the 1950s, swing bowler Devi Chand was granted a new name courtesy of the Maharaja of Patiala. The Southern Punjab bowler only took 11 wickets in seven first-class matches over a ten-year period, but made a name for himself as a youngster bowling to the West Indies legend. Chand said: **"I got Worrell out thrice when he was in Patiala. Bowled over with my performance, Maharaja Yadavendra Singh rechristened me 'Worrell'. The name has stuck with me ever since."**

- Within his first three first-class matches, Desmond Haynes opened the batting for Barbados with two different players who shared the same surname. In his first two matches – in 1976/77 – his opening partner was Gordon Greenidge. In his third match, his partner was the unrelated Alvin Greenidge. After just eight first-class matches, Haynes joined Gordon Greenidge at the top of the order in the West Indies Test side, opening with a stand of 87 against Australia at Port-of-Spain in 1977/78.

- When Tasmania hosted Victoria at Hobart in 1857/58, both of the wicketkeepers shared the same name. In his only first-class appearance, Tasmania's George Marshall achieved a single dismissal, a stumping, while his opposite number George Marshall (32) made the top score in the match during Victoria's first-innings total of 78.

- Two Kenyan players whose surname began with the letter O made their Twenty20 international debuts at Durban in 2007 and both made a duck. David Obuya and debutant Maurice Ouma were both dismissed without scoring opening the batting – against New Zealand at Durban in the ICC World Twenty20 – while Thomas Odoyo and Peter Ongondo opened the bowling. Three others in the Kenya team also had surnames beginning with O – Collins Obuya, Alex Obanda and the other debutant, Nehemiah Odhiambo.

- England's Graeme Swann did a Brian Lara in 2011 by naming a new-born child Sydney. The spinner and his wife named their son Wilfred Richard Sydney Swann, with the second middle name chosen to commemorate England's Ashes win in 2010/11. Swann said: **"It came to me on the spur of the moment and I couldn't help telling the lads I'd be naming our first son after the scene of our achievement."** Lara named his daughter Sydney following an innings of 277 for the West Indies in the Sydney Test of 1992/93.

> **"Actually, I was named after you."**
> West Indies and Kolkata Knight Riders spinner Sunil Narine talking to India's Sunil Gavaskar in 2012

- Despite having one of the most common surnames in the world, when Steven Smith made his Test debut for Australia in 2010, he became only the third Smith to wear the baggy green. The other two who preceded him were Australia's 104th Test player, Dave Smith, who appeared in two Tests in 1912, and their 323rd, Steve Smith, who played in three Tests against the West Indies in 1983/84.

- For the first time in history, the two captains for a Test in 2011/12 had the same surname, and both scored a pair of fifties. Zimbabwe's Brendan Taylor hit 50 and 117 in the match at Bulawayo, while New Zealand skipper Ross Taylor achieved identical knocks of 76. The second player – after Murphy Su'a – of Samoan heritage to play for New Zealand, the Kiwi captain was born with the name Luteru Ross Poutoa Lote Taylor.

- In the second innings of a first-class match at Bloemfontein in 2011/12, Free State's appropriately-named wicketkeeper Rudi Second picked up a record eight dismissals. Second took 12 catches for the match, against North West, becoming just the second keeper to achieve a dozen dismissals in a South African first-class match.

- During the 2008/09 Zimbabwean Logan Cup, four players who possessed unusual Christian names achieved a variety of personal bests in matches played in Harare. Remembrance Nyathi scored a maiden first-class century, with 100 for Centrals versus Westerns, while Freedom Takarusenga (65*) carried his bat for Westerns against Centrals. An Easterns bowler prospered during the tournament, with Prosper Utseya taking ten wickets in two consecutive matches, while the admirably marvellous figures of 18.2-11-15-5 came the way of Admire Marvellous Manyumwa, for Northerns against Westerns.

A SELECTION OF COLOURFULLY-NAMED ZIMBABWEAN FIRST-CLASS CRICKETERS

Player	First-class debut	
Chamunorwa Justice Chibhabha	Mashonaland	2003/04
Lovemore Tatenda Gumunyu-Manatsa	Northerns	2008/09
Romeo Tatenda Kasawaya	Matabeleland	2003/04
Shepherd Tichandepi Makunura	Mashonaland A	2001/02
Admire Marvellous Manyumwa	Northerns	2006/07
Prince Spencer Masvaure	Northerns	2006/07
Silent Mujaji	Easterns	2006/07
Bornaparte Mujuru	Westerns	2006/07
Steady Musoso	Easterns	2006/07
David Travolta Mutendera	Cricket Academy	1998/99
Tinotenda Confidence Mutombodzi	Northerns	2008/09
Waddington Mwayenga	Mashonaland	2001/02
Blessing Ngondo	Mashonaland Under-24s	1993/94
Remembrance Nyathi	Centrals	2006/07
Freedom Takarusenga	Westerns	2006/07
Prosper Tsvanhu	Northerns	2006/07

SOME FROM THE CARIBBEAN

Player		
Hamish Arbeb Gervais Anthony	Leeward Islands	1989/90
Tino la Bertram Best	Barbados	2001/02
Nikolai Gabriel Ramon Charles	Barbados	2008/09
Colwin Brentnol Cort	Guyana	1990/91
Esuan Asqui Crandon	Guyana	2000/01
Royston Tycho Crandon	Guyana	2006/07
Gosnel Cupid	Windward Islands	1993/94
Romel Kwesi Currency	Windward Islands	2000
Darnley Clements Campbell Clairmonte Da Costa	Barbados	1898/99
Bront Arson DeFreitas	Leeward Islands	2007/08
Danza Pacino Hyatt	Jamaica	2003/04
Lindon Omrick Dinsley James	Windward Islands	2003/04
Moreland Moses le Blanc	Windward Islands	2010/11
Javier Springteen Liburd	Barbados	2006/07
Denville St Delmo McKenzie	Jamaica	1995/96
Donovan Jomo Pagon	Jamaica	2002/03
Javon Philip Ramon Scantlebury-Searles	Barbados	2008/09
Lendl Mark Platter Simmons	Trinidad and Tobago	2001/02
Darwin Terrel Telemaque	Windward Islands	1987/88
Charles Harold Lushington Valencia	Jamaica	1901/02

... AND ONE OTHER

Helao Nafidi "Pikky" Ya France	Namibia	2010/11

- A player by the name of Bond, James Bond, played in a final at Lord's in 2008 and batted at number '007'. Bond made the second-highest score of 27 for Malden Wanderers against Kibworth in the final of the Cockspur Cup.

- Indian fast bowler Ishant Sharma had a name change in 2011 in a bid to improve his fortunes on the field. A graphologist had advised him to change the spelling of his name to Ishannt. Sharma said: "**I do not know how and why, but I'm more at peace now since the signature change ... I haven't changed them in my bank account or official papers, as that is a long drawn-out process.**"

- In a County Championship match in 2011, Leicestershire opener Greg Smith was dismissed by Derbyshire's Greg Smith. Later in the summer, opposing players named Smith took each other's wicket in a county match at Lord's. Middlesex's Tom Smith was dismissed by the aforementioned Greg Smith of Derbyshire in the first innings, while Greg was in turn dismissed by Tom.

- History was made at the Adelaide Oval in 2011/12 when Michael Clarke was dismissed for 210 by Indian fast bowler Umesh Yadav. It represented the first occasion in Test history of two batsmen who had made a double-century being dismissed for exactly the same score by a bowler with the same last name. In the famous tied Test against India at Madras in 1986/87, Dean Jones had been dismissed for 210 by Shivlav Yadav.

CENTURIONS DISMISSED BY BOWLERS WITH SAME SURNAME FOR THE SAME SCORE IN A TEST

	Batsmen	Matches
210	Dean Jones b Shivlal Yadav	Australia v India at Madras 1986/87
	Michael Clarke b Umesh Yadav	Australia v India at Adelaide 2011/12
118	Stanley Jackson b Ernie Jones	England v Australia at The Oval 1899
	Clive Lloyd b Jeff Jones	WI v England at Port-of-Spain 1967/68
115	Derek Randall b Geoff Lawson	England v Australia at Perth 1982/83
	Steve Waugh b Jermaine Lawson	Australia v WI at Bridgetown 2002/03
106	Mushtaq Ali lbw Denis Atkinson	Pakistan v WI at Calcutta 1948/49
	Wazir Mohammad lbw Denis Atkinson	Pakistan v WI at Kingston 1957/58

- A club cricketer belied his name in a New South Wales competition in 2006/07, scoring over 500 runs at an average exceeding 500. Playing for the Kurrajong Gypsies, Tim Duck hit three unbeaten centuries (214*, 102*, 129*) and a half-century (86) at 513.00.

- When wicketkeeper Matthew Wade made his Australian debut in 2011/12, his opposite number in the match had the same initials. In the first match of the triangular one-day series at Melbourne, M.S. Wade made 67 against India led by wicketkeeper M.S. Dhoni. It was only the second time in a one-day international involving Australia that the two keepers shared the same initials. The previous occasion was at Sydney in 1982/83 when R.W. Marsh and England's R.W. Taylor kept wicket.

- Upon scoring his maiden Test century in 2011/12, Matthew Wade became the second wicketkeeper with the same surname to achieve a three-figure score at Test level. Matthew's maiden century was one of 106 against the West Indies at Roseau, while South Africa's Billy Wade hit 125 against England at Port Elizabeth in 1948/49.

    Matthew Wade was the sixth keeper whose surname began with the letter W to score a Test century, after Billy Wade, England's Henry Wood, the West Indies' Clyde Walcott, South Africa's John Waite and New Zealand's B.J. Watling.

- During the calendar year of 2002, Sri Lankan fast bowler Dilhara Fernando twice dismissed a batsman thanks to two team-mates with the same surname. During the second Test against Bangladesh at Colombo, Ehsanul Haque was caught by Charitha Fernando off Dilhara Fernando; two Tests later in Centurion, South Africa's Gary Kirsten was caught by Hasantha Fernando off Dilhara.

- A player named Samantha de Mel turned out for Italy in the 1996/97 ICC Trophy. He also appeared in 12 first-class matches in his native Sri Lanka. In 1991/92, a Mandy Yachad played in a one-day international for South Africa, while Chris Mary Kuggeleijn appeared in two Tests for New Zealand in 1988/89.

- During his only series for England, Chris Adams was bowled in consecutive Tests by his namesake Paul Adams. The South African bowler, with his so-called 'frog-in-a-blender' action, dismissed the England batsman for 19 at Durban and for 31 at Johannesburg in the 1999/2000 series.

  During a one-day international series in New Zealand in the same summer, Damien Fleming twice dismissed Stephen Fleming. The Australian fast bowler had previously taken the Kiwi's wicket at Sharjah in 1994, the first example of such a dismissal in a one-day international.

A SELECTION OF FAMOUS CRICKETING NAMESAKES

Don Bradman (Australia)	Shannon Bradman Bakes (Tasmanian 2nd XI), Prince Bradman Ediriweera (Sri Lanka A)
Kapil Dev (India)	Kapil Dev (Jammu and Kashmir Under-16s)
Muttiah Muralitharan (Sri Lanka)	Darwin Muralitharan (Malaysia)
Barry Richards (South Africa)	Barry Richards (Boland)
Garry Sobers (West Indies)	Arul Sobers (Hyderabad Under-19s), David Sobers (Belize)
Sachin Tendulkar (India)	Chandrakanth Tendulkar (Goa)
Shane Warne (Australia)	Tom and Frank Warne (Victoria)
Younis Khan (Pakistan)	Younis Khan (Germany)
Zaheer Abbas (Pakistan)	Zaheer Abbas (Pakistan Under-19s)

- Two cricketers with fast bowling-themed surnames both passed away on the same day in 1990. Andrew Speed, a Warwickshire medium-pacer of the 1920s, and batsman Arnold Quick, who appeared in 19 first-class matches for Essex, both died on 17 July.

- Peter Bowler, a batsman who played for Tasmania and three English counties, took 34 wickets in first-class cricket as a right-arm off-break bowler. Bowler's best with the bat was an unbeaten 241. Chris Batt, who appeared in 12 first-class matches, was better with the ball than the bat, taking a six-wicket haul on his County Championship debut for Middlesex in 1998. In his next match – against Surrey at Guildford – Batt dismissed Jonathan Batty for a duck, on his way to a first-innings haul of 5-51. Batt's best with the bat was 43. Kent's Arthur Fielder, who appeared in six Tests for England between 1904 and 1908, took over 100 catches in a first-class career of 287 matches.

- When the Sri Lankan pair Mahela Jayawardene and Prasanna Jayawardene put on 351 against India at Ahmedabad in 2009/10 it represented the biggest Test match partnership by players with the same surname. Mahela hit 275 and the wicketkeeping Prasanna an unbeaten 154 in a sixth-wicket union as Sri Lanka piled on 760/7 declared.

- A former Sri Lankan captain and his wife named their twins after Sachin Tendulkar. The sons of Hashan Tillakaratne – who appeared in 83 Tests – were named Duvindu Sachin and Ravindu Sachin.

> "Apart from my husband Hashan, Sachin is my favourite cricketer. Even Hashan likes him a lot. When my sons were born, we thought why not name our kids after Sachin. In spite of their first name, I always mention their middle name wherever we go. So, both are commonly called Sachin Tillakaratne."
>
> Apsari Tillakaratne

- In the late 1990s, India awarded consecutive Test caps to two players with the same name, both of whom played just once. Robin Singh, a Trinidad-born all-rounder, appeared in his only Test against Zimbabwe at Harare in 1998/99, while Delhi fast bowler Robin Singh got his one and only chance against New Zealand at Hamilton a few months later.

- In his only one-day international, Rajshahi fast bowler Aminul Islam played alongside another player with the same name. The two Aminul Islams played for Bangladesh against Kenya at Dhaka in the 1998/99 Meril International Cricket Tournament.

- When Leicestershire hosted Loughborough in a first-class match in 2011, one batsman from each side named Taylor hit a century. After Leicestershire lost their first three wickets for six on the first morning, James Taylor became one of the few to score a double-century in his first first-class match as captain with 237, just behind his namesake Herbie Taylor's unbeaten 250 for Natal in 1912/13. Rob Taylor, who had previously played for Leicestershire's second XI, then scored a match-saving maiden century for Loughborough with 101 not out.

  Four months later, Zimbabwe's Brendan Taylor marked his first Test as captain by scoring his maiden Test century, becoming just the seventh player to achieve the feat. Also on the list is Herbie Taylor who followed a century in his initial first-class match in charge with a maiden Test hundred in his first Test as captain in 1913/14.

- In his final Test match innings for England, at Colombo in 1981/82, Derek Underwood was dismissed for a duck by Sri Lanka's Somachandra de Silva. His final Test wicket was a player with the same last name – Ajit de Silva – and he too made a duck.

- Two left-arm fast bowlers with the same first name shared all ten wickets in a Test match in 2012/13. A first in Test cricket, Mitchell Starc took 6-154 and Mitchell Johnson 4-110 against South Africa at the WACA. The only previous instance of a pair of left-arm quicks sharing all ten in a Test innings was South Africa's Gobo Ashley (7-95) and Charles Vintcent (3-88), against England at Cape Town in 1888/89.

- During the Bangladesh–Australia Test at Fatullah in 2005/06, two players who had 'Gil' in their surnames broke records previously held by Kiwi Chris Cairns. Stuart MacGill took 8-108, beating Cairns's 7-53 in 2001/02, previously the best figures in a Test innings against Bangladesh. Adam Gilchrist hit his 88th six in a Test, overtaking Cairns's tally of 87, while another 'Gil', Jason Gillespie, passed the 1,000 run–200 wicket double, joining a number of others, including Cairns.

- The opening match of the 2012 World Twenty20 tournament saw Zimbabwe dismissed for a neat 100 by three players whose surnames began with the letter M. The first nine wickets were taken by a pair of Mendises with the tenth going to Lasith Malinga. Ajantha Mendis posted the record-breaking figures of 6-8 in his first match in nearly a year, becoming the first Sri Lankan to concede less than ten runs in a completed spell on two occasions. The unrelated Jeevan Mendis took 3-24 after scoring an unbeaten 43 off 30 balls.

  In the third match of the tournament, in Colombo, Afghanistan and India included four players whose names began with the letter Z. A first in international cricket, India had Zaheer Khan in their XI, while Afghanistan's last three in the order were players who shared the same last name – Najibullah Zadran, Dawlat Zadran and Shapoor Zadran.

- Richard Halliwell, who appeared in 43 first-class matches in the 1800s, played much of his cricket under a number of names, including 'O.N.E. More'. He also appeared as 'R. Bisset', his middle name, and as 'R. Tessib', his middle name spelt backwards.

- Two players named Michael David Bates appeared in the 2012 Champions League Twenty20 tournament. One played for Auckland, the other for Hampshire, and played against each other in a match at Centurion, on a day that happened to be the latter's 22nd birthday.

- A world first took place in 2009 when every member of an Indian cricket team had the same surname. The Twirupa Bari High School squad that took part in the Polly Umrigar National School Tournament was comprised of 15 players named Jamatia – Saral Mithun Jamatia, Ananda Jamatia, Ananda Sadhan Jamatia, Tantu Kumar Jamatia, Naresh Kumar Jamatia, Gobinda Sadhan Jamatia, Rati Kumar Jamatia, Amal Kishore Jamatia, Bishnu Behari Jamatia, Durga Dayal Jamatia, Chalai Jamatia, Ajit Kumar Jamatia, Budhijoy Jamatia, Gulak Mani Jamatia and Banita Jamatia. The boys, from the Jamatia community – a tribe in Tripura – set a world record for a team taking part in a recognised tournament.

- When Sri Lankan fast bowler Chanaka Welegedara made his debut against England at Galle in 2007/08, he became the first Test cricketer with six initials. With 49 letters in his name, U.W.M.B.C.A. Welegedara claimed the Test record for most initials from fast-bowling team-mate W.P.U.J.C. Vaas (52 letters) and M.K.G.C.P. Lakshitha (45 letters), who, in 2002, became the first Sri Lankan to claim a wicket with his first ball on his Test debut.

Player's full name	Test Debut
Warnakulasuriya Patabendige Ushantha Joseph Chaminda Vaas	3rd Test v Pakistan at Kandy, 1994
Materba Kanatha Gamage Chamila Premanath Lakshitha	2nd Test v Bangladesh at Colombo, 2002
Uda Walawwe Mahim Bandaralage Chanaka Asanga Welegedara	3rd Test v England at Galle, 2007/08

In first-class cricket, the record for most initials – ten – is also held by a Sri Lankan bowler. Amunugama Rajapakse Rajakaruna Abeykoon Panditha Wasalamudiyanse Ralahamilage Rajitha Krishantha Bandara Amunugama, a right-arm medium-pacer, represented the Kurunegala Youth Cricket Club and Tamil Union Cricket and Athletic Club between 1988/89 and 2003/04.

- For the fourth Ashes Test match at Leeds in 1968, England fielded two batsmen who had the letter X in their surname. Roger Prideaux opened the batting in what was his Test debut, with Ted Dexter slotted in behind him at number three.

- Barbados all-rounder B.B.B. Yearwood, who made his first-class debut in 2008/09, was named in honour of a famous cricketer, tennis player and football star. Born in Barbados in 1986, he bears the names Barrington Bjorn Beckenbauer. Another cricketer named after England batsman Ken Barrington has played first-class cricket, with Barrington Rowland appearing in 68 matches for Indian side Karnataka.

154

- When Corey Anderson made his first-class debut for Canterbury in 2006/07 he appeared on the scorecard with his full name to avoid confusion with a similarly-named player, Carl J. Anderson, who was also on the club's books. He also made his New Zealand debut as Corey J. Anderson – not C.J. Anderson – in 2012/13.

- In the wake of V.V.S. Laxman's retirement from international cricket in 2012, his parents thanked a former Australian captain for coining the expression "Very Very Special". Laxman's mother paid tribute to Ian Chappell, saying: **"We must say 'thank you' to Chappell for giving this name to my son. To us, he is very, very special, because, he is very modest and simple. His name is Laxman and God's names like Venkata and Sai were added like to any new-born babies in the family. Vangipurappu is our family surname."**

- The day before Sachin Tendulkar made his one-day international debut in 1989, a baby was born to the Baby family in the Indian state of Kerala. The father watched Sachin's debut, and although the 16-year-old was dismissed for a duck, he decided to name his new-born son in his honour. **"We never imagined how big Tendulkar was going to be. But there was something very impressive about him. I wanted my son to grow up to be like him."**

  Twenty years later, Sachin Baby made his first-class debut, making 32 for Kerala against Andhra at Thalassery in the 2009/10 Ranji Trophy: **"I was interested in cricket from a young age, but it was only later that I realised I was named after Tendulkar."**

- When Pakistan's Mohammad Yousuf made 223 against England at Lahore in 2005/06, he became the first batsman to score Test match double-centuries under two different names. Yousuf, who converted to Islam in 2005, had previously scored two double-hundreds under his birth-name Yousuf Youhana – 203 against New Zealand at Christchurch in 2000/01 and 204 not out against Bangladesh at Chittagong in 2001/02.

- A player with one of the most romantic names in the annals of first-class cricket made his debut at Lord's in 1841. In his only match, for Cambridge against the MCC, Valentine Faithfull made a duck and one.

The Fast and the Slow

- An 11-year-old caused a mini sensation with the ball in his first match in the summer of 2011 by taking wickets with his first three deliveries. Playing for Sutton against Sanderstead in the UK, Sai Patel claimed a hat-trick and finished the match with figures of 4-1-14-4.

- During the course of four first-class matches for Afghanistan in the Intercontinental Cup, fast bowler Hamid Hassan achieved a record three ten-wicket hauls. In 2010, he took 11-154 (6-40 and 5-114) against Scotland at Ayr followed by 11-157 (5-70 and 6-87) in his next appearance, against Kenya in Nairobi. The following year, he then claimed a match haul of 10-85 (7-61 and 3-24) against Canada at King City.

- In 2011, Australia's Mitchell Johnson became the first bowler to achieve a five-wicket haul in his 100th one-day international. Playing against Sri Lanka at Pallekele, Johnson went one better with 6-31. The previous best by a bowler in his 100th ODI was 4-32 by Pakistan's Wasim Akram against New Zealand at Port Elizabeth in 1994/95.

    In the first final of the 2004/05 VB Series in Melbourne, Glenn McGrath took 3-34, becoming the first bowler to mark his 200th ODI with a three-wicket haul. Pakistan's Shoaib Malik – who played in the MCG final – became the second bowler to do so, with 3-6 in his 200th match, against Bangladesh at Chittagong in 2011/12.

- After being labelled "ordinary" by Bangladesh on his Test debut, Zimbabwe fast bowler Brian Vitori responded with two match-winning five-wicket hauls in one-day internationals. In a one-off Test match at Harare in 2011, Bangladesh opening batsman Tamim Iqbal had underplayed Vitori who ended up dismissing both openers in the first innings, and taking five wickets in the match. In their next encounter – a one-day international at Harare – the left-arm Vitori became the first Zimbabwean to take a five-wicket haul on debut with 5-30 off ten overs. He dazzled again in the next ODI, picking up 5-20, the first bowler to achieve a five-for in both of his first two one-day internationals. The previous best start to a career had been by Australia's Ryan Harris, who took five-wicket hauls in his second and third ODIs, while compatriot Gary Gilmour took two lots in his third and fourth matches.

- Medium-pace bowler Trent Copeland made the record books on his first-class debut for New South Wales by picking up eight wickets in the first innings and ten for the match. Playing against Queensland in Sydney in 2009/10, the 23-year-old seamer took a record 8-92 in the first innings with a match haul of 10-149. Appearing in his third match, Luke Feldman won the game for Queensland with a second-innings return of 5-32 and 9-81 in the match. Copeland enjoyed a bumper debut season, taking five wickets in an innings three times in his first four first-class matches and securing a total of 35 wickets in five.

- Just eight months on from being employed as a grounds-man at the Adelaide Oval, Nathan Lyon was called up for Australia's 2011 tour of Sri Lanka and took a wicket with his first ball in a Test. With just four first-class matches under his belt and 12 wickets at 43, Lyon debuted in the first Test at Galle becoming the first Australian bowler since 1894/95 to take a wicket with his first delivery. Remarkably, the other debutant in the Test – New South Wales quick Trent Copeland – took a wicket with his second delivery, claiming the Sri Lankan opener Til-lakaratne Dilshan. Lyon star-

Australia's Arthur Coningham, the first bowler to take a wicket with his first ball on his Test debut

red with 5-34, becoming the 32nd Australian to take a five-wicket haul on Test debut. He also became the first player from any country to take a wicket with his first ball and collect his maiden five-wicket haul in first-class cricket in his first Test.

AUSTRALIAN BOWLERS TO TAKE A WICKET WITH FIRST BALL ON TEST DEBUG

Bowler	Victim	Match		
Arthur Coningham (2-17)	Archie MacLaren	2nd Test v England	Melbourne	1894/95
Nathan Lyon (5-34)	Kumar Sangakkara	1st Test v Sri Lanka	Galle	2011

"For Trent Copeland to get his first wicket was fantastic to see. Someone I grew up with playing country cricket in New South Wales and seeing him get his first wicket was something pretty special. I'm 100 per cent stoked for Trent. To make my debut with someone you watched play cricket when you were younger and come from the same zone in New South Wales cricket was something pretty special.

"It's been one of the best days of my life, best couple of days, receiving the baggy green off Greg Chappell and to be able to take five wickets on debut is something pretty special and something I'm going to hold pretty close to my heart. I couldn't breathe in the huddle [after Sangakkara's dismissal]. I was so full of excitement. I wouldn't say it was the perfect ball, I thought it was a bit wide, but I was quite happy with it in the end."

Nathan Lyon

● Within the space a month in 2011, Sri Lankan fast bowler Shaminda Eranga took a wicket in the first over of his debut in both Test and one-day international cricket. In his first ODI – against Australia at Hambantota – Eranga uprooted the wicket of Brad Haddin with his second delivery, finishing with figures of 2-38. On his Test debut four weeks later – against Australia in Colombo – Elanga removed Phillip Hughes for a duck, becoming the 18th bowler to gain a wicket with his first delivery. With Nathan Lyon doing likewise in the first Test at Galle, it signalled only the second time that two bowlers had both taken a wicket with their first ball during the same Test series. The first occasion was in 1905/06 when South Africa's Bert Vogler and England's Jack Crawford did so in the same Test, the first, at Johannesburg.

In 2012, Eranga became the first bowler to pick up a wicket in his first over in all three forms of international cricket. On his Twenty20 international debut, against India at Pallekele, he dismissed Gautam Gambhir with the fourth ball of his first over.

- During a run of four first-class matches in Sri Lanka in 2009/10, Dinuka Hettiarachchi took six lots of five wickets in an innings. A spinner for the Chilaw Marians side, he began his purple patch with 10-123 (6-40 and 4-83) and a hat-trick against Tamil Union in Colombo. In his next match, he took 5-72 and 8-66, matching Bloomfield's Suraj Randiv by securing 13 wickets, Randiv for the second time in the season. A week later, Hettiaracchi took 13 wickets (6-25 and 7-201) for the second match in a row to total 36 in his last three.

    The slow left-armer – who played in a single Test in 2000/01 – then took seven wickets and another five-wicket haul in his next appearance, against Moors in Colombo. He finished the season as the Premier League's leading wicket-taker, with 66 victims at just under 19 each.

- Ajit Chandila, a tall off-spinner from Haryana, claimed a highly unusual hat-trick in the 2012 IPL in which none of his victims fell for a duck. A virtual unknown with just two first-class matches behind him, Chandila opened the bowling for Rajasthan Royals at Jaipur and disposed of the first three batsmen in the Pune Warriors' line-up. Jesse Ryder went first for one and Sourav Ganguly for two in Chandila's first over and he then picked up Robin Uthappa for six with the first ball of his second.

- A week after Makhaya Ntini took 5-9 in a Supersport Series match in 2008/09, so did South African team-mate Morne Morkel. Representing the Warriors, Ntini – with figures of 10.5-5-9-5 – and Lonwabo Tsotsobe, with 8-6-3-4 – had blasted away the Eagles for a record-low 28 at Port Elizabeth. Morkel, playing for the Titans, took 6-47 and 5-9 and a maiden first-class ten-wicket haul in the match against Ntini's team at East London.

- Upon his retirement from Test match cricket in 2010, Muttiah Muralitharan ended up being responsible for over a third of his country's wickets. In 132 Tests for Sri Lanka, he claimed 795 – or 38.78 per cent – of his country's total of 2,050 wickets. Murali also claimed a further five wickets in a Test for a World XI against Australia at Sydney in 2005/06.

    Of the 493 wickets he took in home Tests, Muralitharan achieved 45 lots of five wickets in an innings. The Test record by a considerable margin, the best by a fast bowler is 17 instances by Ian Botham in England. Dennis Lillee achieved 15 five-fors in 84 innings in Australia, a number matched by Shane Warne in 129 innings at home.

- During a first-class match involving the second-string West Indies B team in 2000/01, a top-order batsman from each side returned bowling figures of 3-9 or better. In Jamaica's first innings in the match at Montego Bay, Kurt Wilkinson had figures of 6.5-3-8-3, while Wavell Hinds responded with a first-innings haul of 6-3-9-3.

- New Zealand's Shane Bond got his chance to play for Hampshire in 2008 after Queenslander Ryan Harris was dropped in light of irregularities concerning his eligibility to play using his British passport. Bond stepped up and took 7-66 against Sussex at Southampton, the best debut innings figures for the county since Charles Llewellyn took 8-32 against the 1899 Australians.

  Imran Tahir – a Pakistan-born leg-spinner who would later represent South Africa – also took 7-66 on his first-class debut in the 2008 County Championship. Imran took 12-189 in his first match for Hampshire, with 5-123 in the first innings against Lancashire at Manchester. His match figures were the best by a Hampshire debutant since 1875, when Arthur Ridley took 12-173 against Sussex.

- In what turned out to be his final appearance in first-class cricket, Trinidad off-spinner Syed Ali was no-balled for throwing on at least 26 occasions in a single innings. Ali switched to bowling underarm in the match – against Barbados at Bridgetown in 1942 – and took a wicket.

- After just two Test matches, Australia's Jason Krejza unwittingly assumed the dubious distinction of the worst economy rate of all time by any bowler in history. He took 12 wickets for 358 on his Test debut – against India at Nagpur in 2008/09 – and leaked 100 runs in his first four innings, which included match figures of 1-204 against South Africa in Perth the following month. His economy rate of 4.53 – 562 runs off 743 deliveries – was the worst for any bowler with a minimum of 100 overs in Test cricket.

- During the Bangladeshi Cricket League tournament in 2008/09, Sylhet left-arm spinner Nabil Samad took 13 wickets in a match twice in a month and both times ended up on the losing side. In his team's first match of the season, he achieved career-best figures of 8-61 and 13-134 in the match, with Khulna victorious by a margin of 35 runs. Four weeks later, Nabil picked up 8-69 and 13-116 against Chittagong, only to see his opponents take the match by 53 runs.

- In the same one-day international that Virender Sehwag paraded a record-breaking double-century, one of his team-mates took three wickets on debut. The fifth bowler used in the match against the West Indies at Indore in 2011/12, leg-spinner Rahul Sharma took 3-43, striking with the last ball of his first three overs and shattering the stumps each time.

- Bangladesh's Abdur Razzak made history during the 2011/12 National Cricket League when he became the first bowler to take 15 wickets in a match. Captaining Khulna, Razzak racked up figures of 15-193 (8-123 and 7-70) against Barisal at Sylhet Stadium, beating the previous best haul of 13-106 by fellow left-arm spinner Elias Sunny in 2008/09. Curiously, only a few days before, Sunny had produced the second-best figures by a Bangladeshi on his Test debut, picking up 6-94 against the West Indies at Chittagong.

BEST BOWLING FIGURES BY LEFT-ARM SPINNERS ON TEST DEBUT

8-104	Alf Valentine	West Indies v England	Manchester	1950
7-56	James Langridge	England v West Indies	Manchester	1933
6-94	Elias Sunny	Bangladesh v West Indies	Chittagong	2011/12
6-103	Dilip Doshi	India v Australia	Madras	1979/80

- When India's Anil Kumble took the wicket of Andrew Strauss at Lord's in 2007, he became the first bowler to dismiss ten batsmen in the nineties in Test match cricket. The previous record of nine had been held by fellow Indian Kapil Dev.

> "The first Test match I ever saw was the first I played in. All I knew was what I had read in books and what my family and friends had told me. I was shattered that opposition players swore and abused me. I have learned to cope now, but I still don't understand it. Test cricket should be on a plane above all other games – a beautiful sport."
>
> Kapil Dev

- Achmat Magiet, a middle-order batsman and occasional slow bowler, only played twice at first-class level, securing the remarkable innings figures of 3-3-0-3 on his debut. Given the ball in his first match for Western Province at Cape Town in 2004/05, Magiet bowled three batsmen as North West slid to an innings defeat in the UCB Provincial Cup. Magiet concluded his first-class career a year later with three wickets at an average of 0.00.

- In a one-day international at the MCG in 1981/82, an opening fast bowler from each side dismissed each other for a first-ball duck.

Pakistan's Imran Khan took 3-23 including the West Indies' Andy Roberts for nought, who later took 3-42, including Imran for nought.

- Auckland pace bowler Don Cleverley made his Test debut for New Zealand against South Africa in 1931/32, but had to wait 14 years for his second, and last, Test. With 99 victims in first-class cricket, Cleverley failed to take a wicket in either Test and died at the age of 94 in Queensland in 2004.

- In 2010, a new one-day cricket team in England gambled on a bowler from the New South Wales town of Casino who hadn't played big-time cricket in five years. Neil Hancock, a left-armer, appeared in 11 List A matches for Devon and Somerset between 1999 and 2005 before getting his big break with the Unicorns, a team of un-contracted players set up specifically for the Clydesdale Bank 40-over tournament. In his final match of the season, Hancock starred with a maiden five-wicket haul of 5-64 against Lancashire at Colwyn Bay.

- During a four-week period in the English summer of 2011, four junior cricketers achieved the unusual feat of twin hat-tricks in a match. The most noteworthy double came from the nephew of the England captain Andrew Strauss, who took his two hat-tricks in a single over. Eleven-year-old Henry Forster performed the feat for Junior King's School Canterbury against St Edmund's.

The other youngsters to achieve two hat-tricks in a match were March Town's 13-year-old fast bowler Josh Fox (pictured) against Waterbeach; 14-year-old off-spinner Joe Braund-Smith, on his debut for the Dalton 1st XI against Cleator 2nds, and 15-year-old left-arm spinner Will Holmes, for the Woodford Under-18s against Stockport Georgians.

Another youngster to achieve the same feat in the same summer was 12-year-old wicketkeeper Owen Price for Westlands against West and Middle Chinook. He finished the Under-12s game with figures of 6-6. Price said: **"I had hurt my finger in a county game a few days before so I asked if I could not be wicketkeeper. I was then brought on to bowl and I just kept taking wickets. My coach said he is going to bowl me every week now."**

- In the calendar year of 2001, Muttiah Muralitharan bowled over 1,000 overs in international cricket and took a record number of wickets for the 12 months. In 45 matches – Tests and one-day internationals – the Sri Lankan claimed 136 wickets, with eight five-fors and four ten-fors. Next on the list is Murali again, who claimed 128 wickets in 2006. In five fewer matches, but this time with the benefit of Twenty20 internationals, Muralitharan took 128 wickets. He also performed the feat of 100 wickets in 1998 and 2000.

Wkts	Year	M	OMdns		Runs	BBI	BBM	Avge	Econ	SR	5WI	10WM
136	2001	45	1089.5	245	2718	8-87	11-170	19.98	2.49	48.0	8	4
128	2006	40	854.2	147	2687	8-70	12-225	20.99	3.14	40.0	9	5
109	2000	31	823.3	166	2143	7-30	13-171	19.66	2.60	45.3	9	3
100	1998	26	720.1	167	1986	9-65	16-220	19.86	2.75	43.2	9	2

- Sri Lanka's Rangana Herath did something with the ball in 2011/12 that Muttiah Muralitharan was never able to achieve when he secured a six-wicket haul in three consecutive Test innings. After a match-winning double of 6-74 and 6-97 against England at Galle, Herath then took 6-133 in the first innings of the following Test in Colombo.

- After struggling with just seven wickets in four Tests in the 2010/11 Ashes and being dropped, Ben Hilfenhaus bristled on his comeback with consecutive five-wicket hauls against India the following summer. A maiden Test match five-for at the MCG was followed by another five in an innings at the SCG and two four-wicket hauls in the third Test at the WACA.

    In a big innings win for the Australians in Perth, all of the bowlers who took a wicket claimed the same number in each innings – Hilfenhaus 4-34 and 4-54, Ryan Harris 1-33 and 1-34, Mitchell Starc 2-39 and 2-31 and Peter Siddle 3-42 and 3-43.

- England's James Anderson had the better of Kumar Sangakkara in Sri Lanka in 2011/12, dismissing the former captain for two first-ball ducks. Sangakkara became just the fourth number three batsman to incur golden ducks in consecutive Tests, but the first to fall to the same bowler.

- New Zealand batsman Martin Guptill, an occasional off-break bowler, extracted a rarity in his first bowling stint in a Test match by dismissing both openers caught-and-bowled. The sixth bowler used in the second innings of the third Test against Pakistan at Napier in 2009/10, Guptill broke a century partnership by dismissing Salman Butt for 66 and then Imran Farhat for 61, both caught-and-bowled. It was only the third such instance in Test cricket, after fellow Kiwi

Hedley Howarth, at Lord's in 1973, and England's Derek Underwood, at Auckland in 1970/71.

- After finishing 2011 with the unique Test match bowling figures of 11-111 and as his country's most successful bowler, Saeed Ajmal began the following year in record style, becoming the first Pakistani to claim five lbws in a Test innings against England. With a first-innings haul of 7-55, Ajmal spun out England for 192 on the opening day of the first Test at Dubai. Six of his victims came without assistance from the field after bowling out Andrew Strauss at the top of the innings. He finished the match with a ten-for, the second of his career.

> **"It is clear Ian Bell couldn't pick Saeed Ajmal. He has more chance of picking his nose than Ajmal's doosra."**
>
> cricket commentator Geoff Boycott

- In a Ryobi One-Day Cup match at Hobart in 2011/12, a bowler from each side claimed a maiden five-wicket haul, with both taking six wickets each, the first such occurrence in Australian domestic limited-overs cricket. In a revamped format in which bowlers were allowed more than ten overs, Tasmanian spinner Jason Krejza took 6-55 off 11.5, while New South Wales paceman Scott Coyte took 6-60 off 12.5. In the very next match, Victorian spinner Jon Holland also claimed a maiden five-wicket haul and went on to take six. Off 13 overs, Holland took 6-29 against South Australia in Adelaide.

- In the calendar year of 2011, fast bowler Pat Cummins made his debut in six major strands of the game. After making his Twenty20 debut for New South Wales in January, Cummins then played his first List A match for the Blues the following month, before making his first-class debut in March. In October, he appeared in his first Twenty20 international and one-day international, before making his Test debut in November.

  Forced out of the big league with a foot injury following a seven-wicket effort in his first Test, Cummins made his debut in a youth one-day international in 2011/12, against the New Zealand Under-19s in Townsville.

- After flying in from grade cricket in Sydney, Australian fast bowler Jackson Bird became an instant hit for Tasmania in 2011/12, reaching the milestone of 50 wickets in his first season of first-class cricket. Named the Sheffield Shield's best player of the year, Bird took 53 wickets at an average of 16.00, with five five-wicket hauls and ten wickets in a match twice, together with a hat-trick against Western Australia in Hobart.

- Nearly a decade on from his last stint at the bowling crease in a Test, West Indies batsman Basil Butcher achieved a maiden five-wicket haul in first-class cricket. His 5-34 – against England at Port-of-Spain in 1967/68 – included four wickets in three overs, and were the only wickets he claimed in his 44-match Test career.

- Despite Australia going down in the final over to Sri Lanka at Melbourne in 2011/12, Daniel Christian took a hat-trick and a maiden five-wicket haul in one-day international cricket. He became the fourth Australian – after Bruce Reid, Anthony Stuart and Brett Lee – to take a hat-trick, but the first to do so in a defeat. Christian's haul of 5-31 improved on his previous best of 3-53, also against Sri Lanka a week before. Appearing in his first match in six months, James Pattinson took 4-51, which provided just the third instance in ODIs of two bowlers taking all the wickets that fell in an all-out innings.

  The others to pick up a hat-trick in a losing cause before Christian were Bangladesh's Shahadat Hossain, New Zealand's Shane Bond, and the unluckiest of them all, Sri Lanka's Lasith Malinga. In the MCG match, Malinga took 4-49, but in the 2007 World Cup had become the first bowler to take four wickets in four balls in a ODI, only to end up on the losing side with 4 for 54 against South Africa at Providence.

- Between 2009 and 2011, Australia's Brett Lee took at least one wicket in 26 consecutive one-day internationals. The best for a bowler taking a minimum of two wickets in the most consecutive ODIs is Sri Lanka's Dilhara Fernando (2-19, 3-47, 2-32, 2-32, 3-43, 2-46, 2-53, 2-38, 2-22, 2-55, 2-33 and 2-21), over a span of 12 matches in the early 2000s.

- When spinner Shakib Al Hasan took a match-winning 4-16 against the West Indies at Chittagong in 2011/12, he became the first Bangladesh bowler to reach the milestone of 150 one-day international wickets without the aid of a five-wicket haul. In doing so, he joined a trio of giants in the game, Steve Waugh (195), Carl Hooper (193) and Malcolm Marshall (157), who also took more than 150 wickets without a five-for.

- West Indies fast bowler Marlon Black appeared in five one-day internationals and bowled over 200 balls without taking a wicket. He sent down 228 balls without success, a number matched by Netherlands spinner Jacob-Jan Esmeijer, who played in six one-day internationals in the early 2000s without taking a wicket. In a 39-match ODI career,

Sri Lankan batsman Athula Samarasekara bowled 338 balls, but failed to claim a wicket.

- During the first Test against New Zealand at Ahmedabad in 2010/11, Sachin Tendulkar became the first player to achieve 100 wicketless innings in Test match cricket. Tendulkar was the seventh bowler used in the visitors' first innings, returning figures of 0-16. The previous record holder was Steve Waugh (98).

- On his way to ten wickets against India at the MCG in 1967/68, Graham McKenzie picked up a record haul before lunch on the opening day. The West Australian fast bowler took 6-34 before the break, beating the previous best of 6-39 by England's Tom Richardson, against Australia at Lord's in 1896.

  In 1950, the West Indies' Alf Valentine marked his Test debut by taking 5-34 before lunch on day one of the first Test against England at Old Trafford. Valentine achieved his pre-lunch five-for despite not opening the bowling, taking 8-104 in the innings, and 11-204 in the match.

- In the first innings of the fifth Test at Durban in 1922/23, England's top seven batsmen in the order were dismissed by a different bowler. A record in Test match cricket, South Africa used seven bowlers in the innings, with each picking up at least one wicket.

- In 1982/83, Geoff Lawson became the first bowler to take more than ten wickets in an Ashes Test match at Brisbane. After taking five wickets on the opening day, he picked up at least one more on each of the other four days, another first in Ashes cricket.

- When Bangladesh's Talha Jubair claimed the first wicket for his country in the first Test against Sri Lanka in Colombo in 2002, he became the youngest wicket-taker of all time. When he dismissed Marvan Atapattu for 20 and then Mahela Jayawardene for a duck on his Test debut, Jubair was aged 16 years and 223 days. The youngest to take a wicket in a one-day international is Pakistan's Aaqib Javed, who was 16 years and 127 days old when he debuted against the West Indies at Adelaide in 1988/89 and dismissed Richie Richardson.

- In the first innings of a first-class match against Badureliya at Katunayake in 2010/11, two of the Lankan Cricket Club bowlers took 5-15. Slow left-armer Roshan Laksiri Illeperuma took his off 11 overs on his first-class debut, while right-arm off-break bowler Rajeeva Weerasinghe matched him in 4.2 overs.

- During his 6-81 at Wellington in 2011/12, South Africa's Vernon Philander reached the 50-wicket milestone in just his seventh Test. He reached the milestone quicker than anyone else had done in more than 100 years, with Australia's Charlie Turner getting there in six in 1888. Coming into the match with a 13.60 average, Philander went past the 50 mark with six five-wicket and two ten-wicket hauls.

Two others picked up a six-for in the same match with team-mate Morne Morkel (6-23) becoming the first bowler to take six wickets in a Test innings in which only six wickets fell. New Zealand's Mark Gillespie secured a maiden six-wicket haul (6-113) to back up a maiden five-for in the previous Test against South Africa at Hamilton. Having not played Test cricket since 2008/09, Gillespie made up for lost time with five-wicket hauls in the first innings of both Tests.

FEWEST TESTS TO FIRST 50 WICKETS IN A CAREER

#	Bowler	Time	Match		
6	Charlie Turner	1y 215d	Australia v England	Manchester	1888
7	Tom Richardson	2y 303d	England v Australia	Lord's	1896
7	Vernon Philander	139d	South Africa v New Zealand	Wellington	2011/12
8	Fred Spofforth	5y 323d	Australia v England	Sydney	1882/83
8	Alf Valentine	1y 206d	West Indies v Australia	Melbourne	1951/52
8	Rodney Hogg	113d	Australia v Pakistan	Perth	1978/79
8	Terry Alderman	162d	Australia v Pakistan	Brisbane	1981/82

- The two best bowling performances by Charlie Turner were the same, and came within the space of just four Tests. In his first seven Tests, Turner took four lots of seven wickets in an innings, with career-best figures of 7-44 against England at The Oval in 1882 and against England at Sydney five months later, in 1882/83.

- When India hosted Pakistan in 1998/99, the spinning fraternity combined to take 50 wickets for the first time in a two-match Test series. Two bowlers stood out with Pakistan's Saqlain Mushtaq taking ten wickets in both Tests – with five wickets in four consecutive innings – and Anil Kumble, who took 21 for the series, starring with 10-74 in the second innings of the second Test at Delhi. The grand total of 55 spinners' wickets obliterated the previous record of 41 set the summer before in a two-match series between Sri Lanka and Zimbabwe.

  In 2011/12, Sri Lanka and England also breached the 50-wicket barrier, with ten-wicket hauls from opposing bowlers – Rangana Herath (12-171) in the first Test in Galle and Graeme Swann (10-181) in the second in Colombo.

- Recalled for his second Test, and his first in more than a year, West Australian slow bowler Michael Beer was given the ball to open the Australian bowling against the West Indies at Port-of-Spain in 2011/12. The left-armer became the first spinner to open the first innings of a Test for Australia since Bill O'Reilly at Nottingham in 1938. He took two wickets in the innings, including opener Adrian Barath, with the West Indies score reading 26/2. It was the earliest an Australian spin-opening bowler had taken a wicket in the first innings of a Test since O'Reilly got England's Herbert Sutcliffe at 16/3 in Adelaide in 1932/33.

- Captaining Multan against Faisalabad in 2010/11, Abdur Rauf claimed a hat-trick and a ten-wicket haul, but ended up on the losing side. The right-arm quick took 8-85 in the first innings of the match at Bahawalpur, dismissing Faisalabad's first three in a hat-trick. With his sixth victim in the first innings, he passed the milestone of 500 first-class wickets.

  Rauf then claimed ten wickets in a losing cause for a second consecutive match, a week later against Sialkot at Okara. Waqas Ahmed took 12 wickets for the winners, while team-mate Prince Abbas claimed a hat-trick. Rauf almost made it three tens in a row, taking nine wickets in vain in his next match, against Rawalpindi. He ended up with 91 wickets for the season, with eight five-wicket hauls, at 20.71.

- Despite not being a member of the original team, Durham's Graham Onions came on during a County Championship match in 2012 and had a hand in all ten first-innings dismissals. Onions achieved career-best first-class bowling figures of 9-67 and effected a run-out with Nottinghamshire dismissed for 154 at Trent Bridge.

  Not required by England for the third Test against South Africa, Onions got in his car and drove 200km to Nottingham where his county side Durham had batted and made 194. Replacing Mitch Claydon in the side he then took the new ball for the best figures of his first-class career to date. Onions said: **"It was almost literally out of the car and on to the field."** With 1-58 in the second innings, Onions collected his third ten-wicket haul in first-class cricket.

- When Corey Collymore took 7-78 and 4-56 against Pakistan at Kingston in 2005, he became the first West Indies bowler to claim ten wickets in a Test in five years. The previous instance was by Courtney Walsh, 59 Tests ago, at Lord's in 2000, with nearly the same number of Tests elapsing until the next ten-for when Kemar Roach snapped up 5-105 and 5-41 against Australia at Port-of-Spain in 2011/12. Roach became just the fifth Windies bowler to take ten in a Test against the Australians, and the first since Curtly Ambrose's 10-120 at Adelaide in 1992/93.

  After going through 58 Tests before Roach's ten, the Windies had no time to wait for their next, with another in their very next match, against Australia at Roseau. Hometown boy Shane Shillingford collected 10-219, his third ten-wicket haul in four consecutive first-class matches. It represented just the fourth occasion in history of at least two bowlers taking ten in a Test for the losing side in a series which generated none for the winner.

- Brought on as seventh bowler in a County Championship match in 1969, Glamorgan's Tony Cordle picked up career-best figures of 9-49. The Barbados-born quick had taken just six wickets in his previous seven Championship matches, claiming another four victims in the second innings for a match haul of 13-110, albeit in a losing cause against Leicestershire at Colwyn Bay.

- After taking a record 8-35 in a first-class match in Bangladesh in 2012/13, fast bowler Talha Jubair was pulled from the attack after 15 overs. Under new rules just introduced in the country, seamers are only permitted to bowl 15 overs per day in a move designed to protect bowlers from injury. Jubair's 8-35 – for Dhaka Metropolis against Rangpur in Bogra – was the first instance of eight in an innings by a Bangladeshi seamer in first-class cricket.

- South African batsman Daryl Cullinan was dubbed Shane Warne's 'bunny' after losing his wicket to the Australian 12 times in 29 Tests. Between 2002 and 2006, fellow South African Ashwell Prince fell to Warne on 11 occasions, but in 20 fewer appearances. Eight of his dismissals came in consecutive innings against Australia – over two Test series in 2002/03 and 2005/06 – a world record.

BATSMEN DISMISSED THE MOST TIMES IN TESTS BY SHANE WARNE

Batsman	Team	Span	M	Dism
Alec Stewart	England	1993–2003	40	16
Hansie Cronje	South Africa	1993–1999	44	15
Craig McMillan	New Zealand	1997–2005	27	14
Nasser Hussain	England	1993–2003	27	13
Jacques Kallis	South Africa/ICC	1997–2006	43	12
Daryl Cullinan	South Africa	1993–2000	29	12
Inzamam-ul-Haq	Pakistan	1994–2005	29	11
Ashwell Prince	South Africa	2002–2006	9	11

England's Mike Atherton marked his final innings in Test cricket by collecting a world record that had been held by Australia's Arthur Morris since 1953. In his farewell appearance at the crease in a Test match – at The Oval in 2001 – Atherton lost his wicket to Glenn McGrath, the 19th occasion the Australian fast bowler had dismissed the England opener. Atherton was also dismissed 17 times in Tests by West Indians Curtly Ambrose and Courtney Walsh, 11 times by South African speedster Allan Donald and ten times by Warne.

A portrait of Glenn McGrath by Australian artist Sally Robinson and one of South Africa's Allan Donald by former Western Province wicketkeeper Richie Ryall

- Nepal's Shakti Gauchan spun some magic in an ICC World Cricket League match in 2012, claiming the extraordinary figures of 3-2 in ten overs against Malaysia. In a spell that included eight maidens, the leg-spinning Gauchan took two wickets in two balls as Malaysia (69) went down by ten wickets in the match at Kuala Lumpur.

- South African youngster Marcello Piedt celebrated his first-class debut in 2012/13 by picking up nine wickets and innings figures of 7-6. A right-arm medium-pacer, Piedt opened the bowling for South West Districts against Western Province (34) at Oudtshoorn, taking two wickets in his second, fourth and fifth overs.

From Pitch to Parliament

● Pakistan's 12th Prime Minister once appeared in a World Cup warm-up match. Nawaz Sharif, PM between 1990 and 1993 and again in the late 1990s, opened the batting for Lahore Gymkhana against England in a practice match at the 1987 World Cup. While his opposite numbers, Graham Gooch and Chris Broad, both retired after scoring half-centuries, the future Prime Minister scored one – bowled by Phillip DeFreitas – in a game England won by 129 runs. Nawaz Sharif also played first-class cricket, scoring a duck in his only innings, for Pakistan International Airways B against Railways at Karachi in 1973/74.

PRIME MINISTERS TO HAVE PLAYED FIRST-CLASS CRICKET								
Player	Prime Ministership	M	Runs	HS	Avge	Wkts	BBI	Avge
Francis Bell	New Zealand 1925	2	2	2	0.66	-	-	-
Grantley Adams	WI Federation 1958–62	1	15	14	7.50	-	-	-
Alec Douglas-Home‡	UK 1963–64	10	147	37*	16.33	12	3-43	30.25
Nawaz Sharif	Pakistan 1990–93, 97–99	1	0	0	0.00	-	-	-

‡ *Played as Lord Dunglass*

"The Indian cricket team should come to Pakistan and the Pakistan team should tour India because cricket can bring the two countries closer. I am ready to do my part in reviving the ties. In fact I want to be part of the Pakistan team when India come to play us!"

Pakistan Opposition Leader Nawaz Sharif, 2012

- Indian batsman Vinod Kambli, who appeared in 17 Tests in the 1990s, turned his attention to politics in 2009. He unsuccessfully contested a seat in Mumbai in the 2009 Vidhan Sabha election for the Lok Bharati Party.

- A future Tasmanian politician scored a half-century on his first-class debut against the famous 1960/61 West Indies team. Darrel Baldock – who represented the Labor Party in the state's House of Assembly from 1972 to 1987 – scored 54 for Tasmania against the West Indians, his first of two first-class matches.

- The Conservative Party's James Morris, who won a seat in Britain's 2010 general election, had previously played first-class cricket. Mr Morris appeared in three first-class games for Oxford in 1991, falling for a duck in one match to Yorkshire's Darren Gough, who, two decades later, would be asked by the Prime Minister to stand for the seat of Barnsley.

  In 2011, David Cameron had phoned Gough to suggest he run in a by-election for the seat, but Gough hung up thinking it was a prank call.

THE FIRST-CLASS CAREER RECORD OF JAMES MORRIS

M	I	NO	R	HS	Avge	Ct
3	5	0	63	28	12.60	3

- In the same year that they won the ICC Intercontinental Cup in 2010, Afghanistan received a pat on the back from a leading US politician. Secretary of State Hillary Clinton spoke glowingly of Afghanistan's new-found success on the cricket field: "**I might suggest that if we are searching for a model of how to meet tough international challenges with skill, dedication and teamwork, we need only look to the Afghan national cricket team. Afghanistan did not even have a cricket team a decade ago ... the team made it to the World Twenty20 championships featuring the best teams in the world. That's incredible progress.**"

> "When I last saw him, he asked me to explain the BMW rule. I said that the first thing he needed to know was that it was called lbw."
>
> Afghanistan coach Kabir Khan following a meeting with the country's President, Hamid Karzai

- Australia's longest-serving federal MP was a cricket fan who once played in a match dressed in his suit. During his time as Prime Minister in 1921, Billy Hughes injured his back when he took a tumble while batting for the Commonwealth Offices XI against the Defence Department in Melbourne.

Australia's seventh Prime Minister, Billy Hughes, with daughter Helen, watching a cricket match at the SCG

- A former cricket-playing Indian MP threatened to starve himself to death in 2012 in protest against the IPL. Kirti Azad, a member of the BJP, said the Twenty20 competition was being tarnished by money laundering, spot fixing and violence. The son of a former Indian minister, Azad appeared in seven Tests in the early 1980s with a top score of 215 in 142 first-class matches.

- Coinciding with the 2011 Commonwealth Heads of Government Meeting in Perth, a visiting British writer and actor backed debate on Australia becoming a republic. Stephen Fry rattled off a few big names

Former Australian wicketkeeper and captain Adam Gilchrist, with Kamla Persad Bissessar, the Prime Minister of Trinidad and Tobago, and Australia's PM of the day Julia Gillard, at the Commonwealth Heads of Government Meeting in Perth in 2011

that might be considered for Australia's first President, including Allan Border and Adam Gilchrist: **"Shane Warne would be amusing ... Adam Gilchrist is a very bright man."**

- In 2011, Lord's hosted a match between MCC and the Lords and Commons cricket team for the first time since 1939. The cross-party parliamentary XI was captained by the Conservative Party's James Morris and included fellow MPs Danny Alexander, Nigel Adams, Crispin Blunt, David Gauke, Matthew Hancock, Jo Johnson, John Redwood, Rob Wilson, Sports Minister Hugh Robertson and Ed Balls, who as shadow Chancellor, assumed the wicketkeeping duties. Mr Balls said: **"I never dreamed that I would one day play at Lord's. It seemed so far beyond what was possible. I did a bit of keeping for my college side at Oxford, but after I played at Lord's you'd think I was more of a goalkeeper than a wicketkeeper. There were a lot of body stops rather than clean takes."**

  In a match ruined by rain, Mr Alexander – then the Chief Secretary to the Treasury – was responsible for the only wicket to fall, dismissing former Sussex second XI batsman Tim Whittome lbw for a duck. It is believed to be the first instance of a serving cabinet minister taking a wicket on the main ground at Lord's.

DAVID GAUKE'S DREAM TEAM

Jack Hobbs (E)
Len Hutton * (E)
John Edrich (E)
Walter Hammond (E)
David Gower (E)
Ian Botham (E)
Alan Knott † (E)
Harold Larwood (E)
Jim Laker (E)
Frank Tyson (E)
Sydney Barnes (E)

British Conservative Party politician David Gauke

- British MP Matthew Hancock is a lifelong cricket fan who became secretary of the Lords and Commons Cricket Club soon after his election to parliament. Five years before he won a seat for the Conservatives in the British election of 2010, he set out on foot to play the northern-most game of cricket on record at the North Pole. And although he failed in his quest after succumbing to frostbite, he did end up playing in, what turned out to be, the most northerly recorded game of cricket.

LORD'S
THE HOME OF CRICKET

60p

M.C.C. v. LORDS & COMMONS
FRIDAY, 10th JUNE, 2011

M.C.C.

			Innings	
1	J. J. J. Brennan		not out	18
2	T. M. B. Whittome		lbw b Alexander	0
3	Miss C. J. Connor		not out	4
4	T. G. Graveney			
5	J. P. Butler			
6	D. J. Otway			
*7	M. V. Fleming			
8	W. F. W. Dudley			
9	G. S. Brooksbank			
10	N. S. Trueman			
†11	T. Hodson			

b , l-b , w , n-b , p ,

Total .... (1 wkt, 11 overs) **22**

FALL OF THE WICKETS
1—9   2—   3—   4—   5—   6—   7—   8—   9—   10—

ANALYSIS OF BOWLING

Name	O.	M.	R.	W.	Wd.	N-b.
Alexander	6	1	11	1	...	...
Johnson	5	2	11	0	...	...
	...	...	...	...	...	...
	...	...	...	...	...	...
	...	...	...	...	...	...
	...	...	...	...	...	...
	...	...	...	...	...	...
	...	...	...	...	...	...

LORDS & COMMONS

			Innings
1	C. J. R. Blunt		
2	H. M. Robertson		
3	R. O. Wilson		
†4	J. G. Morris		
5	J. E. Johnson		
6	M. J. D. Hancock		
*7	E. M. Balls		
8	N. Adams		
9	D. G. Alexander		
10	D. M. Gauke		
11	J. A. Redwood		

b , l-b , w , n-b , p ,

Total ....

FALL OF THE WICKETS
1—   2—   3—   4—   5—   6—   7—   8—   9—   10—

ANALYSIS OF BOWLING

Name	O.	M.	R.	W.	Wd.	N-b.
	...	...	...	...	...	...
	...	...	...	...	...	...
	...	...	...	...	...	...
	...	...	...	...	...	...
	...	...	...	...	...	...
	...	...	...	...	...	...
	...	...	...	...	...	...
	...	...	...	...	...	...

Umpires—R. McLeod & G. Birtwistle   Scorers—C. H. Fellows-Smith & Mrs L. M. Rhodes

†Captain   *Wicket-keeper

Play begins at 11.00 Luncheon Interval 1.00 – 1.40 Tea Interval 3.40 – 4.00

Close of play – 20 overs from 5.00

M.C.C. won the toss

Match abandoned – rain

175

CRICKET IN THE COLD
Matthew Hancock

I've been a cricketer for as long as I can remember. Days of glorious sunshine at Old Trafford watching Lancashire. Afternoons in the pavilion at my Chester club, with rain thudding on the roof. Evenings playing in the rain in the garden. It's safe to say my enthusiasm is better than my ability.

So in 2005, while planning a two-man expedition to the North Pole, when a tentative sponsor offered to back us, if we played cricket at the pole, I leapt at the chance.

My rationale was simple: We'd been planning the trip for several months. We were raising money for Cancer Research UK, and carrying out experiments for the European Space Agency. We needed a sponsor, and wrote to hundreds of companies.

Brit Insurance wrote back, explaining with the air of a classic rejection letter, that they only sponsored cricket. "But can you remember Buzz Aldrin playing golf on the Moon? You can play cricket at the North Pole." With that, our sponsorship was secured, and my passion for cricket became an unlikely world record attempt.

For months we trained, in Norway, and dragging tyres around Hyde Park. We flew to Resolute Bay, in the northern reaches of Canada, and acclimatised at the hut previously frequented by Ranulph Fiennes and other arctic legends.

At last, we set out for the pole.

Dragging everything we needed, for eight hours a day, across the sea ice was torment. The cold wasn't the problem, so much as the constant, unstinting effort. But the sight of the Arctic, the beauty of the desolate landscape, and the freedom that comes with being hundreds of miles from the nearest human, made up for it.

One evening, with the temperature dropping to -40, as we pitched the tent it ripped. Immediately, I went to sew it up, discarding my outer gloves, keen to get the tent up and the fire on inside. The nip of the cold went away after a minute or so, and I got the job done.

But the numbness of my fingers was a warning I should have heeded. Once inside I removed my inner gloves. Four of my fingers were solid. The frozen stumps rang out as I tapped them against my metal water can.

You don't lose fingers to frostbite unless you thaw them out and refreeze them. So to save my fingers, the only option was to call in support, and the next day a rescue plane was summoned.

And while we waited, we made stumps of our ski-poles, and played the most northerly game of cricket in history. I couldn't hold the ball too well, so after scoring a couple of runs batting first, you can imagine my relief when I hit the stumps, and bowled my team-mate for a duck.

My fingers are now mostly recovered, save for mild arthritis in one joint. My cricket continues to be enthusiastic, in the milder environment of the Lords and Commons Cricket Club. The Club plays a full fixture list, including games at Lord's, Wormsley, and Emmerdale, and against other Parliaments from around the world. It's open to all Members and staff to join, and a superb way to represent Parliament.

Arriving in Parliament also taught me a thing or two about world records. Expounding one day about mine, a fellow new MP calmly listened, and told me: "I heard about your record. My mother broke it."

- Eric Bullus was the Tory MP for the seat of Wembley North for 24 years from 1950 and played in 71 matches for the Lords and Commons cricket team. He served as the club's treasurer between 1957 and 1974 and wrote a book about its history in 1959.

- British Conservative Party politician Edward Campbell played cricket for a number of teams, including Surrey's second XI in 1911. First elected to parliament in 1924, he once took a five-wicket haul (5-48) for the Lords and

A HISTORY OF
LORDS AND COMMONS
CRICKET

by
Eric E. Bullus, M.P.

Commons team against MCC at Lord's in 1930, with two England Test players – Gubby Allen and Greville Stevens – among his victims.

- UK politician William Bromley-Davenport, who held the seat of Macclesfield for the Conservatives between 1886 and 1906, had a brother who played Test cricket. Hugh Bromley-Davenport, a Middlesex all-rounder, appeared in four Tests against South Africa in the 1890s.

  William, who was better known as a footballer in his day, also played the occasional game of cricket, turning out for teams such as Eton and Lords and Commons. In a match against a Government XI at Lord's in 1893 he kept wicket for the Opposition, achieving a pair of stumpings.

- Upon the election of the Conservatives' David Cameron as British Prime Minister in 2010, the *Wisden Cricketer* magazine calculated that England had won more Test matches in recent times when a Labour government was in power. Between the end of the Second World War and the ascendancy of Mr Cameron, the magazine estimated that England had won 36.8 per cent of its Tests under Labour and 28.6 per cent under a Conservative government.

> **"Your background has a major bearing on your politics and my father** [a trade unionist] **said, jokingly, he would not speak to me for a month if I did not vote Labour. My mother voted Tory once, as my father likes to remind her."**
>
> Glamorgan batsman Gareth Rees

> **"Thatcher, Major, Cameron – I love them all. I am a true Blue and always have been. My father was a Conservative councillor. I think cricketers have always been that way inclined."**
>
> former England bowler Dominic Cork

- Before he became Britain's Prime Minister, Labour's Harold Wilson once took part in an impromptu game of cricket while in Moscow. In the Soviet capital for a trade meeting, the game was watched over by the secret police. Sir Harold said: **"My second over was interrupted by a gentleman from the NKVD, who was appointed to follow** us around and see that we came to no harm. He stood in the middle of the pitch and remonstrated with us in a very long Russian speech. He was supported by two men who came up on horseback with rifles. I persuaded him, after some negotiation, to take up his position at square leg, out of the way of even my bowling."

- Indian politician Kiran Kumar Reddy was once on the books of the Hyderabad cricket club. Although he never played first-class cricket, Reddy, a wicketkeeper, appeared in a number of Under-22 matches for the state. He became Chief Minister of Andhra Pradesh in 2010.

- Barbadian fast bowler Duncan Carter appeared in three first-class matches over a nine-year period later forging a career in politics. After one match for Barbados in 1964/65, Carter played in two matches for the South African team Eastern Province in 1973/74 before becoming a Labour Party MP back home in the Caribbean. In 1981, he captained a Barbados XI, which included Desmond Haynes, against Yorkshire at Scarborough.

> **"Upon returning to Barbados after living abroad for a number of years, Duncan lost no time in placing his acquired skills at the disposal of the Barbados Labour Party."**
>
> Barbados Labour Party leader Mia Mottley

- MP and former Test cricketer Navjot Singh Sidhu had a run-in with security guards at a highway toll gate in India in 2011 when his driver refused to pull over. On his way to a political function organised by the BJP, a guard threw a rock at his car, damaging a window.

- A warrant was issued against cricketer-turned-politician Mohammad Azharuddin in 2012 after he failed to attend court on a matter concerning a bounced cheque. The former Indian captain said he was busy campaigning for elections in Uttar Pradesh.

> **"Cricket is a foreign game played in white flannels ... it is not our game, wrestling is. In fact, cricket should not be played at all. What baffles me is why Indians are so bothered about watching cricket."**
>
> Uttar Pradesh Chief Minister Mulayam Singh Yadav, 2005

- While a sitting member of the British parliament, Sigmund Freud's grandson once kept wicket in a match at Lord's. Clement Freud – who held a seat for the Liberal Party from 1973 to 1987 – scored seven with the bat in a one-day match for the Lord's Taverners in 1975.

- Thomas Mostyn played first-class cricket for Oxford and MCC and represented the people of Flintshire in parliament between 1854 and 1861. His brother-in-law Edward Bligh also played first-class cricket, mostly for Kent in the 1850s and 1860s.

- When England knocked off India to take the number one spot in Test cricket in 2011, the Prime Minister of the day, David Cameron, paid an impromptu visit to the team's dressing room at The Oval. One of England's players, fast bowler James Anderson, was caught off-guard by the prime ministerial visit: "**They say strange things can happen after a shower. I emerged from mine after play in only a towel to find the Prime Minister in our dressing room. David Cameron was congratulating us on our recent achievements and I was looking for some clothes to put on. He said he was a big cricket fan.**"

> **"I watched the closing overs on the sofa at home and will remember the joy of the crowd at Edgbaston and England getting to number one in such style for a long time to come. The whole nation can be proud of our team of world beaters."**
>
> Britain's Prime Minister David Cameron after England took the No. 1 Test ranking from India in Birmingham in 2011

- During an official visit to the United States in 2012, the British Prime Minister and the US President discussed a number of meaty issues including the war in Afghanistan, violence in Syria, and cricket. While

> Jon Stewart: **Well, I can't wait to hear about his trip. I bet he thinks he hit a home run** [commenting on US President Barack Obama's visit to Asia in 2010].
>
> Barack Obama [on TV news footage]: **Instead of hitting home runs, sometimes we're gonna hit singles, but they're really important singles.**
>
> Stewart: **Oh ... at least he's not using cricket references.**
>
> – from the US Comedy Central's *The Daily Show with Jon Stewart*, 2010

"I was on the phone to Obama the other day. I said, 'There are terrible things happening in the world but at least England is number one at cricket.' But he said, 'You invented the game. That's like saying America is number one at baseball or American football.' I said, 'You don't understand Barack, but I'm not going to argue it out with you now'."

David Cameron revealing what US President Barack Obama had thought when England became number one in Test cricket

"Now, Michelle [Barack Obama's wife], I'm sure that you often wonder what happens when your husband goes for a night out with the guys. So maybe I should come clean about last night. We went to basketball and we had a real man-to-man chat. Barack tried to confuse me by talking about 'bracketology' but I got my own back by running him gently through the rules of cricket. The truth is we have to have a guys' night out because so often we find we are completely overshadowed by our beautiful wives."

David Cameron at a White House state dinner, during which he invited Barack Obama to attend a cricket match

Barack Obama took David Cameron along to a university basketball game, the US President was taught the rules of cricket, just as former West Indies batsman Brian Lara had tried to do a few years previously. Mr Obama said: "**David Cameron is going to teach me cricket. He's going to teach me cricket because I don't understand what's going on.**"

● A leading sports betting agency once offered odds of 750/1 against England all-rounder Andrew Flintoff ever becoming a member of the British Cabinet. In 2007, a Ladbrokes spokesman said: "**We think the only cabinet Freddie is likely to be in is the drinks cabinet.**"

- UK politician and Roman scholar Boris Johnson mentions Shane Warne in his book *The Dream of Rome*, which was published in 2006. A former UK shadow minister who was elected Mayor of London in 2008, Mr Johnson writes of a statue of Augustus, the first Emperor of the Roman Empire: " … and there he is, arm aloft like Shane Warne doing his flipper, effulgent in marble and larger than life."

- The bowler who achieved Tasmania's first first-class hat-trick is the son of a former state Labor politician. In 1982/83, the Sydney-born Peter Clough, a right-arm medium-fast bowler, dismissed John Dyson, Steve Smith and Trevor Chappell in a hat-trick during the Tasmania–New South Wales Sheffield Shield match in Hobart. His father, Mick Clough, represented the electorates of Blue Mountains and Bathurst in the New South Wales parliament between 1976 and 1999.

- When Dwight D. Eisenhower attended a Test match in Pakistan in 1959, the US President met members of the Australian cricket team captained by Richie Benaud and managed by Sam Loxton, a sitting member of the Victorian parliament. General Eisenhower became the first American President to watch Test cricket, witnessing the fourth day's play of the third match in Karachi, the slowest Test day's play on record.

   The President signed a cricket bat and was presented with a Pakistan team blazer. When Benaud saw the President wearing the coat, he light-heartedly commented: **"Mister President … you have joined the other camp."**

US President Dwight D. Eisenhower meets the Australian cricket team at Karachi during the third Test against Pakistan in 1959/60

- Lyndon B. Johnson, who was President of the United States between 1963 and 1969, once mentioned Don Bradman in a critique of Australia's war effort. During a fact-finding trip to Australia in 1942, Congressman Johnson noted: **"Australia has no ideology. Its only heroes are Ned Kelly, the bandit, and Don Bradman, the cricketer – crime and cricket. The national motto, so far as I have been able to determine, is f**k all."**

Richard Nixon – US President between 1969 and 1974 – wields a cricket bat for the cameras at the MCG in 1956

- A leg-break bowler who dismissed Don Bradman for 369 in a first-class match later became the leader of a state Liberal Party. Rex Townley, who took 36 wickets in 16 first-class matches for Tasmania, was leader of the state's opposition from 1950 to 1956. His brother Athol also mixed cricket with politics, playing non-first-class matches for the Prime Minister's XI and South Tasmania. A member of federal parliament, he held a number of ministries, including defence, immigration and civil aviation, in the Liberal government of Robert Menzies.

- A former Barbados fast bowler based in Britain was saved from deportation in 2008 after his case was taken up his local MP. Hartley Alleyne, who had also played first-class cricket for Worcestershire, Kent and Natal, had been refused a work permit despite having lived and worked in England for 30 years. A decision to review Alleyne's case came after an appeal by Julian Brazier, the Tory MP for Canterbury, to the Immigration Minister: **"Hartley's a really good guy, who has given most of his adult life to this country. It's crazy that he was told to go."**

- Former Australian fast bowler Carl Rackemann switched to politics in 2011 by standing for Bob Katter's Australian Party. Rackemann, who appeared in 12 Tests and 52 one-day internationals, stood unsuccessfully for the regional seat of Nanango in the 2012 Queensland state election and said: **"The Australian Party is the only party that will stand up to protect landholders' rights and the only party that will protect the remaining Queensland assets from being sold off. It is determined to restore good government and that is why I have signed up."**

Rackemann's campaign launch suffered a setback when his guest of honour Andrew Symonds bailed at the last minute. Rackemann later said the former Australian all-rounder had probably "lost his mind", and added: **"He's a friend, so it's disappointing he didn't show."**

- As one of his first acts as a new MP, Sachin Tendulkar turned down an offer of free government accommodation in the capital Delhi. Sworn in to the Indian parliament in 2012, Tendulkar said he would prefer to stay in a hotel while in Delhi on parliamentary business: **"I am not keen on staying in any government bungalow when I will be in Delhi for only a few days. I feel this would be a waste of taxpayers' money and it would be better if the bungalow is allotted to someone else who needs the bungalow more than me."**

In the same year that Tendulkar was installed as a MP, one of his former team-mates also embraced political life. Jacob Martin – who appeared in ten one-day internationals – signed up to the Congress Party. He said: **"I want to start playing another innings by joining the Congress Party and serving the community. I liked the ideology of the party, so I joined it."**

- On the day that former Prime Minister Kevin Rudd put his hand up for another tilt at the leadership of the Labor Party in 2012, Australia was playing a one-day international against Sri Lanka in Hobart. A cheeky Channel Nine viewers' poll asked who would make a better Prime Minister – Mr Rudd, the incumbent PM Julia Gillard or Ricky Ponting, who had just been dropped from the Australian one-day side. The poll was inspired by a spectator's placard that asked for Ponting to be PM and displaying a photo of the cricketer wearing glasses similar to those worn by Rudd, a spitting image of the politician who was Prime Minister between 2007 and 2010. A few minutes into the poll, Ponting was a clear favourite with 82 per cent of the vote.

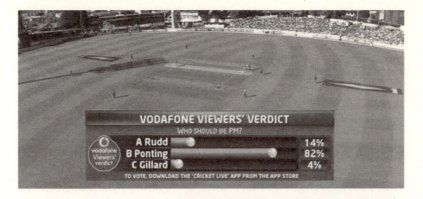

VODAFONE VIEWERS' VERDICT
WHO SHOULD BE PM?

A Rudd		14%
B Ponting		82%
C Gillard		4%

TO VOTE, DOWNLOAD THE 'CRICKET LIVE' APP FROM THE APP STORE

KEVIN RUDD'S DREAM TEAM

Matthew Hayden (A)
Ian Chappell * (A)
Don Bradman (A)
Sachin Tendulkar (I)
Steve Waugh (A)
Imran Khan (P)
Ian Botham (E)
Adam Gilchrist † (A)
Shane Warne (A)
Muttiah Muralitharan (SL)
Glenn McGrath (A)

Kevin Rudd – Australian Prime Minister between 2007 and 2010

THE PHILANTHROPIC CRICKET TEAM
Kevin Rudd

Matthew Hayden: A great Queenslander and captain of my Prime Minister's XI in 2010. But also a timeless supporter of cancer and muscular dystrophy research, and a key player in the World Youth Day campaign.

Ian Chappell: Tough as teak as a leader and a batsman. Now uses his profile to advocate for the world's 16 million refugees.

Don Bradman: There is little more that can be said about one of the world's greatest sportsmen ever. He was a national icon who offered Australia hope at the height of the Great Depression.

Sachin Tendulkar: Widely acknowledged as the greatest modern batsman, he carries the weight of a billion people on his shoulders. But he remains humble and generous in his sponsorship of two hundred underprivileged children each year, and fund raising for cancer treatment and facilities for underfunded government schools.

Steve Waugh: A tough cricketer and keen strategist who led Australia to dominance throughout the 1990s. Named the Australian of the Year in 2004, he invited Australians to enjoy the cultures of other cricketing nations through his tour diaries and his ongoing work for children with rare diseases in Australia and India through his foundation.

Imran Khan: Pakistan's most successful captain with a progressive vision for his country on and off the pitch. His foundation has built a cancer hospital and technical college.

Ian Botham: Tormented touring Australian teams with bat and ball, building on the Ashes legacy. He continues to inspire through his charity walks, which have raised over £12m for various causes.

Adam Gilchrist: Revolutionised the wicketkeeping position with his explosive batting. Admired for his commitment to his ideals by walking when he believed himself to be out and his prominent role as ambassador for World Vision.

Shane Warne: Aside from his 'charity' work helping the Indian Premier League, Warnie has taken a strong interest in helping disadvantaged and sick kids. The Shane Warne Foundation has raised millions of dollars and the list of beneficiaries is huge with more than 70 different charities benefiting.

Muttiah Muralitharan: The highest wicket-taker in both Tests and ODIs. Whatever you think of his action, his work off the field is unblemished – he co-founded the Foundation of Goodness, joined the UN World Food Program as an ambassador, and went above and beyond to help his countrymen during the 2004 tsunami which devastated the region.

Glenn McGrath: The most successful Test fast bowler and the epitome of professionalism. He inspired and stirred the cricketing world through his tireless work with the McGrath Foundation which is dedicated to raising money to fund more breast care nurses in rural and regional Australia.

Brian Lara (12th man): One of the game's most entertaining and dominant batsmen, Brian Lara is also a statesman who represents his country on a diplomatic passport and has established a foundation in his parents' name which works on health and social issues in Trinidad. I presented him with a much deserved Order of Australia in 2009.

- During a trip to India in 2012, Australia's Prime Minister Julia Gillard paid a visit to a cricket clinic in Delhi. The event was marked by her officially announcing that the Indian cricketing MP Sachin Tendulkar would be awarded honorary membership of the Order of Australia: **"This is a very special honour, very rarely awarded to someone who is not an Australian citizen or an Australian national ... a very special recognition of such a great batsman. Cricket is of course a great bond between Australia and India. We are both cricket-mad nations**."

- On the day that Australian captain Michael Clarke brought up his maiden Test match double-century in 2011/12, two former Prime Ministers were on hand to witness the historic moment. John Howard watched proceedings at the SCG from the Victor Trumper Stand, while Labor's Bob Hawke was mobbed by a horde of well-wishers on the lower decks. Video footage of the then-82-year-old former Labor leader accepting a challenge to skol a glass of beer went viral over the internet.

"You've got to love the way in which we Australians engage with our politicians. Hawkie got more press coverage of downing that beer, in what looked to me to be pretty record time, than I got in announcing $95m in cricket infrastructure at Adelaide, Sydney and Hobart."

Australian Prime Minister Julia Gillard

- Alexia Walker, who appeared in three women's one-day internationals for England, once dismissed a future British Sports Minister for a duck. Appearing in a match for England Women against the Lords and Commons cricket team at Roehampton in Surrey in 2002, Walker took 2-7, including the wicket of Conservative Party MP Hugh Robertson for nought.

HUGH ROBERTSON'S DREAM TEAM

Graham Gooch (E)	*Conservative*
Sunil Gavaskar (I)	*MP Hugh*
Viv Richards (WI)	*Robertson*
Sachin Tendulkar (I)	*(right) –*
David Gower * (E)	*appointed*
Ian Botham (E)	*Britain's Sports*
Alan Knott † (E)	*Minister in 2010*
Shane Warne (A)	*– with former*
Muttiah Muralitharan (SL)	*England coach*
Malcolm Marshall (WI)	*Peter Moores*
Dennis Lillee (A)	

- A former Pakistan Foreign Affairs Minister joined forces with Imran Khan's political party in 2011, citing his objection to the country's close relationship with the United States. Shah Mehmood Qureshi, who was Foreign Minister from 2008 until 2011, was described by Imran as a "clean candidate" worthy of his party.

- Leading British author Salman Rushdie lashed out at Imran Khan in 2012, describing the cricketer-turned-politician as a "dictator in waiting". Rushdie made his remarks at a New Delhi conference, from which Imran had withdrawn, saying he "**... did not dream of being seen with Rushdie for the immeasurable hurt he has caused to Muslims.**"

  In an address to the conference, Rushdie – who was accused of insulting the prophet Muhammad in his 1988 novel *The Satanic Verses* – also compared Imran to former Libyan dictator Muammar Gaddafi: **"Have you noticed the physical resemblance between Imran and Gaddafi? ... could cast as a slightly better-looking Gaddafi. I'm not sure Imran Khan has liberal points of view and I think if he ever gets in the seat, we might see the consequences. He has made deals with both the army and the mullahs. I think that's pretty clear in order to be where he is."**

Supporters turn out in large numbers for an Imran Khan political rally at Karachi in 2011

- British conservative politician Alan Haselhurst is a cricket author of some note, penning a number of comic novels on the game. First elected to parliament in 1970, Sir Alan – a chairman of the All-Party Parliamentary Cricket Group – has written five books, *Occasionally Cricket*, *Eventually Cricket*, *Incidentally Cricket*, *Accidentally Cricket* and *Unusually Cricket*.

ALAN HASELHURST'S DREAM TEAM

Barry Richards (SA)
Herbert Sutcliffe (E)
Jack Hobbs (E)
Don Bradman * (A)
Sachin Tendulkar (I)
Ian Botham (E)
Adam Gilchrist † (A)
Imran Khan (P)
Malcolm Marshall (WI)
Hedley Verity (E)
Michael Holding (WI)

British Conservative Party politician Alan Haselhurst

- A number of Prime Ministers from the Caribbean rallied behind West Indies batsman Chris Gayle in 2012, after he had been sidelined from the national team for more than a year. Jamaica's Prime Minister Portia Simpson Miller publicly sought a resolution to a feud between the big-hitting batsman and the West Indies cricket board. Gayle had not played for the Windies since the 2011 World Cup following a scathing critique of the board and its officers. **"Justice delayed is justice denied and we demand that a resolution be found as quickly as possible,"** Mrs Simpson Miller said on the impasse. **"Cricket is too important to the people of Jamaica and the West Indies for this to be left down the wicket."**

  Soon after her impassioned call, an agreement was brokered between Gayle and the board, which included the involvement of St Vincent Prime Minister Ralph Gonsalves and Antigua and Barbuda Prime Minister Baldwin Spencer. Back in the team for the one-day international series against England in 2012, Gayle was at his wrecking-ball best, scoring 53 off 51 balls at The Oval, thumping five massive sixes and three fours.

- During his time as Prime Minister of Australia, Bob Hawke played in a cricket match alongside greats such as Clive Lloyd and Doug Walters. Mr Hawke captained the Prime Minister's XI against an Australian Aboriginals XI at Manly Oval in Sydney in 1988/89, scoring two. He had made a duck in the same match the previous summer, a

189

Australian Prime Minister Bob Hawke hit in the face by a cricket ball during a Parliamentarians v Press cricket match in Canberra in 1984

game that featured Rod Marsh, Max Walker, Ian Chappell and Gary Cosier. Curiously, Hawke had scored two and a duck in his first cricket match of significance, at Oxford in 1954. Hawke batted at number four for the D.C.P.R. Jowett XI against the C.C.P. Williams XI in a three-day Oxford University trial match.

SCOREBOARD
AUSTRALIAN PRIME MINISTER'S XI v AUSTRALIAN ABORIGINALS – MANLY 1988–89
AUSTRALIAN PRIME MINISTER'S XI

D.P. Waugh	c Williams b Gregory	6
I.C. Davis	c Williams b Appoo	28
T.M. Chappell	c Williams b Mainhardt	5
C.H. Lloyd	b Appoo	63
K.D. Walters	c sub (D.M. Thompson) b Appoo	3
R.J.L. Hawke *	b Pearce	2
S. Waddington	b Mainhardt	21
M.H.N. Walker	b Bulger	1
M. Taber †	b Bulger	2
P.F. McLay	not out	1
W.D. Evans	not out	0
Extras		14
Total	(all out – 47 overs)	**146**

- British Prime Minister David Cameron revealed in 2012 that one of his most valued possessions is a cricket bat signed by Sachin Tendulkar. Mr Cameron scored the bat during his first visit as PM to the subcontinent in 2010: "**I found my wife in the garden at Chequers** [the Prime Minister's weekend residence] **the other day playing French cricket with this cricket bat. And I said, 'no darling, put it down, this is probably the most valuable possession I have'.**"

- Former British Prime Minister John Major was on hand for a charity cricket match in 2012 when the Lords and Commons took on a World

WAYNE SWAN'S DREAM TEAM

Matthew Hayden (A)
Bob Simpson (A)
Ian Chappell * (A)
Doug Walters (A)
Steve Waugh (A)
Garry Sobers (WI)
Ian Healy † (A)
Shane Warne (A)
Dennis Lillee (A)
Malcolm Marshall (WI)
Glenn McGrath (A)

Wayne Swan, who became Australia's deputy Prime Minister in 2010

PETER HAIN'S DREAM TEAM

Len Hutton (E)
Sachin Tendulkar (I)
Don Bradman (A)
Viv Richards (WI)
Graeme Pollock (SA)
Garry Sobers * (WI)
Ian Botham (E)
Denis Lindsay † (SA)
Wes Hall (WI)
Frank Tyson (E)
Shane Warne (A)

British Labour Party MP Peter Hain

XI at the Sir Paul Getty Ground in Wormsley. Sir John watched on as the Lashings XI rattled up a match-winning 288/7 off their 25 overs, with a half-century from former England player Phil DeFreitas (68). An innings of 33 from 61-year-old Gordon Greenidge was brought to an end by a catch from Conservative MP and Lords and Commons captain Nigel Adams, who said: **"It was one of the highlights of my cricketing career, which wouldn't be a bad place to retire."**

With an unbeaten 50, Gloucester MP Richard Graham scored the only half-century for Lords and Commons, while John Redwood (1-49) – a minister in John Major's government – opened their bowling, taking the wicket of former New Zealand batsman Lou Vincent (43).

- In 2012, the New Zealand Prime Minister took to the cricket field for the first time in his life during a charity fundraiser in Wellington. John Key faced up to the bowling of Shane Warne in the innings break of a Twenty20 match staged for the victims of an earthquake that had rocked the city of Christchurch. The PM earned $100,000 for the appeal when he hit Warne to one of the shortened boundaries at the Basin Reserve.

- A senior Australian government minister came to the defence of a senior Australian batsman in 2011 who had been dumped by the national selectors. Stephen Smith, the Defence Minister of the day, and member for the seat of Perth, went into bat for the West Australian-born Simon Katich who lost his Cricket Australia contract after 56 Tests and 4,188 runs. Mr Smith said: **"Well, historically of course there have been a series of atrocities committed by the Australian Cricket Board or Cricket Australia or the Australian selectors against Western Australian cricketers but this one is extraordinary. This one is very high at the top of the list.**

  "I mean this is a bloke who over the last 30 Tests he's played has got nearly 3,000 runs, an average of 50 and done better than Ponting and Mike Hussey. So it's an extraordinary decision. And regrettably whilst it's always easy to take a shot at selectors I think it says a lot more about the selectors than it does about Simon Katich and I think frankly it has sent very much a message which has undermined confidence in the selectors that they're really up to the task in terms of managing a transition to the next generation of Australian cricketers.

  "Simon Katich has the resolve and the determination that you want to have during hard times. So it's an extraordinary decision."

STEPHEN SMITH'S DREAM TEAM

Graeme Wood (A) Bruce Laird (A) Justin Langer (A) Kim Hughes (A) Mike Hussey (A) Tom Moody (A) Rod Marsh * † (A) Tony Mann (A) Graham McKenzie (A) Terry Alderman (A) Dennis Lillee (A)	*Australian Labor Party politician Stephen Smith*	

THE BEST OF THE WEST
Stephen Smith

The first time I went to the WACA was with my grandfather for a Sheffield Shield game in the 1967-68 season, not long after we moved to Perth from country Western Australia. In those days, Sheffield Shield games really meant something, were well attended and bristled with Test players past, present and future.

Since then I have gone to the WACA for Shield and Test matches, domestic and one-day internationals, interstate Twenty20 matches and first-grade finals, not to mention AFL football, rugby league and the Rolling Stones!

My WACA membership is now over 20 years old and I take great pleasure that as the local federal member for Perth I represent the WACA. These days my favourite WACA day is the first day of the annual WACA Test match in the company of my son Hugo.

As a consequence, my Dream Team revolves around the WACA and West Australian cricket. My team is an Australian team to play a Test Match at the WACA against the West Indies at the peak of their fast bowling prowess and on a traditional fast-paced WACA pitch.

To be eligible for selection a player must have been captain of a West Australian Sheffield Shield/Pura Cup team who has played Test cricket for Australia and who made their Shield debut for WA. This excludes, for example, notable WA captains like Tony Lock, who played Test cricket for England and Keith Carmody, Adam Gilchrist and Bob Simpson who started their careers with New South Wales, and Ken Meuleman, whose debut was for Victoria.

Nine players eligible for selection were overlooked: pace bowlers Julian and Angel, opening batsmen G.R. Marsh and Veletta, and top-order batsmen Rutherford, Sergeant, Shepherd, Inverarity and Martyn. The pace attack is self-selecting – Lillee, McKenzie and Alderman (who between them captained WA on only five occasions), as is the keeper Rod Marsh. Tony Mann is included as the leg-spinner, a traditional West Indies weakness, with Mann's Test century as a nightwatchman seeing the team bat to eight.

Wood and Laird at their courageous best under West Indies' fire are picked as the openers over the unlucky Geoff Marsh and Langer bats at first drop, giving three effective openers in the case of an early breakthrough, but also a successful and experienced Test No. 3.

Kim Hughes is preferred to Damien Martyn at No. 4, as is Mike Hussey over Martyn and Barry Shepherd at five. Martyn is the unluckiest omission, a potentially controversial call. Moody's bowling record at the WACA sees him as the all-rounder. Against the West Indies, sentimentality cannot find room for John Inverarity, Western Australia's best cricket strategist and captain. Inverarity is coach for the one-off Test match.

MARTIN FERGUSON'S DREAM TEAM

Sunil Gavaskar (I)
Barry Richards (SA)
Don Bradman * (A)
Sachin Tendulkar (I)
Viv Richards (WI)
Garry Sobers (WI)
Ian Botham (E)
Adam Gilchrist † (A)
Shane Warne (A)
Dennis Lillee (A)
Michael Holding (WI)

Martin Ferguson – a long-serving Australian Federal Government minister

JOEL FITZGIBBON'S DREAM TEAM

Sunil Gavaskar (I)
Garry Sobers (WI)
Don Bradman * (A)
Sachin Tendulkar (I)
Allan Border (A)
Viv Richards (WI)
Ian Botham (E)
Adam Gilchrist † (A)
Dennis Lillee (A)
Joel Garner (WI)
Shane Warne (A)

The ALP's Joel Fitzgibbon – Australia's Defence Minister from 2007 to 2009

● The MP for the Sri Lankan district of Matara made a comeback to first-class cricket in 2010/11, appearing in his first such match since entering politics. United People's Freedom Party MP Sanath Jayasuriya turned out for Bloomfield against the Sinhalese Sports Club in Colombo, his first first-class match in 17 months. He also appeared in a one-day international as a sitting MP, scoring two against England at The Oval in 2011 and, in 2012, was one of the top picks for the inaugural Sri Lankan Premier League Twenty20 tournament.

> **"I'm enjoying helping my constituents with developing roads and creating jobs. I promise small things I can deliver ... people are tired of politicians who promise too much and fail."**
>
> Sanath Jayasuriya

All Creatures Great and Small

- Play was held up for a brief moment during a Twenty20 match at Headingley in 2009 when Yorkshire's Jacques Rudolph killed a bird while fielding. Played at the ground which houses a clock dedicated to umpire Dickie Bird, the South African hit a pigeon after throwing the ball back to the wicketkeeper. He then picked up the remains and deposited them over the boundary.

> **"The ball's hit a pigeon and the pigeon is no more. Jacques Rudolph is the man who could have the pigeon's blood on his hands here. Rudolph did the fielding, he gets the ball in the air, and with about as much accuracy as a patriot missile he downs the incoming pigeon … poor old pigeon."**
>
> Sky Sports TV commentators Charles Colvile and Paul Allott

- Play in the opening match of the 2009 IPL in South Africa was dogged by the presence of an animal on the ground at Cape Town. A stray dog eluded capture for some ten minutes during the Mumbai–Chennai match in which opener Sachin Tendulkar scored an unbeaten 59.

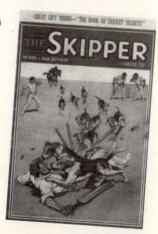

- The estranged wife of Ian Botham's son was arrested in 2011 in connection with the disappearance of a cocker spaniel. The dog, belonging to Liam Botham's girlfriend, went missing from the Botham family home in Yorkshire.

- Matthew Hoggard's autobiography published in 2009 featured a foreword by his dogs. *Hoggy: Welcome to My World* contains a 'paw-word' from his pet doberman and border collie.

- A game of cricket was brought to a close in highly unusual circumstances in England in 2008 when a swarm of flying ants invaded the field. Crouch End Calthorpe's Simon Tanner said the ants had covered every part of the players' clothing: **"If you can imagine ants in your hair, in your ears and in your eyes, and you're trying to concentrate on a cricket ball coming at you. It was very disconcerting."**

- The 2011 England versus India Test at Trent Bridge began rather painfully for South African umpire Marais Erasmus when he was stung by a bee during the first over. He gave no indication of his predicament and battled on without complaint.

- An employee of the Sri Lankan cricket board was injured in 2010 when a car in which she was travelling was attacked by an elephant. The incident took place near Dambulla after she and a colleague had attended a cricket function.

- Coinciding with India's first-ever Test win in England in 1971, an elephant was seen grazing on the edges of The Oval. Some of the players who took part in the match don't recall the incident, including England batsman Keith Fletcher, who scored one and a duck in India's four-wicket victory. Fletcher said: **"An elephant on the outfield? I don't remember no bloody elephant. I just hope it had been to the loo before it got there."** Team-mate Richard Hutton hit 81 in the first innings batting at number eight: **"I remember they brought an elephant into the ground. Not a very big elephant, but, yes there was definitely an elephant."**

- A pair of tiny blue and yellow birds took up residence at a Lancashire cricket club in 2012 building a nest in a wall-mounted ashtray. According to the manager of the Fulwood and Broughton cricket club, Steve Gregson, the blue tits became a local attraction: **"It's a bit of a wildlife magnet here. We are a bit rural with lots of fields with foxes and rabbits running round. It's like a menagerie."**

- Spooked by a run-in with a duck in Perth in 2010/11, Victoria's Andrew McDonald smashed an imposing 163 in the Sheffield Shield match against Western Australia. While taking a walk prior to the match getting underway on the second morning, McDonald inadvertently upset a drake and his ducklings. McDonald said: "**He got on top of my backpack and started chipping away at my head. It was a savage attack, so lucky to survive. I never knew they could be so feisty.**" His innings, off 116 balls, included 21 fours and seven sixes.

- England's Archie MacLaren was dismissed in odd circumstances at Melbourne in 1897/98 when a fly hit him in the eye while facing up to the bowling of Hugh Trumble. Batting at number three in the second innings of the fourth Test, MacLaren was caught by Frank Iredale off Trumble for 45.

- A few months away from reaching the milestone of 6,000 Test runs, Alastair Cook was busy dealing with 6,000 turkeys. Instead of undertaking some warm-weather training in preparation for the 2012 Test series with Pakistan in the United Arab Emirates, the England opener opted to spend time on his family farm in Bedfordshire, preparing the birds for Christmas dinners across the UK. Cook said: "**I've got 6,000 of them. Excellent turkeys they are too. I'll be at the end of the production line, hanging them up when they're goneski.**"

- A pigeon race with starters named in honour of Australian cricket commentators was launched in 2009, with Tubby winning the inaugural contest. Named after Mark Taylor, it beat 11 other contenders, with Scoop – named after Simon O'Donnell – coming second and Warnie third. The race, over a 30km course in New South Wales, was staged to raise funds for the McGrath Foundation.

> "**I've made more friends out of pigeon racing than cricket because when we had rest days, a lot of cricketers play golf and I'd always visit pigeon fanciers. I've got pigeon fancier friends in South Africa, England, Ireland and Scotland and certainly around Australia. It's been very, very good to me.**"
>
> Channel Nine commentator and former Australian captain
> Bill Lawry

- A flock of pink-painted sheep named after Australian cricketers was put up for auction in the New South Wales city of Dubbo in 2011. Tubby Taylor and Warnie both sold for $500 each, while the rest fetched $6,750, with the proceeds going to the McGrath Foundation.

- A flock of Australian sheep was fed a treat in 2012 with a New South Wales wool producer using grass from the Sydney Cricket Ground. A patch of the hallowed turf was dug up and then grown into a paddock to feed a selection of merino sheep, whose wool would later be shorn to be made into suits for members of the Australian cricket team.

> "What a fantastic idea. I can't think of a single sporting fan that wouldn't want a suit made from sheep grazed on Australia's most hallowed turf. For us it's a very special feeling to know where the wool has come from."
>
> Shane Watson

- A club cricketer lost his life in 2011 following a shark attack at a beach in Perth. The 64-year-old Bryn Martin had played for the Western Australians Colts side and the Selkirk club in Scotland in 1974.

- A 26-year-old raised thousands of dollars for a programme to save an endangered Australian marsupial in 2012 when he became the first person in the world to face 15,000 deliveries in a marathon net session. Jade Child batted for 25 hours straight and faced 15,701 balls from bowling machines and local bowlers. Some of the money from the event was handed over to the Save the Tasmanian Devil programme.

- Having lived in Africa as a child, former England Test captain David Gower developed a keen awareness of wildlife preservation, later lending his support to a number of organisations around the world. He became a vice-president of the UK group Nature in Art Trust and a patron of the David Shepherd Wildlife Foundation, a charity set up to fund projects to save endangered mammals. Gower also became a patron of the Save Foundation, a similar organisation based in Australia.

- A number of big-name international cricketers, including Anil Kumble and Wayne Parnell, have lent their names to the noble cause of animal rights by signing up with PETA. In 2012, Indian spinner Murali Kartik took part in a promotion to encourage people not to consume caged chickens, saying: **"Chickens killed for meat spend their entire lives in cages so small they can't even spread their wings."**

- A match in Hampshire was interrupted for 20 minutes in 2011 because of a tiger. Local police launched a large-scale operation involving a helicopter after members of the public reported sighting a white tiger in a field: **"After a brief stalk through the Hedge End savannah, the officer realised the tiger was not moving and the air support using their cameras realised there was a lack of heat source. The tiger then rolled over in the down draft and it was at that point it became obvious it was a stuffed life-size toy. This incident will definitely be the highlight of our day. The CCTV footage convinced us all we were dealing with a real tiger. It's not often an incident leaves our staff with a smile on their face."**

- A Twenty20 match in New Zealand in 2012 came to a halt when a stray horse ran across the pitch. The second-grade match in Blenheim continued after a five-minute delay when the horse and its intoxicated owner were apprehended.

Other animals to interrupt cricket matches include a hedgehog in the Gloucestershire versus Derbyshire County Championship match in 1957, a mouse during the England–Pakistan Test at Lord's in 1962 and a snake in an Under-17s match in suburban Sydney in 2009.

West Indies players Chris Gayle and Reon King and a snake

- During Australia's tour of Zimbabwe in 1999/2000, Steve Waugh paid a visit to a zoo in Bulawayo. While in the lion enclosure, one of the beasts urinated over the Australian captain, which he took as a good omen, predicting he would score a century. He did, hitting an unbeaten 151 in the Test at Harare. It happened to him again during a tour of India 18 months later. After being sprayed at a zoo in Kolkata, Waugh again predicted he would make a century, and did so with 110 in the second Test at Eden Gardens in 2000/01.

- Former England all-rounder Andrew Flintoff went in to the wild in 2012 getting cuddly with killer whales, crocodiles and elephants. A follow-up to a TV documentary he had done in 2011, *Freddie Flintoff Goes Wild* took him to various locations around the world including the Australian outback and the jungles of Borneo for face-to-face meetings with animals in their natural habitat. Flintoff said: "**Each country had different things. In Australia, I went crocodile hunting and in Tanzania we tried to find the wildebeest migration. But spotting the pygmy elephant was a real highlight, just how close we got to them.**"

- Lancashire County Cricket Club sent out a press release in 2012 announcing that six cows had been acquired to trim the Old Trafford ground ahead of the start of the season. Milk from the cows would be used for tea and coffee at the venue, while their droppings would be applied as manure for the ground's gardens.

  On the same day, the England Cricket Board revealed that bulldogs would replace ball boys on the boundaries for an upcoming Twenty20 competition. Both press releases were sent out on April Fools' Day.

- To commemorate a one-day international series win against India in 2012/13, each Pakistan player was awarded a camel. The gift came from a provincial government minister.

A camel and a keeper – the West Indies' Carlton Baugh riding high during a tournament in the subcontinent

Captains Courageous

- Andrew Strauss marked his first Test as England captain by scoring a century, with two of his team-mates in the match later replicating his feat. After Strauss had scored 128 against Pakistan at Lord's in 2006, the next two instances of debut hundreds by Test skippers came from Kevin Pietersen and Alastair Cook.

  Pietersen began his brief tenure as England captain in 2008 with an innings of exactly 100 against South Africa at The Oval. Captain Cook made 173 on his Test captaincy debut, against Bangladesh at Chittagong in 2009/10, backing it up with an unbeaten 109 in the following Test at Mirpur. Cook became the first player since Australia's Clem Hill in 1910/11 to score 150 runs on the first day of his first Test in charge, finishing day one of the Chittagong Test on 158.

  In 2012/13, Cook hit 176 against India at Ahmedabad in his first Test as the official and permanent captain of England. He became the first player to score centuries in his first three Tests as captain and also became the first England skipper to score 150 in a Test in India. He then made it four in a row, with 122 in the second Test at Mumbai, and five in a row with 190 at Kolkata. Cook was run out for the first time in his first-class career, in his 312th innings, a world record.

- Despite scoring a duck in his first Test as Australian captain, Steve Waugh went on to win the match. Only the second Australian captain to do so, after Bob Simpson in 1963/64, Waugh's men triumphed over the West Indies at Port-of-Spain in 1998/99. Waugh scored 14 and a duck in the match, the exact same scores made by Zimbabwe's Stuart Carlisle in his first Test as captain – also a winning one – in 2001/02.

- Kepler Wessels, who hit a century in his first Test, uniquely made 100 runs on his home and away Test debut as both a batsman and as a captain. On his Test debut, the South African-born Wessels hit 162 and 46 for Australia against England at Brisbane in 1982/83 and 141 in his first overseas Test, against Sri Lanka at Kandy, in the same season.

  Elevated to the captaincy after returning to his homeland, he made 59 and 74 for South Africa against the West Indies at Bridgetown in 1991/92 in its first Test after readmission to five-day international competition. In his first Test as skipper in a home Test, Wessels marked the occasion with 118 in the first innings against India at Durban in 1992/93.

- The third Test of the 1955 England–South Africa series featured the first example of opposing captains reaching a century on the same day. Jackie McGlew (104*) and Peter May (117) both brought up a ton on the fourth day of the match at Manchester with the feat not matched again until 2012. On the second day of the second Test at Trent Bridge, the West Indies' Darren Sammy (106) achieved his maiden Test century while Andrew Strauss went on to make 141.

- In a one-day international at Toronto in 2006, both of the captains took three wickets. A unique occurrence in ODIs, Kenya's Steve Tikolo took 3-14, while Canada's opening batsman John Davison claimed 3-43.

- During the New Zealand–South Africa Test at Wellington in 1963/64, the opposing captains both bowled each other out. Trevor Goddard was bowled by John Reid for 40 in the second innings, while Goddard got Reid with the same mode of dismissal for 12 in New Zealand's second innings.

- In Nottinghamshire's all-out 162 at Trent Bridge in 2012, their wicket-keeping captain scored 64 per cent of the runs. Chris Read hit an unbeaten 104 in the first innings of the County Championship match against Somerset, in which the next highest score was ten.

- In 89 one-day internationals that he captained in Australia, Ricky Ponting was victorious on 61 occasions. The record for most wins on home soil is 70 by Allan Border in 114 matches.

- During a match of 35 overs each at Dunedin in 1973/74, New Zealand's Bev Congdon scored 82, the highest innings by a captain in a one-day international to date, only to be pipped by his opposite number Ian Chappell, who made 83. Congdon regained the record the following summer, with 101 against England at Wellington, beating another Chappell innings – after the Australian captain's 83 at Dunedin, he clocked up 86 the following day at Christchurch.

PROGRESSIVE HIGHEST SCORES BY CAPTAINS IN ONE-DAY INTERNATIONALS

1	Ray Illingworth	England v Australia	Melbourne	1970/71
27	Bill Lawry	Australia v England	Melbourne	1970/71
53	Ian Chappell	Australia v England	Manchester	1972
55	Rohan Kanhai	West Indies v England	Leeds	1973
66	Mike Denness	England v West Indies	Leeds	1973
82	Bev Congdon	New Zealand v Australia	Dunedin	1973/74
83	Ian Chappell	Australia v New Zealand	Dunedin	1973/74
86	Ian Chappell	Australia v New Zealand	Christchurch	1973/74
101	Bev Congdon	New Zealand v England	Wellington	1974/75
171*	Glenn Turner	New Zealand v East Africa	Birmingham	1975
175*	Kapil Dev	India v Zimbabwe	Tunbridge Wells	1983
181	Viv Richards	West Indies v Sri Lanka	Karachi	1987/88
186*	Sachin Tendulkar	India v New Zealand	Hyderabad	1999/00
189	Sanath Jayasuriya	Sri Lanka v India	Sharjah	2000/01
219	Virender Sehwag	India v West Indies	Indore	2011/12

- Michael Clarke bowled Australia to victory in the third Test against the West Indies in 2011/12 by claiming the second five-wicket haul of his career, but his first in seven years. After a match-winning 5-86 at Roseau, Clarke became the first captain to record the double of a five-wicket haul and a triple-century in Test match cricket. He achieved both strands of the double within the space of four months, after scoring an unbeaten 329 against India at the SCG, a match in which he had a chance to knock off Brian's Lara's record for highest score in a Test by a captain had he not declared.

PROGRESSIVE HIGHEST SCORES BY CAPTAINS IN TESTS

1	Dave Gregory	Australia v England	Melbourne	1876/77
10	James Lillywhite jnr	England v Australia	Melbourne	1876/77
43	Dave Gregory	Australia v England	Melbourne	1876/77
52	Lord Harris	England v Australia	The Oval	1880
143*	Billy Murdoch	Australia v England	The Oval	1880
211	Billy Murdoch	Australia v England	The Oval	1884
270	Don Bradman	Australia v England	Melbourne	1936/37
285*	Peter May	England v West Indies	Birmingham	1957
311	Bob Simpson	Australia v England	Manchester	1964
333	Graham Gooch	England v India	Lord's	1990
334*	Mark Taylor	Australia v Pakistan	Peshawar	1998/99
400*	Brian Lara	West Indies v England	St John's	2003/04

- In his 15 matches as skipper of the 2010 IPL Mumbai Indians, Sachin Tendulkar became the first captain to score 600 runs in a Twenty20 series. Tendulkar accrued 618 runs in his 15 innings, with five fifties and a highest score of 89 not out. He topped 500 runs in the following IPL as well, scoring 553 with an unbeaten 100 his peak.

- Under a new captain and playing their first Test match in six years, Zimbabwe pulled off a win at Harare in 2011/12 ending a barren trot spanning 11 Tests and almost seven years. Their previous victory had been in 2004, at the same ground and against the same opposition, Bangladesh. With a second-innings 105 not out, Brendan Taylor became the second Zimbabwe captain, after Dave Houghton in 1992/93, to score his maiden Test century in his first match in charge.

MAIDEN TEST CENTURY
IN MAIDEN TEST AS CAPTAIN

153*	Billy Murdoch	Australia v England	The Oval	1880
143	Harry Trott	Australia v England	Lord's	1896
133	Monty Noble	Australia v England	Sydney	1903/04
109	Herbie Taylor	South Africa v England	Durban	1913/14
107	Geoff Rabone	New Zealand v South Africa	Durban	1953/54
121	Dave Houghton ‡	Zimbabwe v India	Harare	1992/93
105*	Brendan Taylor	Zimbabwe v Bangladesh	Harare	2011/12

‡ *On Test debut*

- After scoring a half-century at Old Trafford in 1896, Australia's captain Harry Trott picked up two important wickets when England batted, dismissing Andrew Stoddart and his opposite number W.G. Grace. Both openers were stumped by James Kelly, a unique occurrence in Test match cricket.

- England's Arthur Gilligan made history at Lord's in 1924, when he became the first captain to bowl the first ball of a Test to his rival captain. In a match England won by an innings, Gilligan accounted for his opposite number Herbie Taylor, twice, for scores of four and eight.

- Bowling to the Eagles in the 2006/07 Standard Bank Pro20 Series in South Africa, Arno Jacobs became the first captain to take a five-for on his debut in Twenty20 cricket. He followed up his 5-26 with a top score of 32 for the Warriors, batting at number three.

- In a Twenty20 match against Karnataka in Hyderabad in 2010/11, Tamil Nadu was captained by Dinesh Karthik, who also kept wicket, batted and bowled. He led his side to a 65-run victory, scored 28 off 21 with four boundaries and also took a catch and a wicket (2-0-10-1).

- Alastair Cook, who scored a century in his first Test as captain, had also scored a hundred in his first stint as captain in first-class cricket. Opening the batting for MCC against Sussex at Lord's in 2007, Cook scored 142, while his opposite number, Michael Yardy, was forced to retire hurt with a busted finger one run short of a century.

- The Lord's Test match against South Africa of 2012 was a historic occasion for both captains, with one appearing in his 100th and final Test and the other becoming the most capped captain of all time. Andrew Strauss's 100th Test was also his 50th as England captain, while Graeme Smith broke Allan Border's record of 93 Tests in charge.

  Strauss emulated Border by making his 50th appearance as captain at the same ground where he made his captaincy debut. The only two to achieve such a distinction, Border's first stint as captain came against the West Indies in 1984/85, with his 50th against Pakistan in 1989/90 – both matches came at the Adelaide Oval. Strauss's first time in charge was against Pakistan, also at Lord's, in 2006.

- Australia's captain in the 2012 Under-19 World Cup finished the tournament with a mega batting average of 276.00. Dismissed just once in six innings, William Bosisto made his highest score of 87 not out in the final, which was won by India after a century from his opposing captain, Unmukt Chand. Following a century in the final of the Under-19 Asia Cup the month before, Chand became the first batsman to hit five hundreds in Under-19 one-day internationals with an unbeaten 111, a knock that contained seven fours and six sixes.

  Anamul Haque, the Bangladesh captain, was the only batsman to score two centuries in the tournament and topped the batting charts with 365 runs at 60.83.

- Two future Test captains scored centuries when England hosted the West Indies in a Youth Test at Nottingham in 1993. Michael Vaughan hit 119, while Shivnarine Chanderpaul became only the second batsman to score a double-century on his debut in an Under-19 Test with 203 not out.

  Coincidentally, Chanderpaul also struck an unbeaten 203 in his first Test as captain of the West Indies, against South Africa, at Georgetown in 2004/05. He became only the second captain to mark his first Test in charge with a double-century after New Zealand's Graham Dowling (239) against India at Christchurch in 1967/68.

- There were awkward moments for two iconic cricket grounds in England in 2011 when officials refused access to past and present Test captains. In the first incident, former England skipper Alec Stewart was denied entry to a hospitality box at The Oval during the fourth England–India Test. Later, India's captain Mahendra Singh Dhoni was stopped from attending an official photo shoot at Old Trafford in Manchester because he was wearing spikes.

A former England batsman and county captain also suffered at the hands of officialdom at Old Trafford, with David Lloyd ejected from a bar at the ground during the England v India Twenty20 international. A steward failed to recognise the famous face of the former Lancashire captain, who was forcibly removed from the members' bar. Lloyd said: **"I'm absolutely flipping livid. I'm a life member and ex-captain of the club. I pointed out I was just looking at a few photos, and mentioned that I was in most of them. They asked me whether I was refusing to leave, and when I said I was going nowhere, two of them grabbed me by the arms. I said, 'We're in a stalemate here, because I'm not moving'."**

- When Tasmania hosted Victoria in Hobart in 1889/90, captain Charles McAllen failed to turn up in time to bat, with his team demolished for 39 in a little under an hour. Appearing on his first-class debut, McAllen then made a duck in the second innings as Tasmania followed-on, sustaining an innings-and-147-run defeat. His opposite number in the match, Jack Blackham, also made a duck, and both kept wicket.

- In his only appearance in a Twenty20 international, Shahriar Nafees captained his side to victory. Opening the batting in his country's inaugural Twenty20, Nafees hit 25 at Khulna in 2006/07, with Bangladesh beating Zimbabwe by 43 runs. In Test cricket, England's C. Aubrey Smith, the South African trio of Alf Richards, Henry Taberer and Biddy Anderson and the West Indies' Nelson Betancourt each captained in their only international appearance.

  Taberer and Anderson got their captaincy gigs in the same Test series, against Australia in 1902/03. Taberer led South Africa in the first Test at Johannesburg, while Anderson did so in the second Test at the same venue a week later.

- Michael Clarke made a return to grade cricket in 2012, becoming the first incumbent Australian captain in a decade to do so. Clarke stepped out in his whites for the Western Suburbs club against North Sydney in 2012/13.

  The third Australian skipper after Warren Bardsley and Bob Simpson to hail from the Wests club, Clarke later became the first batsman to score three Test match double-centuries as captain in a calendar year. Clarke began the year with an unbeaten 329 and 210 against India, and added 259 not out against South Africa in Brisbane. At the end of the match, Clarke had edged ahead of the great Don Bradman with the highest average by a captain with 1,000 Test runs in a calendar year. In 1948, Bradman scored 1,025 runs in 13 innings at 113.88. After 11 innings in 2012, Clarke had 1,041 runs at 115.66.

Clarke's 259 was only the third such innings in Test match cricket, with one of the others scored by his opposing captain – Graeme Smith (259), against England at Lord's in 2003. Clarke shared in two 200-run partnerships during his 259, including one of 259 for the fourth wicket with Ed Cowan. His purple patch continued in the following match, at Adelaide, scoring 230, becoming the first batsman to make four Test match double-centuries in a calendar year.

HIGHEST BATTING AVERAGES BY A TEST CAPTAIN IN A YEAR

Qualification: 1000 runs

Captain	Year	M	Runs	Avge	100s	50s
Don Bradman (A)	1948	8	1025	113.88	5	2
Michael Clarke (A)	2012	11	1595	106.33	5	3
Ricky Ponting (A)	2006	10	1333	88.86	7	4

• Oxford University captain Miles Howell made history in 1934 when, for the sake of the game, he declared an innings closed while he was on 99. It happened in the match against Free Foresters at Oxford, a match that ended up being drawn. Transvaal captain Clive Rice did the same thing in a Currie Cup match at Cape Town in 1990/91.

CAPTAINS DECLARING A FIRST-CLASS INNINGS WITH A BATSMAN ON 99 NOT OUT

Captain	Batsman	Match	Result
Miles Howell	Miles Howell	Oxford University v Free Foresters at Oxford, 1934	D
David Graveney	Phil Bainbridge	Gloucestershire v Kent at Bristol, 1983	D
Adrian Kuiper	Terence Lazard	Western Province v N. Transvaal at Cape Town, 1988/89	D
Clive Rice	Clive Rice	Transvaal v Western Province at Cape Town, 1990/91	D
Mark Benson	Neil Taylor	Kent v Nottinghamshire at Nottingham, 1995	L
Paul Reiffel	Michael Klinger	Victoria v Tasmania at Hobart, 2000/01	L
Luke Sutton	Graeme Welch	Derbyshire v Somerset at Taunton, 2005	W

• Australian captain George Bailey lost a Twenty20 international on his birthday in 2012, a fate suffered in the same year by South Africa's skipper A.B. de Villiers. In March 2011, two captains – England's Andrew Strauss and Zimbabwe's Elton Chigumbura – both lost a one-day international on their birthdays.

• Despite not being a member of England's one-day international side, Alastair Cook took over the captaincy of the team from Andrew Strauss in 2011. For the first time, England had a different captain for each form of the game, with Strauss in charge of the Test side and Stuart Broad succeeding Paul Collingwood as skipper of the Twenty20 team.

> **"It's forward thinking, in that other cricket boards might not have the guts to do it."**
>
> England batsman Jonathan Trott

- By scoring 137 and 102 against Pakistan at Abu Dhabi in 2011/12, Alastair Cook became the first England captain to score back-to-back hundreds in one-day internationals. Ricky Ponting is the only captain to date to have twice hit centuries in consecutive ODI innings, with both instances coming in the calendar year of 2007 and all hundreds scored against the same opposition, New Zealand – 111 and 134 not out in January, and an unbeaten 107 and another score of 134 not out, in December, with all innings made on home soil.

- During the 2012/13 Border-Gavaskar Trophy, Michael Clarke became the first captain to declare a first innings of a Test and go on and lose by an innings. On the first day of the second Test at Hyderabad, Clarke pulled his troops in at 237/9, only to watch India pile up 503. Batting again, Australia was spun out for 131 to lose by an innings and 135.

  In the following Test, at Mohali, the pain continued for Clarke, going first ball in the first innings, becoming the first Australian captain to be stumped for a duck by the opposing captain. In the first Test, at Chennai, M.S. Dhoni had become the very first wicketkeeping captain to score a Test match double-century (224), only to have the feat matched just 15 days later, by Bangladesh's Mushfiqur Rahim (200) against Sri Lanka at Galle.

  With Clarke unavailable for the final Test at Delhi with a back complaint, Shane Watson was promoted to the captaincy role, setting an odd record in the process. Having being dropped for the previous Test at Mohali due to disciplinary reasons, Watson left the tour to return home for the birth of his first child, then went back and promptly became Australia's 44th Test captain.

Cricket Records and Cricket Hits

- A number of greats from the world of rock music turned up for the 25th anniversary celebrations of the charity Bunbury Cricket Club in England in 2011. Eric Clapton, Bill Wyman, Ringo Starr and David Essex were on hand for a gala night in London, also attended by members of the Ashes-winning England cricket team. Bill Wyman's Rhythm Kings performed live on stage, as did Eric Clapton, whose set included 'Crossroads', 'Hoochie Coochie Man' and 'Wonderful Tonight'.

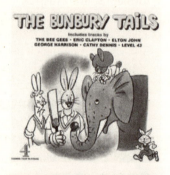

- An album featuring the likes of Eric Clapton and Elton John was released in 1992 to raise funds for the Bunbury Cricket Club. The LP *The Bunbury Tails* kicks off with the single 'We're The Bunburys' by the Bee Gees, and also includes numbers from former Beatle George Harrison and jazz-funk bands Shakatak and Level 42.

- In the same year that he sang at an Andrew Flintoff benefit dinner, Elton John performed a series of concerts at some of England's iconic cricket grounds. In 2006, Sir Elton put on shows in five counties – Sussex, Durham, Worcestershire, Kent and

Somerset – that drew record crowds and much-needed finances for the clubs concerned.

> **"Every musician I've ever known would like to be a sportsman and every sportsman I've known wants to be a musician. They're both great levellers and there is a feeling of togetherness – sport and music, more than anything, bring people together."**
>
> Elton John

- Pankey Alleyne, a Trinidad-born trumpeter and part-time cricketer, was a member of the Caribbean All-Star Orchestra and the Fleetwood cricket club in the UK. It was his love of cricket that cost him his place in the band after turning up late for a concert dressed in his cricket gear. He became professional at Fleetwood in the Ribblesdale League in 1950, and continued playing the game until 1983. Alleyne said: **"They still used to pick me and I felt embarrassed … my hair turning grey**."

- Steven Crook, an Adelaide-born fast bowler and singer, achieved his maiden first-class five-wicket haul at the home of cricket in 2011. A former South Australian Under-19 representative, Crook – who fronts the UK rock band Juliet The Sun – took 5-94 for Middlesex against Northamptonshire at Lord's, only the second five-for of his first-class career which began in 2003.

  In 2009, his band recorded a song, 'Time for Heroes', which became England's unofficial theme song for the Ashes. Crook gave a copy of the song to county team-mates Graeme Swann, Andrew Flintoff, Monty Panesar and James Anderson and said: **"The only problem is that being a proud Australian I'm taking a real ribbing from my band mates."**

- One of Britain's best-known folk bands recorded an album of cricket songs in 1984. *The Sound of Cricket* by The Yetties, and featuring cricket commentator John Arlott, contained tracks such as 'Cricket on The Village Green', 'The Flower Bowler', 'The High Catch', 'Four Jolly Bowlers' and 'Harold Gimblett's Hundred'.

- Indian batsman Sanjay Manjrekar released an album of songs in the 1990s called *Rest Day*. It featured the favourite tunes of Manjrekar's team-mates, including Sachin Tendulkar, Anil Kumble and Javagal Srinath. Vinod Kambli, who appeared in 17 Tests and 104 one-day internationals, also sang on the album.

- Described as a band with a "unique, genre-spanning blend of music they call chap rock", The Don Bradmans is a British group formed in 2003. All members of the band are known as 'Don Bradman' – their debut album *Across the Drewson Sea* was released in 2010.

> "The band's name came about because our erstwhile drummer's childhood friend in Dundee had a pet spider called Don Bradman. I thought that was a brilliant name, so when the band was formed I suggested that as a name. None of us knew of the famous cricketer. We'd never heard of him."
>
> Don Bradmans band member 'Don Bradman'

- An organ recital staged at the Sydney Town Hall in 1931 recognised the world's number one cricketer of the day. The initial letters of the composers of the items performed – from Balfe to Nemerowsky – spelt out the surname of Don Bradman.

- The debut album by Don Bradman's granddaughter Greta was nominated for an award by the Australian Recording Industry Association in 2010.

    Her follow-up CD to *Forest of Dreams* was a hit, debuting at number six on the ARIA classical music chart in 2011. *Grace* contained tracks as diverse as 'Pie Jesu' from Andrew Lloyd Webber's *Requiem* and 'Can You Feel the Love Tonight' from the animated Walt Disney film *The Lion King*.

> **Bradman's voice has great range – a top E or thereabouts was on the menu – and a rich dynamic intensity. She is also capable of managing Handel's crazily ornamented vocal lines with aplomb.**
>
> Rodney Smith, *The Advertiser*, 2009

Soprano Greta Bradman with the Zephyr Quartet at a concert in Adelaide in 2010

- Rick Astley, a British pop star from the 1980s, met his first girlfriend at a local cricket club. The singer later made Top 40 charts around the world with a string of hits including 'Never Gonna Give You Up' and 'Take Me to Your Heart'. He said: **"At the cricket club disco I asked Jackie to dance and she said 'no' because she didn't like the record. I walked off thinking, 'you're a mug'. Later, 'Tainted Love' by Soft Cell came on, and I thought 'that's it, should I go and ask again?' I was going, 'go on, go on, no don't, no don't' and I ended up walking over, saying 'you dancing now or what?' So we had a dance and that was it. I've been going out with her ever since."**

- Garry Sobers was immortalised in song in the 1960s with at least two singles, one by a legendary West Indies calypso singer, the other by a British actor. 'Sir Garfield Sobers' by Mighty Sparrow asked: "Who's the greatest cricketer on Earth or Mars?/Anyone can tell you, it's the great Garfield Sobers/This handsome Barbadian lad really knows his work."

  Cy Grant, a West Indies-born UK-based actor, also recorded a song in honour of Sobers in 1966 called 'King Cricket'.

  Shivnarine Chanderpaul has also been the subject of a number of songs over the years. One by Guyanese calypso star Dave Martins also pays tribute to Carl Hooper. 'Hooper and Chanderpaul' is a track included on one of his band's greatest hits albums with the lyrics: "We must play Carl and Shiv/That's how we have to live/For us to win this game/Guyana must combine Hooper and Shivnarine/This match is make or break."

- To celebrate the 2007 World Cup in the Caribbean, West Indies calypso singer Alston Becket Cyrus released a cricket-themed album that includes musical tributes to Brian Lara and Courtney Walsh. Some of the tracks on the *Cricket Is We Ting* album include 'Everybody Loves Courtney', 'Laramania' and 'Lara Again'.

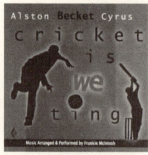

    Fellow calypso star David Rudder also released a cricket album – *The Cricket Chronicles* – in the same year. He said: **"Calypso is still part of the cricket landscape but it's more celebratory as opposed to the topical and heavy social commentary of the past. Caribbean cricket to many now is a huge party with a game taking place on the side."**

- In 2011, a former West Indies Test cricketer formed his own reggae band which he called Eleven. Spinner Omari Banks – the first player from Anguilla to appear in a Test – and his band released their first single 'Move On' in 2012. Banks said: **"My dad, Bankie Banx, is a well-known and respected reggae musician, and musicians like Cat Coore and Tony Ruption of Third World, Junior Jazz of Inner Circle and Benjy Myaz and so many other great reggae musicians have mentored me since I was a young boy."**

Omari Banks with his band Eleven

Banks appeared in ten Tests and five one-day internationals for the West Indies during the 2000s, adding: **"Since I was 11 years old cricket was my job, my priority and something I was blessed to do on the highest professional level. I really enjoyed my time playing cricket, but my passion is music."**

- A tweet was fired off during 2012 declaring that Australian batsman David Warner was recording an album. Another David Warner from New South Wales found fame in music, with Dave Warner forming the 1970s rock band From the Suburbs. Dave Warner also wrote a cricket book, *Cricket's Hall of Shame*, which contained a foreword from former Australian captain Greg Chappell.

David Warner
@davidwarner31 🐦 Follow

Just recording my first album!! Can't say anymore. @ValentinaStoj
pic.twitter.com/2c4v5pm7

← Reply ↻ Retweet ★ Favorite

● Two first-class cricketers from the West Indies carry the name of one of pop music's greatest. Joseph Elvis appeared in two matches for British Guiana in the 1940s, while Elvis Reifer shook his hips as a fast bowler for Barbados and Hampshire in the 1980s. A player named A. Presley represented St Cyprians in the Toronto and District Cricket Council League in Canada in the early 1920s.

● The year 2012 saw the names of two classical music composers join a Strauss on the international stage. A Wagner – Neil Wagner – made his debut for New Zealand, while an Elgar – Dean Elgar – made his debut for South Africa. During the previous year, the names of a Bach and a Holst appeared in junior cricket matches in Australia. Victoria Bach played for the South Australia Under-17s Women, while Brett Holst played for the Victoria Under-17s in 2010/11.

A player named James Taylor made his Test debut in 2012 for England. The eighth such-named cricketer to have played the first-class game, Taylor shares his name with the American singer-songwriter who had a number one hit with 'You've Got a Friend' in 1971.

A SELECTION OF INTERNATIONAL CRICKETERS WHO SHARE THEIR NAMES WITH MUSIC ICONS

Cricketer	Country	FC debut	Musician
Geoff Arnold	England	1963	Malcolm Arnold, British composer
Russel Arnold	Sri Lanka	1993/94	Malcolm Arnold, British composer
Dean Elgar	South Africa	2005/06	Edward Elgar, British composer
Ghulam Ali	Pakistan	1989/90	Ghulam Ali, Indian classical singer
Chris Martin	New Zealand	1997/98	Chris Martin, Coldplay frontman
Andrew Strauss	England	1998	Johann Strauss, Austrian composer
Charlie Parker	England	1903	Charlie Parker, American jazz saxophonist
James Taylor	England	2008	James Taylor, US singer-songwriter
Neil Wagner	New Zealand	2005/06	Richard Wagner, German composer
David Warner	Australia	2008/09	Dave Warner, Australian rock musician

... AND SOME WHO PLAYED FIRST-CLASS CRICKET ONLY

George Harrison	Oxford University	1880	George Harrison, Beatles lead guitarist
Robbie Williams	Middlesex	2007	Robbie Williams, British pop singer
Vaughan Williams	New South Wales	2001/02	Vaughan Williams, British composer

Two other players named George Harrison also played first-class cricket

- Adrian Wykes, who recorded a number of songs in the UK under the name Percy Pavilion, played cricket for Luxembourg. He also appeared in three matches for Cambridgeshire in the NatWest Trophy in the late 1980s, taking five wickets at 15.60.

  Good enough to have once dismissed Steve Waugh, Wykes recorded two cricket-themed 45s in the 1980s. The *Cricket E.P.* was released in 1983, with 'Calypso Intro', 'Cricket in the Jungle', 'Dolly Mixture', 'Mercenaries Cricket Club', 'You're an Extra, Baby!' and 'Brian Johnston's Nose'. He followed it up with 'Gower Power' in 1984.

- Members of a UK rock band stopped by to lend support to a charity cricket event in 2012 which witnessed the first non-stop cricket match to last 150 hours. Staff from Loughborough University played through wind, rain and hail to beat the previous world record by 45 hours. While a number of former England players acted as umpires, Graham Lambert and Stephen Holt from the alternative band Inspiral Carpets turned up to watch.

"Way back in 1992, the team I played for, CWS Manchester, had a midweek game against Delph second XI on a rainy Thursday tucked away north of Manchester in the rolling Saddleworth hills. We were a man short so I called Graeme Fowler, a friend of the band, to see if he fancied a game. He was free so a couple of hours later we turned up in the rain and cracked on with the 20-overs-a-side game.

"They batted first and scored around 90. Myself and Graeme opened the batting. It was a momentous occasion for me opening with 'The Fox'. I was determined whatever happened I would still be batting when he had gone. He pushed, hooked and pulled before holing out on the boundary. I marvelled from the other end leaning on my bat.

"We knocked them off easily. I was nine not out off about 30 balls, but I wasn't concerned with my slow scoring. I'd batted with a guy who had notched a double-hundred for England in India.

"For my cricket career, it just didn't get any better than that."

Inspiral Carpets guitarist Graham Lambert

GRAHAM LAMBERT'S DREAM TEAM

Mike Atherton * (E)
Graeme Fowler (E)
Stuart Law (A)
Carl Hooper (WI)
Andrew Symonds (A)
Andrew Flintoff (E)
Wasim Akram (P)
Warren Hegg † (E)
Paul Allott (E)
Muttiah Muralitharan (SL)
Peter Lever (E)

Inspiral Carpets band member Graham Lambert (right) with former England batsman Graeme Fowler

- The daughter of a famous Test cricketer who played for two countries released a critically-acclaimed debut CD in 2008. Singer-songwriter Catherine Traicos, whose father John appeared in seven Tests, has supported a number of international acts that have toured Australia including award-winning British folk singer Beth Orton.

Singer-songwriter Catherine Traicos – daughter of a Test cricketer – with the band Starry Night

- UK classical ensemble Cantabile, also known as The London Quartet, paid tribute to the game in 2011 with the release of an album called *Songs of Cricket*. The four-member group recorded an eclectic array of musical items from Richard Stilgoe's 'Lillian Thomson' to a medley of TV cricket themes and the England cricket team song 'Jerusalem'.

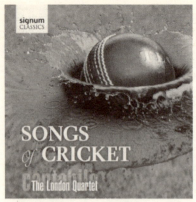

● An album by a British folk singer that contained a cricket song was renamed and redesigned for the US market, with the front cover featuring a half-naked Roy Harper carrying a cricket bat. Harper's 1975 release *HQ* was titled *When an Old Cricketer Leaves the Crease* in the United States.

His biggest-selling single, the seven-minute-long tribute to village cricket, was released twice, in 1975 and 1978. Harper said: "**My childhood memories of the heroic stature of the footballers and cricketers of the day invoke the sounds that went along with them. Paramount among these was the traditional Northern English brass band, which was a functional social component through all four seasons, being seen and heard in many different contexts. My use of that style of music on 'Old Cricketer' is a tribute to those distant memories.**"

The song makes reference to two famous England cricketers in the lyrics – batsman Geoff Boycott and fast bowler John Snow: "When an old cricketer leaves the crease, well you never know he's gone/If sometimes you're catching a fleeting glimpse of a twelfth man at silly mid-on/And it could be Geoff and it could be John with a new-ball sting in his tail/And it could be me and it could be thee and it could be the sting in the ale, the sting in the ale."

A SELECTION OF 45RPM AND CD SINGLES WITH CRICKET ON THE FRONT COVER

'When an Old Cricketer Leaves the Crease' Roy Harper		1975
'C'mon Aussie C'mon'	The Mojo Singers	1979
'Dashing Dougie'	Nash Chase	1981
'The Cricket E.P.'	Percy Pavilion	1983
'Gower Power'	Percy Pavilion	1984
'Cricket'	1st Eleven	1985
'N-N-Nineteen Not Out'	The Commentators	1985
'We're the Bunburys'	The Bunburys	1986

'Better to Bat' (EP)	Blyth Power	1989
'Runs in the Family'	Tim Finn	1994
'Where Would We Be Without A.B.'	Doug Parkinson	1994
'Sir Don'	John Williamson	1996
'Bowlin' Shane'	Haskel Daniel vs Sideshow	2000
'Can't Bowl, Can't Throw'	Six and Out	2000
'Horny Warnie'	Horny Warnie and The Whites	2003
'Was Sport Better in the 70's?' (EP)	The Drugs	2003
'You're Never Gone'	Mark Butcher	2003
'C'mon Aussie C'mon'	Shannon Noll	2004
'Jerusalem'	Keedie and the England Cricket Team	2005
'Murali'	Alston Koch	2007
'Shane Warne' (EP)	Handsome Young Strangers	2007
'I Was a Mate of Don Bradman'	Kamahl (featuring Greg Champion)	2008
'The Ashes Song'	Phil Tufnell and The Wooden Urns	2009
'Deep Backward Square Leg'	New Windsor Porn Stars vs The Pussy Willows	2009
'Meeting Mr Miandad'	The Duckworth Lewis Method	2009
'Bodyline'	Red Jezebel	2010

A SELECTION OF ALBUMS AND CDs WITH CRICKET ON THE FRONT COVER

Plays On	Climax Blues Band	1969
Stones in the Park (Bootleg LP)	The Rolling Stones	1969
There's the Rub	Wishbone Ash	1974
When an Old Cricketer Leaves the Crease	Roy Harper	1975
Greatest Hits Volume II	Elton John	1977
Render Your Heart	Tony Tuff	1984
Los London	The Coal Porters	1996
Slightly Odway	Jebediah	1997
Songs from the South	Paul Kelly	1997
Not Out	The Bats	1999
The Cropredy Box	Fairport Convention	2003
The Elephant	The White Stripes	2003
Love Hits ... Like a Cricket Bat-out-of-Hell	XUK	2005
The Young Cricketer	Chris Corsano	2006
A Perfect Action	The Cavaliers	2007
The Cricket Chronicles	David Rudder	2007
Cricket Is We Ting	Alston Becket Cyrus	2007
The Good, The Bad and The Googly	Geoffrey Oi!Cott	2008

● A county cricketer who was once touted as a future England Test wicketkeeper later became a full-time musician. Given his marching orders by Lancashire in 1954, Frank Parr – a trombonist with the Merseysippi Jazz Band – moved to London where he joined the Mick Mulligan Band: **"All jazzmen are kicking against something and it comes out when they blow. If they knew what they were kicking against, they wouldn't blow nearly so well."**

The trombone-playing Lancashire wicketkeeper Frank Parr

After the demise of the Mulligan band in the early 1960s, Parr became manager of clarinettist Acker Bilk who topped the charts around the world with his single 'Stranger on the Shore': **"I've been extraordinarily lucky. I've made a living out of the two things I loved."**

"The professional cricketer is not just a man who plays cricket for money. He has a social role. He is expected to behave within certain defined limits. He can be a 'rough diamond', even 'a bit of a character', but he must know his place. If he smells of sweat, it must be fresh sweat. He must dress neatly and acceptably. His drinking must be under control. He must know when to say 'sir'.

"Frank, we were soon to discover, had none of these qualifications. He was an extreme social risk, a complicated rebel whose world swarmed with demons. He concealed a formidable and well-read intelligence behind a stylised oafishness. He used every weapon to alienate acceptance. Even within the jazz world, that natural refuge for the anti-social, Frank stood out as an exception. We never knew the reason for his quarrel with the captain of Lancashire, but after a month or two in his company we realised it must have been inevitable."

British jazz legend George Melly

● The award-winning blind British jazz pianist George Shearing was a cricket lover who retained his interest in the game after basing himself in the United States. The leader of the famous George Shearing Quintet, he often insisted that concerts in London be booked to coincide with Test matches. He was also noted for inserting cricketers' names into songs – a Johnny Mercer composition made famous by Judy Garland, 'On the Atchison, Topeka and the Santa Fe' became 'Atherton, Topeka and the Santa Fe'.

> **"It was obvious that if I was going to go out in the street to play cricket with a bunch of sighted kids, I was going to have to have somebody to help me. The main person who did so was a boy called Freddy. Going out with me to play cricket involved Freddy and me holding the bat together. Just holding the bat together is, of course, no guarantee that there's going to be smooth contact with the ball, because Freddy has to move his arms when he sees which way the ball is coming. He sees it and I don't. However, once in a while my anticipation is wrong. On one famous occasion, I remember an incident which – if it ever happened in a real game of cricket – would probably be described as 'jaw before wicket'.**
>
> **"Now most of us know about leg before wicket, but jaw before cricket is virtually unknown. In just the same way that a cricketer would make an unconscious move, for some reason I stood there fully conscious after this ball had hit me smack on the jaw – I repeat, fully conscious – and said 'I'm out!' In retrospect, I'm not sure if that meant I was out as a batsman, or I was out physically."**
>
> George Shearing

- Australian pop singer Casey Barnes, who had a No. 1 dance hit with Elton John's 'Tiny Dancer' in the UK in 2008, once took 7-22 for his high school in Tasmania. A fast bowler, Barnes made a number of appearances in junior representative cricket teams in the Apple Isle: **"... was the worst batsmen you've ever seen ... don't think I ever scored over fifty."**

  Barnes's father coached a young Ricky Ponting at football, while his mother worked in the same bank as David Boon.

- An episode of the long-running BBC radio comedy *The Goon Show* which was later released on record features a cricket reference. 'The Affair of the Lone Banana', featuring Spike Milligan, Peter Sellers and Harry Secombe, was first broadcast in 1954.

[A lone cricket chirping]

Bloodnok: **Listen … what's making that noise?**

Seagoon: **A cricket.**

Bloodnok: **How can they see to bat in this light?**

Eccles: **Major, Major. A man's just climbed over the garden wall.**

Bloodnok: **A boundary! Well played, sir!**

Seagoon: **Bloodnok, you fool. That's no cricketer, he's possibly a rebel assassin.**

Eccles: **Oooh!**

Bloodnok: **Then one of us must volunteer to go out and get him.**

Seagoon: **Yes, one of us must volunteer.**

Eccles: **Yer, yes. One of us must volunteer.**

Seagoon, Bloodnok and Eccles: **England for ever!**

– from 'The Affair of the Lone Banana' episode of *The Goon Show*, 1954

Another comedy sketch about cricket featuring Spike Milligan – first broadcast on radio in the early 1960s – was also released on vinyl. Two episodes from the third series of the ABC radio show *The Idiot Weekly* – 'The Ashes' and 'The Flying Dustman of the Outback' – were released on a Parlophone LP in 1962.

● The name of a famous cricketer gets a mention in a famous song of the 1960s. '$1000 Wedding' by American singer-songwriter Gram Parsons, a member of the rock band the Flying Burrito Brothers, includes a reference to Doctor W.G. Grace.

● The Scotland-born Australian folk singer Eric Bogle, famed for his 1971 song 'And the Band Played Waltzing Matilda', released an album in 1992 called *It's Not Cricket*. The record kicks off with his best-known composition and ends with the title track: "Tubby and Heals are giving Ricky Ponting tips from the comfort of the commentary box/Chappelli's making awful jokes without moving his lips/He only opens his big mouth to change his socks/And I think that they're the reason why I'm a cricketer hater/Those pontificating, self-inflating bloody commentators."

JASON REBELLO'S DREAM TEAM

Alvin Kallicharran (WI)
Sunil Gavaskar (I)
Viv Richards (WI)
Garry Sobers * (WI)
Ian Botham (E)
Derek Randall (E)
Rod Marsh † (A)
Bishan Bedi (I)
Dennis Lillee (A)
Jeff Thomson (A)
Malcolm Marshall (WI)

British jazz pianist Jason Rebello

MIKE WALKER'S DREAM TEAM

Sachin Tendulkar (I)
Adam Gilchrist † (A)
Don Bradman * (A)
Rahul Dravid (I)
Viv Richards (WI)
Brian Lara (WI)
Jonty Rhodes (SA)
Garry Sobers (WI)
Ian Botham (E)
Andrew Flintoff (E)
Shane Warne (A)

British jazz guitarist Mike Walker

- A decade on after scoring a top 40 hit in 1973 with the single 'Gaye', British balladeer Clifford T. Ward released a song about cricket. Included on his album *Sometime Next Year*, the song called 'Cricket' was released as a single in the UK in 1986.

- Irish musician and fast bowler Roger Whelan appeared in two one-day internationals for his country, dismissing two victims, one of whom would later release an album. Whelan took a single wicket in each match, with both being big-name Test players – India's Sachin Tendulkar and South Africa's A.B. de Villiers in ODIs played in Belfast in 2007. Later in the year, Whelan retired from all forms of the game to concentrate on his music career with rock band The Stimulants. In 2010, de Villiers appeared on the album *Make Your Dreams Come True* with South African singer Ampie du Preez, playing guitar and singing two songs.

- Blues legend Eric Clapton once gave his imprimatur to the singing style of a former England Test cricketer. The cricket-loving Clapton gave the thumbs-up to Surrey batsman Mark Butcher in the wake of his 12-track 2009 album *Songs from the Sun House*: "**Great stuff, especially your vocals.**"

Former England batsman Mark Butcher performing at a cricket match at Wormsley in the UK in 2011

"I met Eric Clapton through the Bunburys which is run by David English who used to be part of the management team that looked after Clapton in the early 1970s with RSO Records. He knew how much I admired him and he sat me next to him [at a cricket dinner]. **After not being able to say anything for a good ten minutes I said, 'Eric, I need to get this out there and then we can get on with the dinner … look, basically, I love you'. He laughed, then the ice was broken and we got on with dinner."**

Mark Butcher

- At the age of 70, former England batsman Geoffrey Boycott revealed that he's a big fan of pop music with a particular fondness for Katy Perry. Boycott spoke of his musical tastes during the BBC's commentary of the 2011 Test between England and India at Trent

Bridge. He said: **"I'm a good fan of pop music. I like that Katy Perry. She's a good singer. 'Firework' … that was a good record that. I like the pop music. She's nice, her. She's tops for me. She just has something about her voice. It's good, it's clear, it's strong. I don't think I'll ever meet her, she's American."**

- On the advice of eminent lyricist Tim Rice, American rock sensation Alice Cooper attended his first game of cricket in 2012. Coinciding with the 40th anniversary of the song 'School's Out' which went to number one in the UK in 1972, Cooper paid a visit to Lord's to watch the third Test between England and South Africa. He said: **"When you watch a game on television like we do in the United States, you kind of get an idea of what it's about. When you actually come to the place where it's sort of born, and watch it, I suddenly know how this game is played now. I'm watching the strategy … I now have an appreciation for the game."**

Geoff Boycott (right) meets American rock star
Alice Cooper in 2012

- West Indies star Dwayne Bravo teamed up with one of Jamaica's best-known reggae musicians in 2011 to record a CD. The Test-playing all-rounder and Grammy Award-winner Beenie Man recorded 'Beenie Man and Bravo' that also features the vocals of Guyanese songstress Timeka Marshall.

- Before moving from Western Australia to New South Wales to further his cricketing career, Stuart MacGill was a part-time musician in Perth. The spin bowler sang with a band called The Dot Balls.

- Greg Page, an original member of the Australian children's music group The Wiggles, played cricket as a teenager, once taking 50 wickets in a season. In 1987/88, a 15-year-old Page took 52 wickets at 11.00 in a junior tournament in New South Wales, winning an end-of-season trophy presented by Mark Taylor. Page said: **"I'll never forget that. I'm sure Mark's forgotten it. Actually I've reminded him of it a few times. Yeah, he doesn't remember it. He only remembers that I remind him about it."**

Wiggles member Greg Page, who took a hat-trick during a celebrity fundraising cricket match in the New South Wales city of Wollongong in 2010. Australian rockers Tim Farriss – from INXS – and Mark Callaghan – from Gang Gajang – also played, with the latter dismissing former England batsman Robin Smith

- Indian speedster and self-confessed rock star Shanthakumaran Sreesanth penned a song for the 2011 World Cup which he dedicated to his national team-mates. Sreesanth and his band S36 made its concert debut in the same year, a few weeks prior to the commencement of the showcase 50-over tournament.

- British violinist Nigel Kennedy is a big cricket fan, playing the occasional game for the Bunbury charity group. According to the club, the chart-topping Kennedy is: **" … a 'monster' performer. Borrows**

everyone's gear, runs around like crazy. Batting, bowling, laughing, a genius."

- A classical ensemble that rose to prominence at the Australian Chamber Music competition in 2005 took its name from a former Test captain. The Benaud Trio – named after Richie Benaud – has performed with a number of high-profile soloists and groups, and was a star attraction at the Boxing Day Test match at the MCG in 2006/07.

THE BENAUD TRIO'S DREAM TEAM

Don Bradman (A)
Brian Lara (WI)
Sachin Tendulkar (I)
Viv Richards (WI)
Richie Benaud * (A)
Steve Waugh (A)
Ian Botham (E)
Adam Gilchrist † (A)
Shane Warne (A)
Glenn McGrath (A)
Dennis Lillee (A)

Australian classical group The Benaud Trio

"**Although we named ourselves after cricketing patriarch Richie Benaud, it doesn't mean that we are not one hundred per cent serious about classical music. We spend a lot more time practising our scales than our bowling!**"

Benaud Trio violinist Lachlan Bramble

- American singer Andy Williams, best known for his song 'Moon River', appeared in a celebrity cricket match at The Oval in 1972. Williams (pictured) turned out in a testimonial match for Surrey's Micky Stewart representing the Vic Lewis XI. He opened the bowling after scoring 24 not out in his first-ever game of cricket.

  The leader of the Vic Lewis XI was a famous British jazz guitarist and bandleader. Lewis was also a member of the Middlesex club committee for a quarter of a century from 1976. He said: "**Cricket is just not another sport. Cricket is a religion, a way of life, a brotherhood.**"

- When British politician Boris Johnson appeared on the BBC's long-running radio show *Desert Island Discs* in 2005, he chose the network's cricket theme as one of his favourite pieces of music. 'Soul Limbo' was an international hit in 1968 for American instrumental R&B band Booker T and the MG's.

- West Indies superstar Chris Gayle did a new dance move on the pitch in 2012, going 'Gangnam Style' during the World Twenty20 tournament. After dismissing England's Jonny Bairstow in Pallekele, Gayle broke out with the dance made popular by South Korean pop star PSY in his 'Gangnam Style' music video.

  When the West Indies beat Sri Lanka in the final in Colombo, the entire team did the dance as the song was pumped out over the ground's sound system. Gayle said: **"When it came out, there was a lot of talk about it. That's how I got into it. It depends what sort of mood I'm in. It's a good dance to be honest. I enjoy it. Everybody does."**

Chris Gayle and team-mates bust a move 'Gangnam Style' after winning the 2012 World Twenty20 tournament in Sri Lanka

- While Ricky Ponting had no satisfaction with the bat in the opening Test of the 2012 Frank Worrell Trophy series, his spirits were lifted when he ran into Rolling Stones frontman Mick Jagger in a hotel in Trinidad. Jagger, a cricket tragic, and Ponting spent some time discussing the finer points of the game in the foyer of the hotel where Jagger and the Australian team had been staying.

The cricket-loving Mick Jagger with local children at Gros Islet during a West Indies v Pakistan one-day international in 2011

• Bill Wyman picked up a few big names as a bowler for the Bunbury cricket club, once claiming a hat-trick at The Oval. In 1993 – the year that he left The Rolling Stones – he took the wicket of West Indies fast bowler Michael Holding with a googly. Wyman said: **"I bowled Graeme Hick once, and he was really pissed. That's what happened with Mark Ramprakash too … bowled middle stump by a leg-break that I don't think he expected to spin that much."**

BILL WYMAN'S DREAM TEAM

Jack Hobbs (E)
Sachin Tendulkar (I)
Don Bradman (A)
Garry Sobers (WI)
Viv Richards * (WI)
Ian Botham (E)
Alan Knott † (E)
Shane Warne (A)
Fred Trueman (E)
Jim Laker (E)
Harold Larwood (E)

Former Rolling Stones bass player Bill Wyman

- Padmakar Shivalkar, who appeared in over 100 first-class matches as a spinner for Mumbai, recorded an EP in 1981 which featured the singing talents of Sunil Gavaskar. The four-track record was titled *Life is Cricket*. Shivalkar said: **"I sang two songs on one side and Sunil crooned on the other. The numbers were often played on the radio, though I have no idea how many records were sold."**

- An award-winning pop group scored a nets session with the England cricket team at Lord's in 2010. All members of Scouting For Girls are dedicated cricket junkies having played the game while at school.

"We are honoured to play the England team at Lord's. It is the stuff that childhood dreams are made of. We've loved the game since we started playing at school, since then we've done much more spectating than playing so we look forward to humiliating ourselves in front of the best bowlers in the world!"

Scouting For Girls lead singer
Roy Stride

Greg Churchouse and Roy Stride of the London pop band Scouting For Girls talking cricket and music in the BBC commentary box in 2010

- Somerset's Dar Lyon, a high-scoring batsman who also played first-class cricket for Cambridge, had a musical flair composing items for a series of popular revues staged in London. The right-hander, who later became a Chief Justice of the Seychelles, appeared in 158 matches in the 1920s and '30s with a highest score of 219.

- Released in 2013, David Bowie's first album in a decade contains a reference to cricket. 'Dirty Boys', the second track on *The Next Day*, includes the lines: "I will buy a feather hat/I will steal a cricket bat/ Smash some windows, make a noise/We will run with Dirty Boys."

Crime and Punishment

- In his last match of any importance, the man who became a suspect in a major murder case took a five-wicket haul and top-scored for his team Bournemouth. Montague Druitt, who also played for MCC – and alongside some of the greats of the game including W.G. Grace – was a suspect in the 'Jack the Ripper' murders that gripped London in 1888. Druitt's drowning death in the Thames in December roughly coincided with the last of the murders, which, to this day, remain unsolved.

- A police officer-son of the New South Wales Assistant Police Commissioner came under investigation in 2012 after repeatedly punching a cricket fan at a Big Bash League match at the SCG. The incident took place when the spectator refused to leave the ground and subsequently resisted arrest. Later in the night, a spectator at the same match was stabbed five times in the chest. After watching the Sydney Sixers–Perth Scorchers match, the 22-year-old was attacked with a military-style knife following a road rage incident on a major Sydney thoroughfare.

- Lorrie Wilmot, who appeared in 147 first-class matches with a top score of 222 not out, committed suicide in 2004 by shooting himself on his farm. The year before, Wilmot had been convicted of raping a 13-year-old girl and was awaiting a lengthy jail sentence.

  During the 1972/73 Currie Cup, Wilmot, the captain of Eastern Province, staged a walk-off at Bulawayo with Rhodesia six runs shy of victory. With a minimum of 20 overs to be bowled in the final hour, Wilmot claimed his team had done so and left the field, refusing to return. Despite a win being handed to Rhodesia, the decision was later overturned with the match declared a draw.

- A memorial in honour of the late Australian batsman David Hookes was stolen from a suburban cricket ground in Adelaide on the eve of its unveiling in 2012. The $12,000 brass and bronze sculpture featuring three stumps, a bat and a baggy green cap was commissioned to honour Hookes's time playing cricket at Thebarton Oval during his time with the West Torrens Cricket Club.

- Australian slow bowler Nathan Hauritz was hospitalised in 2011 following a punch in the face at a Queensland nightclub. Hauritz underwent surgery after the incident with the matter investigated by police. He said: **"I can tell you that I was really, really lucky because it could have been a lot worse. Originally, I thought I'd just have a black eye and a few stitches but it turned out to be a lot more than that. I was just out having a bit of fun with friends and obviously this person wasn't impressed. I still don't understand why what happened, happened. I considered pressing charges but decided against it because it's such a long, slow process nowadays. I want to focus on playing cricket."**

    In the same year, his then-New South Wales team-mate Phillip Hughes was also involved in a scuffle, at a hotel in suburban Sydney. Hughes was punched by another patron at the pub but the incident was not referred to police.

- On the eve of his Test debut for Australia in 2011/12, Ed Cowan's parents were the victims of a siege at their home in Sydney. A man broke into the residence at Darling Point, barricading himself inside until police stormed the home and arrested him.

- In 2012, the first Aboriginal cricketer to appear in domestic limited-overs cricket in Australia was sent to prison. Ian King, a fast bowler, was sentenced to 12 years in jail after he was found guilty of charges relating to the sexual assault of a number of young boys while he was a junior cricket coach in Canberra in the 1980s and 1990s. King appeared in eight first-class matches for Queensland, taking 30 wickets at 28.36 with two five-fors. In his only limited-overs match, against New South Wales at Sydney in 1969/70, King took 5-33.

- A village cricket match in Kent was disrupted in 2011 when a nearby resident ran on to the pitch to complain about balls being hit into her garden. But much to her surprise, Maria Chiappini was handcuffed by two of the players, who happened to be off-duty police officers. She was then held in a police cell for six hours, had her fingerprints and DNA taken and issued with an £80 penalty notice for public disorder and offensive language: **"It was awful. I am a law-abiding citizen. I have worked with the public since I was 15. I felt shocked and**

humiliated, it's an absolute violation. Me and my family do not deserve this treatment. This dreadful encounter has severely shaken my confidence in the police."

- A teenage cricket fan was killed by an umpire in Bangladesh in 2012 after running on to the pitch upset over a batsman's dismissal. After being berated by the 15-year-old, the umpire grabbed a bat from a batsman and hit the youngster over the head. He later died in hospital.

- Police seized a haul of historic cricket cards during a raid on a house in Perth in 2012. West Australian police were searching the home of a man who had been arrested for burglary and discovered a number of cards that dated back to 1914.

- A down-and-out couple caught having sex on a cricket pitch in Britain was taken to court in 2011 and charged with 'outraging public decency'. The two 30-plus-year-olds, described as homeless alcoholics, were both fined £50 plus costs.

- Play in the Cape Town Test match between South Africa and India in 2010/11 was soured when a former first-class cricketer was killed outside the ground. Luke Fairweather, who appeared in two matches for Western Province in the early 1980s, was shot in the stomach by a traffic officer following a dispute over a parking fine. A charge of murder against Ian Sinclair was later withdrawn.

- The body of a former Bangladesh Under-19 player was found in a dam in 2012, presumed murdered. Kuntal Chandra was found with wounds to several parts of his body. He had appeared in three first-class matches with a top score of 71.

- A batsman who played for the USA in the 1990 ICC Trophy was murdered in Florida in 2012. The Jamaican-born Errol Peart was shot while coming to the aid of a customer during an attempted armed hold-up at his car cleaning business in Miami. Peart had been the USA's leading run-scorer in the 1990 ICC Trophy with 209 runs at 41.80, which included 101 against East and Central Africa on his debut.

  In 2012, another cricketer had been shot dead during an armed robbery. Louis Vorster, who appeared in 95 first-class matches – the last one for Namibia in 2009/10 – was shot by robbers at a petrol station in Gauteng.

- During a run of three first-class matches in Pakistan's Quaid-e-Azam Trophy in 2007/08, Peshawar included two fast bowlers who were both later murdered. In the second innings of his debut match – against Quetta at Peshawar – Rahatullah took 4-104, while his opening partner Nauman Habib took 1-19. Two months after his third first-class match, the 18-year-old Rahatullah was shot dead by unknown assailants.

In the 2011/12 season, Nauman went missing just a few days after taking seven wickets (4-27 and 3-32) in a first-class match against Multan. After leaving his house in Hyderabad, the 32-year-old was reportedly kidnapped, axed to death and found in a sack. In 63 first-class matches, Nauman took 221 wickets with nine five-wicket hauls and three ten-fors.

FIRST-CLASS CRICKETERS KNOWN OR BELIEVED TO HAVE BEEN MURDERED

Player	Main teams	M	Date died	Age
Edward Wright	British Guiana, Jamaica	18	23/11/1904	46y 257d
Claude Tozer	New South Wales	7	21/12/1920	30y 85d
Jeffrey Stollmeyer	West Indies	117	10/09/1989	68y 183d
Muni Lal	Southern Punjab	20	08/01/1990	76y 362d
Haseeb-ul-Hasan	Karachi, Sind	32	18/04/1990	25y 342d
William Strydom	Orange Free State	80	20/02/1995	52y 336d
Mahinda Jayaratne	NW Province, Kurunegala	6	15/03/1997	29y 308d
Ashley Harvey-Walker	Derbyshire	81	28/04/1997	52y 281d
Francois Weideman	Northern Transvaal, Transvaal	40	04/06/2001	40y 258d
Rahatullah	Peshawar	3	11/02/2008	18y 233d
Nauman Habib	Peshawar	63	11/11/2011	32y 28d
Louis Vorster	Northern Transvaal, Namibia	95	17/04/2012	45y 167d
Kuntal Chandra	Chittagong, Sylhet	3	03/12/2012	28y 25d
John Commins	Western Province	10	03/01/2013	71y 119d

The list does not include cricketers who died as a result of acts of terrorism

The body of New South Wales batsman Claude Tozer following his murder by Dorothy Mort at her home in Sydney in 1920

- In 2012, a former South Africa captain called for a re-examination of the deaths of another former captain and a coach in the wake of match fixing. Clive Rice claimed the deaths of Hansie Cronje and Bob Woolmer were the result of the mafia. He said: **"These mafia betting syndicates do not stop at anything and they do not care who gets in their way. People have been murdered because of it in the past."**

  Woolmer, who had coached South Africa and Pakistan, was found dead in a hotel in Jamaica during the 2007 World Cup, following Pakistan's unexpected loss to Ireland. Cronje, who had been banned for life for his role in a match-fixing scandal, died in a plane crash in 2002. Rice suggested that the plane had been tampered with and added: **"I am convinced his death wasn't an accident."**

- An Indian man was arrested in 2012 for biting off an opponent's ear during a game of cricket in a town near Chennai. Following a verbal stoush between the pair on the pitch, the dispute flared again at the end of the match.

- The home of Pakistan fast bowler Umar Gul was raided in 2012 with a family member arrested on suspicion of harbouring a wanted militant. Pakistan army commandos broke into Gul's home in Peshawar and took away three men who were accused of providing shelter to a member of the outlawed Lashkar-e-Islam group.

- The British government denied the baby son of jailed Pakistan cricketer Salman Butt a visa in 2012. Butt, who, along with Mohammad Asif, was jailed for spot fixing during the 2010 Lord's Test against England, became a father for a second time minutes after his sentencing in 2011 and had never seen his son.

TEST CRICKET JAILBIRDS

Player	Sentence	Year
Arthur Coningham (Australia)	Six months for fraud	1903
Vallance Jupp (England)	Nine months for manslaughter while driving dangerously	1934
Bertie Clarke (West Indies)	Three years for performing abortions	1962
Terry Jenner (Australia)	Six-and-a-half years for embezzlement	1988
Chris Lewis (England)	Thirteen years for drug smuggling	2008
Salman Butt (Pakistan)	Thirty months for conspiracy to cheat and accept corrupt payments	2011
Mohammad Asif (Pakistan)	Twelve months for conspiracy to cheat and accept corrupt payments	2011

Jenner was released after serving 18 months of his sentence, while Butt and Mohammad Asif were released in 2012 midway through their terms. India's Navjot Singh Sidhu was arrested in 1988 after the death of a motorist in a road rage incident and spent several days in jail upon his arrest. He was later found guilty of culpable homicide and sentenced to a three-year prison term; India's Supreme Court stayed the conviction in 2007. Pakistan's Ijaz Ahmed spent six weeks in jail in 2009 accused of writing a bad cheque before being released on bail.

- Big-hitting Australian batsman Luke Pomersbach fainted in a court in Delhi in 2012 when facing charges of molesting a woman and assaulting her fiancé. The incident allegedly occurred while Pomersbach had been partying with members of the Royal Challengers Bangalore IPL team at a city hotel following a win over the Delhi Daredevils. According to K.C. Diwedi, an investigating officer, "**The couple had met Pomersbach at a party and they all went to a room in the hotel for drinks. It is here that Pomersbach assaulted the woman. The woman's fiancé tried to push the cricketer out of the room** [and he] **retaliated by hitting him in the face.**"

  While the case was later withdrawn, it was not Pomersbach's first brush with the law. In 2009, he fled the scene of two hit-and-run incidents in Perth. He pleaded guilty to a number of charges, including drink-driving and assaulting a police officer; he was fined, and had his driving licence suspended.

- An Indian teenager was beaten to death by a group of boys in 2012 after dropping a catch during a game of cricket in Mumbai. After being bashed with cricket bats, the 16-year-old was taken to hospital but later died.

Stumpers and Thumpers

- After scoring a century on his county debut in 2007 at the age of 47, Tim Riley packed it in. A late call-up for a Minor Counties Championship match, Riley made his debut as wicketkeeper for Herefordshire against Devon and said: **"I think I was about ninth choice".** He scored an unbeaten 120 in the first innings and, promoted up the order for the second innings, hit 49. With an average of 169.00 in the competition, he announced he would not be available for selection again, adding: **"My real love is Colwall club cricket and if I played another match for Herefordshire, I'd be barred from the Village Cup … I want to play for them at Lord's."**

- Daniel Smith, a chunky wicketkeeper from New South Wales, lit up the picturesque North Sydney Oval in 2011/12 by spanking the highest unbeaten innings in Australian domestic one-day cricket. Opening the batting against Victoria, Smith achieved his first hundred for the state in any form of cricket with an undefeated 185, becoming the first batsman to hit ten sixes in an innings. His dozen big ones beat the previous record of nine, while the Blues' 15 sixes also set a new benchmark in domestic one-day cricket.

- After an innings of 56 by New Zealand's wicketkeeping captain Brendon McCullum at Wellington in 2011/12, his opposite number responded with a fifty of his own. A.B. de Villiers hit a man-of-the-match unbeaten 106, supplying just the third instance of opposing wicketkeeping captains both scoring a half-century in the same one-day international. The previous occasions both involved India's M.S. Dhoni and Sri Lanka's Kumar Sangakkara, at Rajkot in 2009/10, and at Dambulla in 2010.

McCullum's 56 followed 119 against Zimbabwe at Napier, and with an 85, also at Napier, he put together three consecutive fifties for the first time in his 200-match career. With his innings of 85 against South Africa, McCullum became the first player to score 80 or more in his 200th one-day international.

- During the second Test of the 2011/12 Test series against the West Indies, India's wicketkeeper M.S. Dhoni and V.V.S. Laxman became the first pair of batsmen to achieve two double-century partnerships for the seventh wicket. During their top-class innings of 631/7 declared at Kolkata, Laxman (176*) and Dhoni (144) combined for a 224-run stand, having put on an unbroken 259-run partnership for the same wicket against South Africa, also in Kolkata, in 2009/10. While Laxman became the highest individual run-scorer in Tests at Kolkata, Dhoni became the first wicketkeeping captain to score a Test century on four occasions, overtaking Zimbabwe's Andy Flower.

- During a three-day match in Bloemfontein in 2006/07, Free State's Lefa Mosena secured the wicketkeeper double of a fifty and five dismissals in an innings. With six catches in all against Limpopo, Mosena scored 54 opening the batting after being dismissed handled the ball for six in the first innings. It was the second instance of such a dismissal in successive first-class matches at the Goodyear Park ground, after Cape Cobras No.10 Monde Zondeki against Eagles.

- Indian wicketkeeper Farokh Engineer scored his maiden Test century as an opener, crunching 94 runs before lunch on the opening day. Going in first in the third Test against the West Indies at Chennai in 1966/67, he hit 109 in 155 minutes with 18 boundaries. He believes it was the fastest-ever century scored in a Test match and said: "**I have a strong belief that I scored the fastest century, off just 46 balls. That was against an attack comprising Wesley Hall, Charlie Griffith and the great off-spinner Lance Gibbs.**"

- Despite raising a 500-run total in a first-class match in 2010, Canada finished up the losers following a wicketkeeper's double-century. Their record high of 566 – against Afghanistan in the Intercontinental Cup at Sharjah – included a century from the 41-year-old Sunil Dhaniram and 93 from their wicketkeeping captain Ashish Bagai. After trailing by a whopping 302 after the first innings and set 494 to win, the Afghans sailed home with a record-breaking double-century from their 18-year-old keeper Mohammad Shahzad. Improving on his previous highest score of 88 in first-class cricket, Mohammad struck an unbeaten 214, with 16 fours off 258 balls.

- Afsar Zazai played the perfect innings on his first-class debut in 2011/12, gliding his country to an improbable win against the

Netherlands in the Intercontinental Cup. With Afghanistan needing 122 to win on the final day of the match at Sharjah, but with just four wickets in hand, the 18-year-old wicketkeeper took his country home with an unbeaten 84 off 156 balls, an innings that contained 13 boundaries.

- The Cape Cobras pulled off a big win over the Knights in South Africa's domestic first-class competition in 2011/12 after a record-breaking spurt from their wicketkeeper Dane Vilas. With ten catches behind the stumps and an innings of 187 in front, he became the first keeper to produce such a double in first-class cricket.

- In the space of two Tests in 1971, England wicketkeeper Allan Knott missed out by four runs on scoring three consecutive centuries. After 101 and 96 against New Zealand at Auckland in 1970/71, Knott struck a record-breaking 116 against Pakistan at Birmingham. He hit 12 fours in reaching 52, and 21 fours in reaching 101, with his first 78 runs containing 18 boundaries.

- When Jack Russell was promoted up the batting order on his Test debut in 1988, the England wicketkeeper responded with the highest score of England's innings. Russell hit 94 out of 429 against Sri Lanka at Lord's in his maiden Test knock. He also top-scored with 55 when batting as a nightwatchman against the West Indies at Bridgetown in 1989/90.

- In the fourth one-day international against Australia at Melbourne in 1978/79, England's wicketkeeper David Bairstow was run out attempting a sixth run off a shot from the bat of his captain Mike Brearley. England was dismissed for 94 in 31.7 overs, with Bairstow making three, while Brearley top-scored with 46 opening the batting.

- Australian wicketkeeper Ian Healy hit four centuries in 231 first-class matches, all of which came in Tests. His highest first-class score was an unbeaten 161 against the West Indies at Brisbane in 1996/97.

- Brad Haddin achieved a rarity behind the stumps at Hobart in 2011/12 when he made a stumping off a medium-pacer. Haddin (pictured) got rid of New Zealand's Jesse Ryder via the bowling of Mike Hussey, who took 1-15.

- During the second Test against South Africa at Durban in 2011/12, wicketkeeper Dinesh Chandimal became the first Sri Lankan to score a pair of fifties on debut. With a near

60-run average in first-class cricket, Chandimal was the 35th player to achieve the feat of two fifties on debut, making 58 and 54.

- Michael Spurway, a hard-hitting batsman who kept wicket in three first-class matches for Somerset, once played an eye-catching knock in Singapore hitting the first four balls he received out of the ground. Nicknamed "Slogger", Spurway had joined the colonial service, also playing for Nigeria, but made a duck for the African nation against Gold Coast in Lagos in 1936.

- During a South African ODI battering of Kenya at Cape Town in 2001/02, wicketkeeper Mark Boucher brought up a half-century by scoring a run off every ball he faced. After centuries from Gary Kirsten (124) and Neil McKenzie (131*), Boucher (51*) flexed his muscles with a fifty off 19 balls, scoring off all 20 deliveries he received (2, 2, 1, 6, 1/1, 2, 1/2, 1, 6, 4/1, 2, 1/4, 1, 6, 6, 1).

- Indian wicketkeeper Nayan Mongia appeared in 140 one-day internationals, but never won a man-of-the-match award. In 96 innings, Mongia scored 1,272 runs with a best of 69, and behind the stumps achieved 110 catches and 44 stumpings.

- Two wicketkeepers rescued Essex in a County Championship match in 2011 by sharing a record double-century partnership. After slumping to 63/5 in the match at Chelmsford, Adam Wheater and James Foster – a pair of wicketkeepers both born in the same hospital in Essex – added 253, a record-county stand for the sixth wicket. On a king pair, the 21-year-old Wheater scored 164, while Foster, the appointed match keeper, hit 103.

- The first dismissal by India's Dinesh Karthik behind the stumps in all three forms of international cricket was a stumping. In his first one-day international, he broke the wicket of England's Michael Vaughan at Lord's in 2004; on his Test debut, two months later, his first dismissal was the stumping of Australia's Michael Clarke at Mumbai. In a Twenty20 international – against South Africa at Durban in 2007/08 – Karthik began the match as a batsman – as he had done in all of his previous matches – and ended it as a wicketkeeper. Karthik took the gloves following an injury to M.S. Dhoni and pulled off two stumpings – Vernon Philander, off Harbhajan Singh for two, and Johan van der Wath, also off Harbhajan for two.

- During a run of seven consecutive one-day internationals in 2011, no bowler was able to dismiss India's M.S. Dhoni. In six innings in which Dhoni batted – all of them against England – he scored 78, 50, 87, 35, 15 and 75, all unbeaten. With nine not outs in 24 one-day internationals played throughout the calendar year, Dhoni topped the world averages with 58.76 from a total of 764 runs in 22 innings.

- David Obuya pulled off a first for Kenya during the 2002 ICC Champions Trophy when he dismissed the top four of the order in a match in Colombo. Standing behind the stumps in the match against South Africa, Obuya stumped three and caught the other.

  The first wicketkeeper to dismiss the top five in the order in a one-day international was Australia's Adam Gilchrist – with five catches – against New Zealand at Christchurch in 2004/05.

- After scoring a pair of centuries in the 1978/79 Ranji Trophy final, Delhi's Surinder Khanna became the first Indian wicketkeeper to make a duck on his one-day international debut. In the first of his ten ODIs for India – against the West Indies at Edgbaston in the 1979 World Cup – Khanna faced 12 balls before falling to Michael Holding.

- Pakistan wicketkeeper Zulqarnain Haider was reportedly banned from Facebook in 2010 for spamming. In his quest to oust Kamran Akmal as Pakistan's number one stumper, he set up a page on Facebook to boost his profile, but when the number of followers passed 5,000 in double-quick time, alarm bells rang. Facebook removed his profile, but he set up another later in the year.

- During a six-match Twenty20 series in Pakistan in 2005/06, Karachi wicketkeeper Amin-ur-Rehman pouched a record number of stumpings. From 11 dismissals in the ABN-AMRO Twenty20 Cup, Amin claimed nine stumpings, including three in a match against the Multan Tigers at Karachi.

- After becoming the first wicketkeeper to achieve 12 dismissals in a first-class match in South Africa, Thami Tsolekile impressed again in his next game by not conceding a bye in an innings of 500. Playing for the Lions club against Dolphins at Johannesburg in 2010/11, Tsolekile made six dismissals in each innings, then left the field at Potchefstroom unblemished after Titans made 513.

- During the 1995/96 Sheffield Shield, two wicketkeepers ended the summer with 54 dismissals each. Western Australia's Adam Gilchrist and Queensland's Wade Seccombe shared a then-new record for most dismissals in a Sheffield Shield season, which Seccombe ultimately called his own in 2000/01, when he picked up 58 dismissals. Another Wade – Victoria's Matthew Wade – came close in 2008/09 with 57 scalps.

- Batting in the unaccustomed role of opener, Gujranwala wicketkeeper Khalid Mahmood struck a first-class 50 in less than 15 minutes in the

2000/01 Quaid-e-Azam Trophy. Batting against Sargodha, Mahmood (56) reached his 50 in 13 minutes off 15 balls. Facing a single over from Naved Latif, he smacked him for five consecutive sixes and a two. Mahmood's knock was two minutes off the world record held by Middlesex's Jim Smith (66) against Gloucestershire at Bristol in 1938.

- Standing behind the stumps in his 44th first-class match, Hyderabad's Ibrahim Khaleel established a new world record by snapping up 14 dismissals. In a 2011/12 Ranji Trophy match against Assam, Khaleel achieved seven dismissals in each innings to break the previous best of 13 in a match by Matabeleland's Wayne James in 1995/96. The previous best in Indian first-class cricket had been 11 by Samarjit Nath in his only first-class match, for Assam against Tripura at Guwahati in 2001/02.

> "I just didn't know what was happening. The edges kept coming my way and I was happy to snap them up. I was soaking up our win after the game when I began to receive updates about my feat. First they said the Indian record stood at 11 and I was happy, then I was told that I had surpassed the world mark ... couldn't believe it."
>
> Hyderabad wicketkeeper Ibrahim Khaleel

- In 2000/01, Western Australia's Ryan Campbell achieved record back-to-back hauls of six dismissals in the 50-over Mercantile Mutual Cup. His first lot – of five catches and a stumping – against New South Wales at Perth was followed by six catches against Tasmania at the same venue a week later.

- Humayun Farhat played for Pakistan in the early 2000s, and remains the only wicketkeeper in Test history not to record a dismissal. Humayun made just one Test appearance, in 2000/01 at Hamilton, where New Zealand (407/4 declared) secured an innings victory over the visitors.

- When Brendon McCullum scored 225 against India at Hyderabad in 2010/11, it represented the 100th double-century by an opening batsman in Test match cricket. The former wicketkeeper's double-hundred was the first for a NZ opener since occasional stumper Bryan Young hit an unbeaten 267 against Sri Lanka at Dunedin in 1996/97.

- Appearing in his penultimate one-day international, Bermuda's Dean Minors achieved a major feat by becoming the first wicketkeeper not to concede a single bye in a World Cup innings that exceeded 400.

His record was established in the 2007 tournament in the Caribbean, when India built a formidable 413/5 at Port-of-Spain, an innings that contained 31 extras, but no byes.

- The 2011 World Cup match between India and the West Indies at Chennai provided the first instance of rival wicketkeepers being stumped in a one-day international. Mahendra Singh Dhoni got to 22, while his opposite number, Devon Thomas, made two.

- During a 50-over match at Scarborough in 1990, wicketkeeper Steve Rhodes struck an unbeaten 66 with two sixes hitting a spectator. The same patron was hit twice within five minutes, with one of the players offering the spectator the use of a helmet.

- As many as six wicketkeepers were called upon to stand behind the stumps during a single County Championship match in 2009. In the game against Leicestershire at Southgate, Middlesex used five, after their appointed keeper Ben Scott fell ill on the third day. Batsman Eoin Morgan took his place until David Nash turned up from a second XI game but he too was sidelined after sustaining an injury in warm-ups the following morning. Neil Dexter then took over until John Simpson was summoned, also from second XI duties.

- When a Combined XI played New South Wales in 1939/40, their wicketkeeper Don Tallon scored a century and a half-century, while his opposite number equalled a world record behind the stumps. Tallon hit 55 in the first innings of the match played at the Gabba, with a whirlwind 152 in the second, scoring 100 runs before lunch on the third day.

  Ron Saggers also scored a first-innings half-century, and equalled Tallon's then-world record of seven dismissals in an innings, finishing with ten in the match.

- The Sri Lanka–Canada one-day international played at Hambantota in 2010/11 was a history-making affair with both of the wicketkeepers captaining their side. This was the first occasion it had happened in the World Cup, with Kumar Sangakkara and Ashish Bagai the keepers concerned.

- Following a century from B.J. Watling in his first Test match as a wicketkeeper, New Zealand played another South African after the Northern Districts gloveman sustained a hip injury. In a one-off Test against Zimbabwe at Napier in 2011/12, the Durban-born Watling scored an unbeaten 102, his maiden Test ton in his seventh appearance. For New Zealand's next assignment – a few weeks later in Dunedin – they chose Canterbury's Kruger van Wyk. Appearing in his 100th first-class match, van Wyk made his Test debut against the country of his birth, scoring a patient 36 off 92 deliveries.

Van Wyk's Test debut came at a time when Western Australia's big-hitting wicketkeeper Luke Ronchi had announced he was packing his bags and heading to New Zealand in the hope of playing Test cricket. Ronchi – who was born in NZ – appeared in four one-day internationals and three Twenty20s for Australia, scoring one half-century, a 64 in a ODI against the West Indies at Basseterre in 2008. He made an immediate impact upon his arrival, scoring a century on his first-class debut for Wellington. Batting at number seven against Central Districts, Ronchi hit 111 off just 91 balls, with 13 fours and four sixes.

One month out from qualifying for New Zealand, Ronchi had a record-breaking match against Northern Districts in Wellington in 2012/13. Although he ended up on the losing side, Ronchi scored a pair of centuries (113 and 108) and took eight catches in the match, with six in the first innings.

- India's Mahendra Singh Dhoni pulled off a history-making stumping at Kolkata in 2012/13 when England opener Alastair Cook was dismissed for a second-innings score of one. It was just the second stumping in the first over of a Test innings since Australia's Affie Jarvis got rid of England's Archie MacLaren – also for a score of one - in the first innings of the fourth Test at the SCG in 1894/95.

- During a 2011 World Cup match at Chennai, both of the wicketkeepers were stumped. A unique occurrence in international cricket, the West Indies' Devon Thomas stumped M.S. Dhoni, who then did the same to Thomas.

- During its tour of Australia in 2012/13, Sri Lanka used the services of four wicketkeepers in the wake of a series of injuries. Their number one choice Prasanna Jayawardene suffered a fractured thumb while batting in the second Test in Melbourne, while his replacement Kumar Sangakkara broke his hand later in the match.

  Dinesh Chandimal then took over for the third Test at the SCG, but didn't last long, out with a hamstring injury incurred during the opening one-day international in Melbourne. Kushal Perera was called up for the second ODI, in Adelaide, and made the record books with four catches. He became only the third keeper to achieve the feat on debut in ODIs, after Australia's Richie Robinson, against England at The Oval in 1977, and the West Indies' Chadwick Walton, against Pakistan at Johannesburg in the 2009 ICC Champions Trophy.

Medical Matters

- Two doctors scored big centuries in the same innings against MCC at Crystal Palace Park in 1902, while another MD made the highest score of his first-class career. Playing for London County, New South Wales batsman Les Poidevin made 161 batting at number four, while Doctor W.G. Grace made 131 at five. For the MCC, the Sherlock Holmes creator Arthur Conan Doyle, who studied medicine at the University of Edinburgh, hit 43 at number six in the first innings, but made a duck when opening the second.

  Poidevin, once 12th man in a Test match for Australia, undertook medical studies in Sydney and in Manchester and scored over 7,000 runs in first-class cricket with 14 centuries.

- A cricket match between a team of doctors and a football team in Devon in 2011 had to be called off after one of the players suffered a heart attack while batting. When Harry Parkin, a local businessman, slumped to the ground unconscious, a doctor team-mate rushed to his car to get a defibrillator which ultimately revived the ailing batsman.

- Former England Test cricketer Phil Tufnell joined a campaign in 2012 that aimed to raise awareness of gut disorders and the importance of good digestive health. As part of the UK's annual Gut Week, a survey revealed that Britons' increased time spent on the toilet while reading, eating and surfing the net contributed greatly to an array of conditions, including cramps, pins and needles and haemorrhoids.

- Frederick Buckle, who made 15 first-class appearances for Surrey, had an odd match against Middlesex in 1869, failing to bat in either innings. Representing Young Surrey, Buckle appeared in the scorebook as 'absent, not sent for in time – 0' in the first innings and 'absent, unwell – 0' in the second.

- A bomb blast near a first-class match in Colombo in 2009 resulted in three players sustaining damage to their eardrums. Play in the game, between Air Force and Seeduwa in the 2008/09 Premier League, was delayed for two weeks after the bomb went off on the second day.

- New Zealand bowler Iain O'Brien used the occasion of his 35th birthday in 2011 to announce that he had suffered from depression. Joining a growing list of cricketers with the condition, O'Brien said it hit him hard during a tour of South Africa in 2007/08, explaining: "**I'd just got back into the Test team after two-and-a-half years out of the mix, but for the first two weeks of our tour to South Africa, I didn't really leave my room. I was just too scared. I went and played cricket, went to training and did a bit of shopping. But most nights I'd eat by myself and order room service.**

  "**The rest of the time I'd either hang out in my room or sit by the pool. Wrapped up in it is how you value and see yourself. I didn't feel as though the guys I was on tour with were equals by any means. I didn't want to bother them so I looked after myself. That's still how I deal with it sometimes even now. If I'm having a few bad days, I'll try to get away from people. I can still go and play cricket and have good days on the park, but the rest of it can be quite hard work. I probably should have piped up about it earlier on, just around the team and that sort of thing. But it's not an easy thing to talk about.**"

  Earlier in 2011, England's spinning all-rounder Michael Yardy pulled out of the World Cup on the subcontinent because of depression, saying: "**Leaving a World Cup campaign was a very difficult decision to make but I felt that it was the only sensible option for me and I wanted to be honest about the reason behind that decision.**"

  > "**I was awake 24 hours a day with things going around in my head. I was beyond miserable. It felt like I had this duvet that was soaking wet wrapped around me, and I couldn't get it off.**"
  >
  > Australian-born England wicketkeeper Tim Ambrose in 2012, revealing his battle with depression

- In 2007, a group of doctors in England started using x-rays and photographs of a wicketkeeper's hand to show students what happens if broken bones are left to heal without medical assistance. Dave Morrison from the Barton Cricket Club in Yorkshire said he had broken every finger while standing behind the stumps, but had only once attended hospital. He said: **"I hate hospitals, so I won't go. They heal by themselves. That's why they're so crooked. My fingers still work, more or less. I can bend them all from the first knuckle, although I do have a physio who manipulates the joints to soften the tissue."**

- Indian batsman V.V.S. Laxman is the son of parents who are both doctors. The elegant right-hander enrolled as a medical student but gave it away when cricket took hold.

- Former England captain Chris Cowdrey suffered a minor heart attack in 2011 while attending a hospital in Ashford. The then-53-year-old had been there to have an injured knee looked at when he complained of feeling unwell. He said: **"People always said I was a lucky player – well if you're going to have a heart attack anywhere, then the middle of a hospital is probably it"**. Cowdrey's younger brother Graham also suffered a mild heart attack, in 2008, while their father Colin died following a heart attack in 2000.

- New South Wales spinner Beau Casson, who appeared in a single Test match, retired from first-class cricket at the age of 28 in 2011 because of a heart condition. Casson knew his cricketing days were numbered when he was hospitalised on the opening day of his state's opening Sheffield Shield match in 2011/12.

- After an enthusiastic appeal for lbw during a seniors match in England, an Australian cricketer ended up dislocating a shoulder. Playing for the Birstall Village team in 2009, Julian Saye was rewarded with the wicket in the match against the Bharat Sports XI.

- New Zealand captain Ross Taylor made history in a painful way in 2011/12, ending up in hospital for different injuries during a run of four Tests at home. With a calf strain suffered during the Napier Test against Zimbabwe, Taylor became just the second captain to retire hurt after scoring a century (122*). A few weeks later, he was forced out of the third Test against South Africa at Wellington with a broken arm, becoming the first captain to retire with an injury in the first innings of two Tests and not return to the field in either.

- In 2011, India's Gautam Gambhir pledged to donate his body to a private hospital in Delhi in an initiative supported by a transplant organisation. He did so at the launch of an organ donation website, saying: **"I hereby pledge to donate my kidney, heart, liver, pancreas, small bowel, eyes, lungs and tissues after my death."**

- Kenya beat Canada in a one-day international at Mombasa in 2006/07 without a single ball being bowled. Canada was unable to field a fit XI with at least five of the team laid low with a viral stomach infection. It was the first instance of forfeiture in the history of one-day international cricket.

- On the eve of a Sheffield Shield match in Hobart in 2011/12, half of the Tasmanian squad came down with food poisoning. The outbreak forced three changes to the starting XI with Alex Doolan, Matt Johnston and Jeremy Smith unavailable and a number of players spending time in hospital.

- An Indian cricket fan offered to give up a kidney in 2011 in exchange for a ticket to the World Cup. Sanjay Kumar stood outside a cricket ground in Mohali with a placard outlining his unusual request in the hope of obtaining a ticket for the India–Pakistan semi-final. His plea followed a similar one by another Indian fan who wanted to attend the 2007 World Cup.

- A Gloucestershire batsman of the 1970s was later recognised by the medical fraternity with his name used in children's health research. Simon Eaton, a senior lecturer at London's Institute of Child Health, and a fan of Jim Foat, named an aspect of cellular metabolism after the batsman, who scored five centuries in 91 first-class matches. He said: **"My research is to do with fat breakdown in children. It is called FOAT. It stands for fat oxidation-activation transport. This does not quite make biological sense … it should be FATO, strictly."**

- A South Australian batsman who had to wait five years for his maiden first-class half-century is a qualified doctor. Daniel Harris, who made his debut for the state in 1999/2000, had plenty of patience too when it came to scoring his maiden first-class century, which took eight years.

- Pakistan batsman Zahid Fazal denied himself the chance to score a maiden century in one-day international cricket in 1991 when he limped off the field at Sharjah with a severe bout of cramps. Two runs shy of the 100-mark in the match against India, Zahid's undefeated 98 remained his highest score in 19 one-day internationals.

- Former Kent bowler Alan Igglesden, who appeared in three Tests for England, was diagnosed with brain cancer in 1999. After undergoing a routine MRI scan that followed an epileptic fit while playing for Berkshire, a cricket ball-sized brain tumour was discovered. Igglesden said: **"It was horrendous. You get told you've got cancer, and cancer of the brain … you think how long have I got to live?"**
  Igglesden underwent a major brain operation ten years later, and although successful, it left him partially paralysed. With his love for the game still strong, he later sent down the first over in a Bunbury club charity match in Essex.

- After being diagnosed with cancer in 2012, Indian batsman Yuvraj Singh was back in the national team just a few months later. The 30-year-old underwent a series of successful chemotherapy treatments in the United States, which he labelled the "toughest battle of his life".

> **"Hope he [Yuvraj] recovers well in time and captains India one day. In 1999, during the World Cup it was revealed that my husband had colon cancer. He immediately left his coaching job to begin treatment, but that proved unsuccessful. Malcolm underwent surgery and the operation was thought to have been a success, but ..."**
>
> Malcolm Marshall's wife Connie Marshall

- An Australian-born cricketer lost his life to skin cancer in 2012 after forgetting just once to apply sun cream while playing. Mark Jasper – who represented Devon – suffered sunburn after a game in New Zealand in 2001. Two years later doctors removed a mole on his shoulder with tests revealing it was cancerous. Jasper said: **"It was the one time in my life when I forgot to put sun cream on. I played cricket all the time but I was always very careful. I was wearing a vest and I could feel my skin burning. I remember vividly coming off the pitch and my skin being blistered. The game ended and I had sunburn for the first time in my life. I had no idea it would end up costing me everything."**

- Two giants of cricket broadcasting passed away within four days of each other in 2012/13 due to cancer. Channel Nine's Tony Greig died at the age of 66 on 29 December in 2012 following a heart attack after earlier being diagnosed with lung cancer. The BBC's Christopher Martin-Jenkins succumbed to cancer aged 67 on New Year's Day. The then 67-year-old Robin Jackman, who appeared in four Tests for England in the early 1980s, was missing from the commentary box in South Africa at the same time, battling cancer that was also revealed in 2012.

> **"It was probably for him [Tony Greig] a merciful release because the last stage of any cancer is often hell on earth."**
>
> broadcaster and journalist Christopher Martin-Jenkins

- Former England captain Michael Vaughan took part in a walk along a section of the Great Wall of China in 2011 to raise money for a hospital in Yorkshire. Vaughan, his wife, and 22 friends walked approximately 35 kilometres in the hope of raising £250,000. He said: **"The scenery was absolutely stunning, some of it through beautiful woodland and some of it felt like we were on the top of the world. Some of the wall was incredibly steep and we were scrambling up these steps. It was hard in physical terms, but the whole idea was to raise the profile of Sheffield Hospital."**

- A rose bush named after the late wife of fast bowler Glenn McGrath went on sale across Australia in 2009 to help support breast cancer. A pale pink English-style floribunda, the Jane McGrath Rose was launched at the Melbourne International Flower and Garden Show.

A Jane McGrath breast cancer fundraising day at the SCG in 2010

- Hampshire batsman Michael Carberry was unable to make a tour of Australia in 2010 after he was diagnosed with blood clots on his lungs. The left-hander, who made his England Test debut in 2009/10, was sidelined for a number of months which forced his exclusion from the second-string England Performance Squad that travelled to Australia. Carberry said: **"It has been well documented that I had blood clots and it has taken nine months out of my life."**

- In 2004, a team of British club cricketers, all of whom had been the recipient of a liver, heart, bone marrow or lung transplant, took on their Australian counterparts in the inaugural series for the David Hookes Memorial Shield. The Australian Transplant Cricket Club defeated the tourists, and, in 2005, was named Australian Cricket Club of the Year after winning a competition on ABC Radio.

> **"Who else could boast a team full of legitimate steroid users? At least half of the team have used the high-performance drug known as EPO – legally, of course – for treatment of chronic kidney disease."**
> Australian Liberal Party MHR Margaret May on the 2006
> Australian Transplant Cricket Club team

- Despite orders not to play cricket because of an ankle injury, Afghanistan fast bowler Hamid Hassan picked up a maiden ten-wicket haul in a first-class match in 2010. Playing against Scotland at Ayr, Hamid claimed a match-winning 11-154, which included a spell of three wickets in five balls: **"The doctor told me not to bowl, but I wanted to, so he bandaged my ankle up to my knee."**

- An Indian eye specialist once revealed that nearly half of all eye injuries presented to hospitals in Mumbai were caused by cricket balls. And almost half had been injuries sustained by passers-by.

- In 2005, Pakistan coach Bob Woolmer opened an operating theatre named after him at a hospital in the Indian city of Kanpur where he was born. Two year later, Woolmer – who appeared in 19 Tests for England – died in mysterious circumstances in Jamaica during the 2007 World Cup.

Food and Drink

- A British umpire was reportedly ejected from a hotel in 2005 after asking for a plate of fruit. Steve Kuhlmann, who was in Torquay for a Minor Counties match between Devon and Berkshire, claimed he was told to pack his bags and leave after requesting fresh fruit instead of the normal cooked breakfast.

- An elderly couple was refused admission to a 40-over match at Swansea in 2010 after stewards discovered metal eating utensils during a search of their bag. Mike and Carol Russell decided not to attend the game between Glamorgan and Lancashire as a result. **"Our friend gave us some strawberries and cream and two spoons to eat them with,"** explained Mrs Russell. **"The spoons didn't belong to us, so I couldn't risk leaving them, and we decided not to go in."**

> **"I want to speak to the general or the brigadier, whoever's in charge, 'cause I'm taking my bloody sandwiches in."**
>
> England batsman-turned commentator Geoff Boycott after security staff at the Feroz Shah Kotla ground in Delhi insisted on confiscating his packed lunch in 2011

- Pakistan legends Imzamam-ul-Haq and Saeed Anwar branched out in to the international food market in 2012 by opening up meat shops in Dubai. Branded as One Meat, the business venture had already proved a success in Karachi.

- After scoring a century against New Zealand in 2011/12, his first Test ton in six years, South Africa's Jacques Rudolph paid tribute to his batting partner Jacques Kallis. Given out lbw on 12, Kallis convinced him to ask for a referral which came down in his favour. Upon his dismissal for 113, Kallis hinted to Rudolph that if he, too, got a century, "**... then I want a Double** [Johnnie Walker] **Blue Label.**" Although it was one of the most expensive whiskies in the world, Rudolph was happy to oblige: "**No problem. I'll buy him a bottle if he wants.**"

- England batsman Jonathan Trott revealed a love of alcohol had almost derailed his career. In 2011, Trott – who possessed a 50-plus average in both Tests and one-day internationals at the time – admitted that drinking could have become a major problem had he not nipped it in the bud. He said: "**I used to go nuts and it affected the image people had of me. It used to cloud my judgement, not just that night, but for days afterwards. I still have the occasional beer or glass of wine but, when it comes to nights out, you probably won't find me.**"

- To celebrate his former team-mate Doug Walters living to the ripe old age of 60, Greg Chappell, a non-smoking, non-drinking vegetarian, fulfilled part of a promise that included eating some steak and having a beer. Walters, who turned 60 in 2005 and who later gave up smoking, said Chappell had honoured the bet. He added: "**He didn't go with the smoking part, but he had the steak and he had the beers. I think he enjoyed it. I'm sure it did him the world of good.**"

- South African spinner Paul Harris was unwittingly embroiled in a scam in 2012 when a conman pretending to be the cricketer attempted to hoodwink restaurants in Cape Town. After making large group bookings at eateries around the city, the con artist would claim he had overpaid and then seek reimbursement.

> **"I don't think there's enough beer in all of Australia to satisfy us."**
> South African slow bowler Paul Harris after South Africa beat Australia in 2008/09

- After Wellington had secured the Shell Trophy with a first-innings lead at the Basin Reserve in 2000/01, Northern Districts all-rounder Joseph Yovich marked the occasion by bowling a red apple. In ND's second innings, ten Wellington players had a bowl, four for the first time in first-class cricket.

- During a sweet half-century at Cheltenham in 2005, a six off the bat of Sussex wicketkeeper Matt Prior hit a spectator holding an ice cream which ended up over his face. Prior scored 52 in the County Championship match against Gloucestershire, helping himself to 109 in the second innings.

- The internationally-renowned UK chef Heston Blumenthal once injured the tools of his trade in a staff cricket match. During the game, played in 2008, he dived for the last ball of the day and landed on his fingers. He said: "**My index finger twisted 90 degrees, so it bent to touch my thumb.**"

- A cricket-playing former captain of Scotland's rugby team won Britain's National Cheese Lovers' Trophy in 2006. The Dorset-based cheese-maker Peter Kininmonth, who played for the famous I Zingari cricket team, came second in his school's bowling averages in 1942.

- Shane Warne was almost a late scratching for the start of the Australian domestic Twenty20 competition in 2011/12 after a mishap in the kitchen. The Melbourne Stars spinner suffered burns to his bowling hand while cooking bacon. Warne said: "**No more trying to be a master chef.**"

- India's Rahul Dravid earned the nickname "Jammy" while he was at high school because his father worked for a company that made jams and preserves. The nickname also spawned a junior cricket tournament in Bangalore called the Jammy Cup.

- England fast bowler Harold Larwood, who terrorised Australia's batsmen in the 1932/33 Ashes series, later made Australia his home, gaining a job with the Pepsi-Cola soft drink company. Larwood worked on the production line and as a driver (pictured).

- Simon Sainsbury, a member of the famous British grocery family, once scored a century at Lord's batting as a nightwatchman. Playing for Eton College, Sainsbury hit exactly 100 against Harrow.

- A batch of mangoes planted in honour of India's most fruitful batsman failed to mature in time in 2012 to be presented to Sachin Tendulkar on his birthday. Recognised as one of India's top growers, Haji

Kalimullah Khan named his new variety of mango 'Sachin', and said: **"The tree was grafted a few years ago and I expected 40 to 50 mangoes to be ready this year, but it may take one more month to be delivered to Sachin Tendulkar. I don't know whether Sachin likes this fruit, but he is a son of India and this is my humble effort to name this mango after the master blaster."**

"Sometimes I cook breakfast. Earlier it was on a regular basis, but now it's only on special occasions. I cook various things like prawn masala and stuff that I learnt from my mother. At times I have tried cooking fish curry, and Anjali [his wife] **told me it's the best fish curry she has had in her life."**

Sachin Tendulkar

- Two Sri Lankan captains joined forces off the field in 2011 by opening a restaurant in Colombo. Mahela Jayawardene and Kumar Sangakkara teamed up with a well-known restaurateur at the Ministry of Crab seafood eatery.

Mahela Jayawardene, chef Dharshan Munidasa and Kumar Sangakkara at their Ministry of Crab restaurant in Colombo

- Veteran cricket commentator Richie Benaud revealed in 2012 that he and his wife skip a meal each day. Benaud was the subject of an article in the *Australian Gourmet Traveller* magazine stating: **"We limit ourselves to 14 meals a week – six of fish, three of pasta, two of meat, two of prosciutto and one melon and one of eggs."**

- Former England all-rounder Andrew Flintoff put his tummy to the test in 2012 when he undertook a series of gastronomic challenges in aid of charity. Flintoff broke a number of world records, including most peas eaten with a cocktail stick in 30 seconds (30) and the fastest time to drink a cup of hot chocolate (5.45 seconds).

- A Canadian cricket official staged a hunger strike in 2010 after the country's national body declined to host the 2012 Under-19 World Cup. Pandit Maharaj, the president of the Maple Leaf Cricket Club near Toronto, refused food for a week to try and pressure the ICC, but his protest fell on deaf ears.

- The father of British chef Ainsley Harriott mixed in show-business circles in his native Jamaica, often entertaining cricketers at their home. A second cousin of West Indies wicketkeeper Jeff Dujon, Harriott recalls Garry Sobers playing cricket in his back yard: **"My**

Former England captain Mike Gatting and TV chef Ainsley Harriott in a charity cooking event staged for the Chance to Shine organisation in 2012

dad was in show business so we knew a few of the players. That's how I got into cooking. My mum was always cooking as we were constantly entertaining around the cricket."

BRIAN TURNER'S DREAM TEAM

Geoff Boycott (E)
John Edrich (E)
Michael Vaughan * (E)
Brian Lara (WI)
Garry Sobers (WI)
Ian Botham (E)
Adam Gilchrist † (A)
Shane Warne (A)
Derek Underwood (E)
Fred Trueman (E)
Glenn McGrath (A)

British chef Brian Turner, a frequent contributor to Ainsley Harriott's TV show Ready Steady Cook

---

- As Michael Clarke approached a triple-century during the SCG's 100th Test in 2011/12, things hotted up in the ABC commentary box with two broadcasters engaged in a chilli-eating challenge. Egged on by *ABC Grandstand* listeners seated near the commentary position, Indian broadcaster Harsha Bhogle (pictured) nibbled on a Naga Jolokia – the hottest chilli in the world – while Kerry O'Keeffe chickened out: **"I love it when you talk hot … no I'm not eating it. I'm sorry, Harsha, I don't know anything about chillies, but I know that there's danger."**

• In 2012, former England wicketkeeper Phil Mustard was chosen to officially launch a mustard-themed restaurant in Durham. The city is famed for being the first-known place in the world to use mustard powder in cooking.

A SELECTION OF FOODIE DISMISSALS IN FIRST-CLASS CRICKET

H.P. Chaplin c Beet b Root	Sussex v Derbyshire	Derby	1913
A.J. Lamb c Cook b Rice	Western Province v Transvaal	Cape Town	1980/81
S.J. Cook c Mustard b Onions	Kent v Durham	Canterbury	2007

• Australian food-lover Kumar Pereira once turned up to a junior cricket match with his sons and was immediately signed up as a coach, simply because he was Sri Lankan. Pereira, who competed on the third edition of Australia's *MasterChef* TV show, had to concede his knowledge of cricket was minimal: **"The coach took one look at me and decided that I was going to assist. For the morning I was given a small group and asked to take them through batting, bowling and fielding. My cricket career ended that morning. Can't bowl, can't throw ... can cook though."**

KUMAR PEREIRA'S DREAM TEAM

Jack Hobbs (E)
Herbert Sutcliffe (E)
Don Bradman * (A)
Viv Richards (WI)
Sachin Tendulkar (I)
Garry Sobers (WI)
Imran Khan (P)
Adam Gilchrist † (A)
Shane Warne (A)
Muttiah Muralitharan (SL)
Glenn McGrath (A)

Australian chef Kumar Pereira

Number Crunching

● Two cricket teams from the same club in Surrey recorded the same number of runs off the same number of balls with identical results on consecutive days in 2011. During the month of July, Stoke D'Abernon made 113/9 in 31.2 overs to defeat Warlingham by one wicket. The following day, the club's Sunday team, playing on the same pitch, also scored 113/9 off 31.2 overs to beat Ashtead's 112.

Stoke D'Abernon's first team included the services of two first-class cricketers – Paul Prichard, who appeared in 330 first-class matches for Essex, made a duck, while their overseas player, Mumbai's Hiken Shah, opened the batting and made four.

- During the calendar year of 2000, Pakistan's Mohammad Yousuf scored exactly 2,000 runs in international appearances. In 53 games – Tests and one-day internationals – Mohammad equalled the world record of most matches in a calendar year that Rahul Dravid established in 1999.

- In the tenth match of the 2012 IPL played at Bangalore, the top three batsmen for the Kolkata Knight Riders all passed ten, with the middle order posting a unique numerical sequence. Batsmen four through eight had consecutive scores of 1, 2, 3, 4 and 5 in the match against Royal Challengers.

  In a 40-over match against Nottinghamshire at Guildford in 2012, the first three batsmen on the Surrey team sheet were dismissed for scores of 1, 2 and 3 with the side all out for 123.

- During the 2007/08 Quaid-e-Azam Trophy in Pakistan, Sialkot produced the first instance of a first-class team scoring the "devil's number" 666. In response to Hyderabad's 415 in a drawn match in Sialkot, the home team reached 666/7.

- India's Gopal Sharma earned an unusual record by posting the same number of runs, wickets and catches in both Test and one-day international cricket. Sharma appeared in five Tests and 11 one-day internationals, and scored the same number of runs – 11 – and claimed the same number of wickets – ten – and catches – two – in both formats. With a Test debut in 1984/85, Sharma became the first player from the state of Uttar Pradesh to represent India since the Maharajkumar of Vizianagram in 1936.

- Appearing in his 73rd Test, South Africa's A.B. de Villiers batted in his 123rd innings, matching the 123 innings he had played in one-day internationals at the same time. His 83 in the Test – against New Zealand at Hamilton in 2011/12 – was his 28th fifty at Test level to match the 28 he had scored up to that point in ODIs. At the same time, de Villiers also possessed the same number of centuries (13) in Tests and ODIs and the same average (49) in both formats.

- At the end of the Australia–Sri Lanka one-day international in Perth in 2011/12, Mike Hussey's batting average was exactly the same in Tests. After scoring 4,930 runs in 168 ODIs and 5,489 in 70 Tests, Hussey's average at the time in both forms was 50.82.

- During a Test match at Centurion in 2011/12, Mahela Jayawardene was run out going for what would have been his 10,000th run in Test match cricket. The Sri Lankan number four was dismissed for 15, courtesy of Jacques Kallis, and trudged off the field with 9,999 runs beside his name in a match the visitors lost by an innings and 81.

- Sporting the number 66 on his shirt, Peter Forrest made 66 in his first match for Australia. The first Australian batsman to score 66 on his one-day international debut, Forrest later became the first Australian to score three 50-plus scores in his first four ODI innings.

- During the third Test at Melbourne in 1928/29, Jack Ryder became the first batsman to end the first day of a Test match unbeaten on 111. He managed to add just one run to his 111 the following morning. Michael Clarke (166) was the second batsman to be 111 not out at stumps on day one of a Test, against Pakistan at Hobart in 2009/10. Two seasons later, the West Indies' Shivnarine Chanderpaul (118) and New Zealand's Ross Taylor (122*) added their names to the list.

- Australia ended day three of the Hamilton Test against New Zealand in 2009/10 with 333 runs on the board in their second innings. It was the third time Australia had finished the third day of a Test with the same number of runs, with the first instance of 333/3 against England at Melbourne in 1965/66.

- In the Lord's Test against England in 1996, Pakistan spinner Mushtaq Ahmed bowled an identical number of overs in each innings. His two returns of 38 overs (38-5-92-1 and 38-15-57-5) represented the greatest number of identical lots in a Test, beating South Africa's Hugh Tayfield with 37 (37-15-79-4 and 37-11-113-9), also against England, at Johannesburg in 1956/57.

- During the first Test against Australia at Melbourne in 2007/08, Sachin Tendulkar had a bowl, returning identical numbers of 1-0-2-0 in both innings. It was the second time he had done so in his career, posting twin lots of 2-0-4-0 the month before, against Pakistan in Delhi.

- Indian wicketkeeper Dinesh Karthik scored exactly 1,000 runs in Test cricket off 2,000 balls faced at a strike rate of 50.00. He appeared in 23 Tests, his first in 2004/05.

- When Usman Khawaja scored 100 for the Blues against Tasmania in 2011/12, he brought up the 1,000th century for New South Wales. Khawaja's neat 100 at Hobart was the 43rd ton for the state in domestic limited-overs cricket, which sat together with 957 first-class centuries scored by New South Wales batsmen at the time.

- A numerical first took place in the first Test against England at Galle in 2011/12 with Sri Lanka's numbers ten and 11 both dismissed for 13 in the second innings. With England's number 11 Monty Panesar (13 and 0) also out for 13, he matched Sri Lanka's last man Suranga Lakmal (0* and 13) with an identical number of runs in each innings.

Rangana Herath delighted with a dozen with both bat and ball in the same match, taking 6-74 and 6-97 and scoring five and seven.

- On the eve of India's 2011/12 tour of Australia, front-line bowler Zaheer Khan possessed exactly the same number of wickets in both Tests and one-day internationals. In 79 Tests since his first in 2000/01, Zaheer had 273 wickets at an average of 31.78 – in 191 ODIs at the time he had 273 wickets at 28.84.

- In a one-day international against Kenya at Nairobi in 2009/10, the Netherlands lost its six last wickets with the score on a multiple of ten. The fifth wicket fell on 130, the sixth and seventh on 150, the eighth on 190 and their ninth and tenth on 200.

- During Chris Gayle's mammoth 333 at Galle in 2010/11, a record number of his runs had come off one bowler. The West Indies opener scored 143 of his runs off Sri Lankan spinner Suraj Randiv, who took 3-183 in the innings.

  During his unbeaten 365 at Kingston in 1957/58, Garry Sobers hit an equal number of runs – 118 – off two Pakistanis, Fazal Mahmood and Khan Mohammad.

- When Sri Lanka hosted Zimbabwe in 2001/02, the tourists were dismissed for the same total in all three Tests. In the opening match at Colombo, the Zimbabweans were bundled out for 236 after following-on. They then made 236 in the first innings of the second Test at Kandy, and made it a hat-trick when dismissed for 236 in the first innings of the third Test at Galle.

- After scoring 150 in the second innings at Brisbane in 2011/12, New Zealand made the same score in their next innings at Hobart. The first time a country had made identical totals of 150 in consecutive Test knocks, New Zealand went on to beat Australia by the slender margin of seven runs.

  The previous instance of the same total in two innings was also by New Zealand, in 2008/09 when they made twin lots of 279 against India at Hamilton. On Australian soil, New Zealand had completed a similar feat in 1993/94 at Hobart. In the second Test at Bellerive, the Kiwis scored 161 in the first innings and following-on, made 161 in the second.

- During their chase of 282 for victory over Pakistan at Lahore in 2003/04, New Zealand lost a record number of wickets on the same score to lose the match by 124 runs. In the second one-day international, the Kiwis surrendered five wickets on 155, before being bundled out for 157. Mohammad Sami was in irresistible form on the day, taking five wickets for two runs in 11 balls, blasting away three batsmen for a duck in a single over.

A first in one-day internationals, at the time New Zealand was the only country to lose five wickets on the same score in a Test innings – from 37/3 to 37/7 against Australia at Wellington in 1945/46 and 59/5 to 59/9 against Pakistan at Rawalpindi in 1964/65.

The Kiwis did it again in a Test in 2011/12 against South Africa at Hamilton, giving up wickets three through seven on 133. For the tourists, the last three wickets in their first innings of 253 each realised the same number of runs – 34. The trio of identical partnerships for consecutive wickets represented a new record in Test match cricket, beating three lots of 12 runs – for the third, fourth and fifth wickets – by the West Indies in the second innings against Pakistan at Providence in 2011. The Windies also put on 12 for the seventh wicket.

- Chasing 120 to beat the West Indies in the third Test at Bridgetown in 1996/97, India folded for just 81, an innings that contained an assortment of single-figure scores. They included 0, 1, 2, 3, 4, 5, 6 not out, 8 and 9.

- The Barbados-raised Mark Alleyne, who appeared in ten one-day internationals for England, took the same number of wickets in first-class and List A cricket. He claimed 415 wickets in 328 first-class games and 415 wickets in 436 limited-overs matches.

- During the opening Test of the Sir Vivian Richards Trophy in 2003/04, the first three batsmen to lose their wickets in the third innings all fell for the same score of 44. Graeme Smith, and the two Jacques, Kallis and Rudolph, all fell six runs short of a half-century in South Africa's second innings at Johannesburg. Another famous example of multiple batsmen falling for the same score in the same Test innings also occurred in South Africa, in 1949/50. During Australia's first-innings total of 75 in the third Test in Durban, five batsmen – Ian Johnson, Keith Miller, Lindsay Hassett, Ron Saggers and Neil Harvey – were all dismissed for two, while the number 11 Bill Johnston remained unbeaten on two.

- In a semi-final of the 2012/13 Asian Cricket Council Trophy against the UAE at Dubai, Afghanistan was dismissed for 70, with five batsmen dismissed for four. On the same day, four Queensland batsmen were dismissed for 11 in their first-innings total of 149 in the Sheffield Shield match against Victoria at Brisbane. In the same match, three bowlers reached the milestone of 100 Sheffield Shield wickets. Ben Cutting did so for Queensland in his 26th Shield match, while Peter Siddle (21) and Clint McKay (28) did so for Victoria.

- At the end of his 333rd one-day international, Pakistan's Shahid Afridi had taken 333 wickets at an average of 33. In his 334th match – his first against Afghanistan, at Sharjah in 2011/12, Afridi took 5-36, his seventh five-for on debut against a particular country – after Australia, Bangladesh, Canada, England, Kenya and Sri Lanka – joining the great Muttiah Muralitharan, who took all of his against Test-playing opponents (Bangladesh, England, India, New Zealand, Pakistan, South Africa and Zimbabwe).

- During the second one-day international against New Zealand at Moratuwa in 1983/84, there were five pairs of distinct scores in Sri Lanka's innings. Two batsmen made 13 with one not out, while two made 12, together with doubles of 11, nine and five.

- In a one-day international at Mombasa in 2011/12, four batsmen from both sides made an identical score. Ireland's Andrew White and Kenya's Shem Ngoche made 28, William Porterfield and Alex Obanda 14, the Australian-born pair Trent Johnston and Duncan Allen three and Alex Cusack and Tanmay Mishra two.

- The Australian-born Somer-set cricketer Sammy Woods appeared in the same number of Tests and took the same number of wickets for two different countries. He appeared in three Tests for Australia in England in 1888, taking five wickets, and then took five wickets in three Tests for England in South Africa in 1895/96.

- During the third Test against Sri Lanka in Colombo in 2009, five batsmen in Pakistan's second innings each progressively scored more runs than the one before. The scores of openers Khurram Manzoor (2) and Fawad Alam (16) were followed in the order by 19 from Younis Khan, 23 from Mohammad Yousuf, 65 from Misbah-ul-Haq and 134 from Shoaib Malik. A similar pattern emerged with Australia's top six – Alec Bannerman (2), Tom Garrett (5), George Giffen (12) Sammy Jones (17), Tom Horan (20) and William Bruce (35) – in their second innings against England at Melbourne in 1884/85.

- The South Africa–Australia Cape Town Test match of 2011/12 has been described as one of the most drama-packed and statistically-significant encounters of all time. The second day of the match saw both sides bundled out for less than 100 with a total of 23 wickets taken. The third day was also memorable. At 11 minutes to 11 on the 11th day of the 11th month of the 11th year, South Africa were 111/1, and at 11 minutes past 11, they needed 111 runs for victory.

- When the West Indies' long-serving Shivnarine Chanderpaul scored his 10,000th run in Test match cricket, his career batting average clicked over to exactly 50.00. Aged 37 at the time, Chanderpaul was the tenth batsman to reach the 10,000-run milestone, achieving the feat during the third Test against Australia at Roseau in 2011/12.

- The last year that contained more Tests than one-day internationals was 1980. Tests accounted for 54 per cent of all international matches in 1980, a number that had shrunk to 30 per cent in 1990, to 26 per cent by 2000 and to as low as 17 per cent in 2010..

- Two Tests that began on Boxing Day in 2011 went down a similar path with the corresponding innings in each match separated by a handful of runs. In the first Test between Australia and India at Melbourne, the scores were 333, 282, 240 and 169. The second Test between South Africa and Sri Lanka at Durban – which ended on the same day, the fourth – produced totals of 338, 279, 241 and 168. The difference between each innings was five runs, three, one and one.

- Three matches on from conceding 91 runs in a one-day international at Sydney in 2010/11, England's James Anderson was hammered for the same number in a World Cup match. In the same month – February – Anderson went for 91 off ten overs against Australia at the SCG, and for 91 off 9.5 in a tied match against India at Bangalore.

- Opening the batting for Glamorgan in 2011, Alviro Petersen struck a maiden first-class double-century which contained every scoring shot from one to seven. His 210 against Surrey at The Oval was assisted by some sloppy fielding with overthrows contributing a five and a seven to the South African batsman's innings.

- After being dismissed for 100 by Sri Lanka in the first innings at Galle in 2012, Pakistan went for 300 in the second. It was the first time in history that a team had been bowled out twice in the same Test for a round-figure total.

- England won the first Test against Pakistan at Nottingham in 2010 by 354 runs after scoring the same number of runs in their first innings. In 1950, the West Indies beat England at Lord's by 326 runs on the back of a first-innings 326.

- Chasing a victory target of 231 to win the first Test against Australia at Brisbane in 1992/93, the West Indies' openers were dismissed for the same score off the same number of balls. Desmond Haynes and Phil Simmons were both caught behind by Ian Healy for a score of one off five balls. They slumped to be 9/4, with the next two batsmen dismissed – Brian Lara and Keith Arthurton – both making a duck.

- During his 20th innings in his 20th Twenty20 international, Zimbabwe's Hamilton Masakadza scored his 20th six in the shortened format. Later in the same year – 2012 – Masakadza finished a game against a South African XI in Harare with exactly 2,000 career runs in all Twenty20 matches.

- England's Alec Stewart scored the same number of runs in Tests as his birthdate. Born on 08/04/1963, Stewart scored 8,463 runs.

- Australia's Arthur Morris had an identical number of centuries and half-centuries in both first-class and Test match cricket. In a first-class career of 162 matches in the 1940s and 1950s, Morris had 46 centuries and 46 fifties. In 46 Tests he scored 12 hundreds and 12 fifties.

- In 1939/40, Victoria's Lindsay Hassett marked what would be the final Sheffield Shield match until 1946/47 with a pair of identical centuries. Batting at number four against New South Wales at Sydney, Hassett scored 122 in the first innings and 122 in the second.

  Three scores of 125 were made in a first-class match in South Africa in 2007/08, with two off the bat of Neil Bredenkamp. Numbers four and five (Jimmy Kgamadi – 125*) both made 125 in the first innings for North West against Namibia at Windhoek, with Bredenkamp repeating the feat in the second.

INSTANCES OF IDENTICAL CENTURIES IN SAME FIRST-CLASS MATCH

122 and 122	Lindsay Hassett	Victoria v New South Wales	Sydney	1939/40
146 and 146*	John Langridge	Sussex v Derbyshire	Worthing	1949
121* and 121	Mark Waugh	Essex v Derbyshire	Derbyshire	1995
125 and 125	Neil Bredenkamp	North West v Namibia	Windhoek	2007/08
127* and 127	Craig Cumming	Otago v Canterbury	Queenstown	2010/11

In 1971/72, New Zealand batsman Glenn Turner scored 259 in consecutive first-class innings on the same ground – against Guyana and against West Indies, both at Bourda.

- During Australia's clash with South Africa at Johannesburg in 2011/12, Phillip Hughes and Shane Watson became the first pair of batsmen to make identical fifties during the scoring of a 150-run Test match opening partnership. Both batsmen hit 88 in a 174-run stand, becoming just the fourth pair of openers to score identical half-centuries in a Test innings. Hughes, at 22 years and 353 days, also became the fourth-youngest Australian – after Don Bradman, Neil Harvey and Doug Walters – to reach the milestone of 1,000 Test runs.

OPENERS SCORING IDENTICAL HALF-CENTURIES IN A TEST INNINGS

Jim Christy and Bruce Mitchell	53 South Africa v New Zealand at Wellington	1931/32
Vijay Merchant and Mushtaq Ali	52 India v England at The Oval	1936
Bill Lawry and Keith Stackpole	62 Australia v West Indies at Adelaide	1968/69
Shane Watson and Phillip Hughes	88 Australia v South Africa at Johannesburg	2011/12

- The first batsman to exit the game with exactly 100 Test caps had a highest score of 200. England's Graham Thorpe appeared in 100 Tests between 1993 and 2005 and made his highest score of 200 not out against New Zealand at Christchurch in 2001/02.

  The second batsman to go after 100 Tests was fellow Englishman Andrew Strauss, who announced his retirement in 2012 after leading his country in exactly 50 Tests. The Lord's Test against South Africa was also Stuart Broad's 50th Test match and his 100th in first-class cricket.

- In their defeat of Essex at Southend in 2010, Warwickshire made identical totals of 155. Just nine runs separated all four innings in the match – Essex 150 and 159; Warwickshire 155 and 155/3.

- When Virender Sehwag made a double-century in a one-day international in 2011/12, he had a highest score of 219 in ODIs, 319 in Tests and 119 in Twenty20s. His 119 for the Delhi Daredevils was his maiden century in the format, scored against the Deccan Chargers in the 2011 IPL.

- In India's second-innings 216 at Bangalore in 2010/11, each of the Australian bowlers' economy rate was a whole number. The only previous instance – in which at least four bowlers were used – had been at Calcutta in 1952/53 when India needed just six overs to beat Pakistan.

Bowler	Overs	Mdns	Runs	Wkts	Econ
Ben Hilfenhaus	19	3	57	4	3.00
Doug Bollinger	8	0	32	3	4.00
Mitchell Johnson	16.4	2	50	0	3.00
Nathan Hauritz	9	1	45	1	5.00
Marcus North	4	0	8	0	2.00
Shane Watson	2	0	6	0	3.00

- South Africa's Mark Boucher retired from international cricket in 2012, one wicketkeeping dismissal shy of the magic number of 1,000. Of his 999 dismissals behind the stumps, 555 came in Tests and 444 in one-day and Twenty20 internationals.

- Following an innings of 33 in a one-day international against India at Sharjah in 1986/87, Sri Lanka's Aravinda de Silva then put together successive innings of 3, 3, 3 and 3. His run of threes came in ODIs against Pakistan, the West Indies and India.

- The number 96 turned out to be a recurring theme in the Test career of England opener John Edrich. On three occasions in his 77 Tests, Edrich was dismissed in the 90s, and each time for the same score of 96 – against the West Indies at Kingston in 1967/68, against India at Lord's in 1974 and against Australia at The Oval the following year.

- Appearing in his 191st innings at number three for India, Rahul Dravid was dismissed for 191 by New Zealand at Nagpur in 2010/11. He became the second Indian batsman – after Mohammad Azharuddin – to be dismissed in the 190s twice in Test cricket.

- One run away from what would have been his maiden first-class century, Australia's number nine Mitchell Starc was dismissed for 99 in his ninth Test with the score on 399/9 against India at Mohali in 2012/13. The first number nine to score a Test match 99,

Cricket on Twitter
Tweets from a list by ESPNcricinfo

Aakash Chopra @cricketaakash 6m
If cricket wasn't a game obsessed with numbers, Starc would be celebrating the 99 runs he scored & not the one that he didn't. Well played!!
Expand

his New South Wales team-mate Steven Smith (92) also perished in the nineties earlier in the innings seeking his maiden Test ton. With 86 to another New South Wales player, Ed Cowan, it was the just the ninth time that three batsmen had scored between 85 and 99 in the same Test innings.

When India batted, Shikhar Dhawan hit 187, reaching his first hundred in 85 balls, the fastest-ever century by a batsman on his Test debut. The first Indian opener to score a century in his first Test, and the first Indian to pass 150 on debut, Dhawan took part in an opening stand of 289 with Murali Vijay (153), the second-highest first-wicket partnership by any country against Australia. Coming into the Test, Vijay had uniquely taken part in a triple-century partnership during the scoring of his first two Test centuries. In the previous Test at Hyderabad, he hit 167 and put on 370 for the second wicket with Cheteshwar Pujara (204). While scoring his maiden Test ton of 139 – also against Australia, at Bangalore in 2010/11 – he had shared in a 308-run third-wicket stand with Sachin Tendulkar.

- After an odd sequence of three consecutive ducks followed by three consecutive centuries in his first six Tests, England's Ravi Bopara failed to reach 50 in his next set of six. After 0, 0, 0, 104, 143 and 108, Bopara's next lot of scores were 35, 1, 18, 27, 23, 1, 0, 7 and 44 not out.

Cars, Boats, Planes and Trains

- The Lancashire County Cricket Club made aviation history in 1935 by becoming the first cricket team to travel by air. The historic flight took place when the Lancastrians travelled from Cardiff to Southampton for a match against Hampshire.

- After surviving stumps in a first-class match at The Oval in 1921, Leicestershire's Thomas Sidwell was unable to add to his score after becoming lost on London's underground train system. Sidwell (1*) was not allowed to resume his innings when he eventually turned up, and is listed in the scorebook as 'retired out'.

- On their return home from a Twenty20 tournament in Darwin in 2010, the Victorian cricket team was told to prepare for a bumpy landing. On its descent into Adelaide, their Qantas jet encountered a problem with its wheels, but ended up landing safely with all players unharmed.

> "As we came down towards the runway we went back up again very suddenly. Some of the guys are worse flyers than others and were probably a bit more distressed. But we were all sitting together and all got into the brace position."
>
> Victorian cricket team media manager Jessica Cook

> "Very nerve racking! Just got down safely! Very shaken! Fire engines on runway!"
>
> a tweet from Victorian all-rounder Andrew McDonald

- During a flight from London to Las Vegas in 2010, Shane Warne used Twitter to express his frustrations with British Airways. Warne vented his spleen on a number of issues, from the bad breath of a nearby passenger to the rudeness of staff: **"I hate British Airways, way too arrogant and rude towards people!! Will not be flying with them again after my return from Vegas."**

- Derrick Bailey, who appeared in 60 first-class matches for Gloucestershire, was an airman awarded the Distinguished Flying Cross for services during the Second World War. In 1968, the cricketing pilot set up his own airline after British United Airways pulled out of a route servicing the islands of Alderney and Guernsey.

- The Pakistan-born Australian batsman Usman Khawaja is a qualified pilot. He lists flying as his second passion, just behind cricket: **"There's nothing like a great landing – it's a great feeling. But I don't think there's anything in the world like scoring a hundred or winning a big title for your team. Cricket has always taken that mantle."**

"I started taking flying lessons when I was playing club cricket in Perth. I've loved flying since I first flew on a family holiday when I was four. I just love the whole idea of air travel, although I am a nightmare to travel with. As soon as we get to the airport I sit near the window and look at the planes."

Northamptonshire fast bowler Luke Evans

- Before entering first-class cricket, Mahendra Singh Dhoni worked as a ticket collector at the Kharagpur train station in West Bengal. It was here that he got his big break in cricket, making his first-class debut for Bihar in 1999/2000.

- Indian spinner and car lover Harbhajan Singh attracted a police fine in 2009 after taking his new Hummer for a spin without its number plates. Harbhajan was the second member of the Indian cricket team, after Mahendra Singh Dhoni, to purchase one of the monster SUVs.

- Fed up with cricket balls landing in his garden, a British man drove his car on to the wicket during a village cricket match in 2010 and walked away. The incident took place at St Helens on the Isle of Wight with the man saying he took the unusual step over concerns for the safety of his children.

- A former first-class cricketer received a knighthood in 2005 for his services to the aviation industry. A former head of Australia's Ansett airlines and British Airways, Rod Eddington appeared in eight first-class matches for Oxford University and made his debut against Sussex in 1975. He played in the same team as Test cricketers Imran Khan, Chris Tavaré and Vic Marks, and claimed Tony Greig as his maiden first-class wicket.

ROD EDDINGTON'S DREAM TEAM

Jack Hobbs (E)
Sunil Gavaskar (I)
Don Bradman * (A)
Viv Richards (WI)
Sachin Tendulkar (I)
Garry Sobers (WI)
Adam Gilchrist † (A)
Ian Botham (E)
Shane Warne (A)
Malcolm Marshall (WI)
Dennis Lillee (A)

Former head of British Airways and first-class cricketer Rod Eddington

- Austria's leading airline once named one of its jets in honour of Don Bradman. The Boeing 777 (pictured), which flew the skies for Lauda Air from 2002, was rebadged by Austrian Airlines in 2007.

- Former New Zealand all-rounder Chris Cairns set up a charitable foundation in 2006 after his sister Louise lost her life following an accident at a level crossing. In 1993, a cement truck failed to stop at the crossing in Rolleston and collided with a train. Cairns's sister and two other women died in the accident.

- New Zealand cricket officials were forced to deny a claim that fast bowler Tim Southee had joined the 'mile-high club' en route to the 2011 World Cup. A fellow passenger in the first-class compartment on the flight from Sydney had complained of 'lewd behaviour', a claim rejected by Justin Vaughan, the chief executive of New Zealand Cricket, who said: **"I think Tim met a female passenger and struck up a conversation. They spent a bit of time and had a drink together on the plane. At some stage the female passenger came to Tim's** seat and perhaps spent a maximum of 30 seconds with Tim, and there may well have been, dare I say it, a kiss on the cheek, but that was it. She went back to her seat, and Tim is adamant that nothing inappropriate, nothing untoward, occurred."

- To mark the running of the 2007 World Cup, an Indian transport enthusiast built a car in the shape of a cricket bat. The contraption was 7.6 metres in length and took K. Sudhakar six months to build. He produced a similarly unusual car for the 2003 World Cup, one shaped like a cricket ball.

A car in India dolled up cricket-style for the 2011 World Cup

- A schoolboy cricket match in Sydney was brought to an unexpected halt in 1932 when a plane made a forced landing next to the pitch. After a mechanical problem was rectified the plane then resumed its journey to nearby Mascot airport.

- West Indies batsman Chris Gayle caused a flutter in 2009 after claiming he had been forced to catch a commercial flight to Australia because his pilot was too drunk to fly his private jet. Upon his arrival at Brisbane he admitted that his postings on Twitter were in jest: "**I was mucking around.**"

- A club cricketer put the game before all else in 2008 when he left a family holiday in Europe to catch a plane back to England to play for his local XI. But after flying back home, Rob Marchant wasn't even required to bat – his team had already won.

- So confident was Malcolm Marshall that the West Indies would beat India to claim the 1983 World Cup, he put down a deposit on a luxury car. The fast bowler placed an order for a BMW on the belief he could pay for the vehicle from his winners' cheque. He said: "**I was sure we were going to win that World Cup. I ordered the new BMW car on the misguided belief that I could pay for it out of my winnings. What utter folly! I cannot now comprehend my arrogance and stupidity. To say I was in a relaxed mood** [after India made 183] **would be an understatement.**

"**I could visualise myself sitting behind the wheel of that flashy sports car and I hardly paid much attention to the cricket when we went out to get those 184 runs. Others were**

in a similar state of mind … there was no way we could fail."
The West Indies were bowled out for 140 in 52 overs.

- In the wake of an injury that kept him out of the England Test side, fast bowler Andrew Caddick took to the skies and became a fully certified helicopter pilot. In 2008, Caddick played in a benefit match for former England batsman Marcus Trescothick, arriving in grand style by chopper at the ground in Somerset (pictured).

> **"It's a nightmare. Andrew Caddick's helicopter is not big enough to ferry us around and Sanath Jayasuriya is exhausted already."**
>
> Somerset chief executive Peter Anderson bemoaning long trips his club was forced to undertake in 2005

- Play in a match in regional Victoria was suspended in 2010/11 when an air ambulance landed on the field. The helicopter caused a two-and-a-half-hour delay to the match as preparations were made to transfer a patient from Camperdown hospital to Geelong.

- A number of Australian cricketing legends turned up for a function in 2010 to celebrate the last time an Australian team had travelled to England by ship. The last boat to carry an Australian cricket team was the P&O *Himalaya* in 1961, and most of them – Richie Benaud, Neil Harvey, Bob Simpson, Brian Booth, Colin McDonald, Alan Davidson, Barry Jarman, Lindsay Kline, Frank Misson and Graham McKenzie – attended the event on board the P&O *Oriana* in Sydney.

- Shane Warne took delivery of a brand new Lamborghini in 2010, provided on loan as part of his contract as Australia's first brand ambassador for the Italian car maker. During the 2010/11 Ashes series, Warne had arranged for Kevin Pietersen to test drive one of the cars on the open road in Victoria. The England batsman was nabbed by the boys in blue when he was caught driving over the speed limit on the Great Ocean Road and fined $239. His misdemeanour coincided with another motoring mishap for the tourists on the same day when England's bowling coach, David Saker, damaged the team's bus while vacating the MCG car park.

- Three months before he launched a road safety campaign in Victoria in 2012, Shane Warne had been charged with speeding in Scotland. The previous year, Warne was involved in a road rage incident with a cyclist in Melbourne that sparked a police report.

- A promotional film on road safety featuring Don Bradman was canned in 1948 after a number of traffic rules were broken during its filming. The Australian Road Safety Council rejected the film *Children on the Roads* on the grounds that it contained glaring examples of disregard for safety.

A car acts as a makeshift scoreboard showing off the latest Don Bradman Test score – 232 versus England at The Oval in 1930

- A County Championship match was enlivened in 2010 when part of a plane came crashing to the ground hitting a cricket fan in the chest. A piece of concrete, thought to have fallen from the undercarriage of a plane, crashed into the ground during the Sussex versus Middlesex match at Uxbridge, bouncing into the body of a spectator on the opening day of the match.

Extras

- A County Championship match at Blackpool in 2006 was twice interrupted by water bombs catapulted on to the field from outside the ground. Batting against Warwickshire, Lancashire opener Iain Sutcliffe (159) had his innings upset by the first of the water bombs on the opening day, while a second was launched onto the pitch two days later. The club groundsman used a bar towel to dry the pitch, with the miscreants believed to be local teenagers.

- A six off the bat of Paul Collingwood in a one-day international in 2010 knocked over the wheelchair of a disabled patron at Chester-le-Street. All smiles after his mishap, he was helped back into his chair and resumed watching the match, between England and Pakistan.

- Sam Loxton, who lived to the age of 90, suffered a double tragedy in 2000 when his wife Jo drowned in the pool at their Gold Coast home on the same day that his son Michael was taken by a shark in Fiji. Loxton was one of Don Bradman's "Invincibles" and appeared in 12 Tests between 1948 and 1951.

- Thirumalai Sekhar was a medium-pacer from Chennai who appeared in two Tests for India without scoring a run or taking a wicket or a catch. Sekhar played twice against Pakistan in 1982/83, returning figures of 0-80 on his debut at Lahore and 0-43 at Karachi.

- England's 12th man came a cropper at Lord's in 2011 during a match that celebrated the game's 2,000th Test. Middlesex's Tom Hampton was left a little worse for wear after tripping over a tin of white paint near the pitch during some fielding practice. Covered in paint from head to toe, he managed to get cleaned up just in time for the start of play in the match, the first Test between England and India.

- As Afghanistan prepared for their first one-day international against a Test-playing nation in 2011/12, the team received a message of support from the Taliban. The match – won by Pakistan at Sharjah – was the first ODI between an affiliate member of the ICC and a full member.

- An unusual commemorative cricket match was staged in 2012 to pay tribute to a navy officer who had led Britain's first expedition to the South Pole 100 years before. The mission, which took place between 1910 and 1912, resulted in the death of Robert Falcon Scott and all of his crew. Played in temperatures of -35 degrees Celsius, a team of Britons beat a Rest of the World side at the South Pole in a game organised by Neil Laughton, a Special Air Service officer: "**I thought it was quintessentially British, I wanted to do something that does not happen down here very often, if at all. Obviously it was very cold and difficult with all the bulky clothing to bat and bowl, but we managed it fine.**"

- In 2012, Pakistan's Abdur Rehman appeared in a one-day international and in a first-class match on different continents on the same day. After taking two wickets against Australia at Sharjah in a one-day international that finished in the early hours of the morning, Rehman boarded a plane and turned out for Somerset. Barely 12 hours after completing the ODI, Rehman took 3-30 on the opening day of the County Championship match against Sussex at Hove.

  In 1988, England's Graham Gooch made history by appearing on the field in two first-class matches on the same day. After completing a Test victory over Sri Lanka at Lord's on 30 August, he then played for Essex against Surrey in a County Championship match six miles away at The Oval.

- When the USA lined up for the 2011 Women's World Cup qualifying 50-over tournament, two of their players were aged in their 50s. Captained by 42-year-old Test player Doris Francis, the squad included Grace Chadderton-Richards, 54, and Joan Alexander-Serrano, 50.

- Soon after taking out the ICC Spirit of Cricket award in 2011, India's Mahendra Singh Dhoni was made an honorary lieutenant-colonel in a voluntary division of the country's armed forces. The previous month, Dhoni (pictured) had been awarded an honorary doctor of letters from De Montfort University in Leicester.

- A Mumbai lawyer launched a court case against the CIA in 2010, claiming the American intelligence agency was behind a plot to embarrass the Indian cricket team. Prabhakar Pradhan alleged in the High Court that the Central Intelligence Agency was responsible for

India's Mahendra Singh Dhoni

Former South African Test batsman Neil McKenzie with his Maasai Warrior team-mates at Cape Town in 2012

"tiring out" the country's players and causing shame to the national team. He also claimed that students were unable to concentrate on schoolwork because of a busy international cricket calendar. Mr Pradhan said: **"It is a CIA mischief. It wants to humiliate our players in international matches. It is for the citizens to play or see matches. When I was a student, I never watched matches when there were exams."** The case was struck down by the presiding judge Anil Dave, who said: **"It is not necessary. We are rejecting it."**

- One of the most colourful and unusual cricket teams emerged in the 2000s with tribesmen from the Maasai clan in Kenya swapping their spears for cricket bats. The Maasai Cricket Warriors were formed to foster sport amongst the clan's youth and to target social problems in its community. They played their first official match against the Dol Dol Boys Secondary School in 2009, gaining a 125-run victory in a 40-over game.

  In 2012, the Maasai Warriors were invited to take part in the Last Man Stands World Championships in South Africa, a Twenty20 competition made up of amateur teams from around the world. Famed for playing their cricket in traditional tribal attire of sandals, beads and a 'shuka' wrap, the team's trainer, former Kenya captain Steve Tikolo, insisted they turn up for matches in whites. He said: **"Cricket has its own rules that have to be followed. I appreciate they want to sell the image of Kenya, but they must play in the normal cricket uniform and not their traditional attire."**

  They ended up playing in their garb, and took part in four matches in the competition staged in Cape Town. After three consecutive losses, they peaked in their fourth encounter after acquiring the services of Neil McKenzie. The former South African batsman – who also played in their traditional clothing – hit 34 off 17 balls, while Papai Simon Ole Mamai struck a maiden Twenty20 fifty for the Maasai Warriors in a memorable tie.

- Former Australian fast bowler Max Walker is an avid collector of fountain pens. Regarded as one of the country's top-selling authors, Walker still writes books with a pen: **"It's hard to define what it is about writing that I love. To me, it's just the feel of an extension of your fingers through the pen on the paper. It's the smell of the ink. I've always loved to see a graphic representation of a thought."**

- Sri Lankan fast bowler Chaminda Vaas was fined a day's allowance by team management after a masseur was discovered in his hotel room during the 2001/02 Sharjah Cup. On the eve of the final, in which Sri

Lanka was flogged by Pakistan, Vaas was caught with a male masseur in his room after a 10pm curfew imposed by team officials.

- On the eve of the 1999 World Cup final against Australia, Pakistani spinner Saqlain Mushtaq hid his wife in a hotel cupboard. With wives and other family members banned towards the end of the tournament, Saqlain had to take swift action when a team official knocked on his door.

- A group of daring, but inebriated, Sydneysiders made news around the world in 2012 after playing a game of nude cricket in the hallway of a hostel in Darwin. Sent to bed after being caught on the facility's cameras, the group lost their bond after checking out.

> **"They were really good about it, they knew they were being punished for what they had been doing. It is not that extreme. It is quite a traditional Australian male thing, playing cricket naked."**
>
> hostel employee Joe Manning

- Batting against South Africa at Johannesburg in 2011/12, Usman Khawaja brought up his maiden half-century in Test match cricket. The Pakistan-born Australian was dismissed by the South African spinner Imran Tahir, who was also born in Pakistan. A similar type of dismissal took place in 1993 when Brendon Julian – born in New Zealand and playing for Australia – took the wicket of Andrew Caddick – born in New Zealand and representing England – in the third Ashes Test in Nottingham. Another truly 'international' dismissal came about in a Test at Adelaide in 1910/11 as Sammy Carter – born in England but playing for Australia – fell to the bowling of Reggie Schwarz, who was also born in England, and playing for South Africa.

- Bangladesh's Enamul Haque jnr appeared in ten one-day internationals over a five-year period, all against the same opposition. After three games against Zimbabwe in Bangladesh in 2004/05, he played the remaining seven against the Zimbabweans in the calendar year of 2009.

- Of the final 22 one-day internationals played by Aaqib Javed, 20 came against the same country. After a run of 12 ODIs against India that began in 1997, the Pakistani quick then played against Bangladesh. His next eight games were all against India, with his final ODI against Zimbabwe in 1998/99.

- Dutch batsman Jelte Schoonheim had one of the shortest, and unluckiest, international careers on record with his only match abandoned without a ball bowled. On his debut for the Netherlands – a Twenty20 international against Ireland in Belfast in 2008 – the captains made the toss but the rains came and the match was called off. He was never selected for his country again.

- In the same week that an offer to play in the 2011 World Cup was withdrawn, a West Australian batsman was found guilty of assaulting a player during a club match in Perth. Michael Swart, who later played one-day internationals and first-class cricket for the Netherlands, was involved in a physical clash with Essex import Billy Godleman in a Perth grade match in 2010/11. Although a three-match ban was overturned, suffered the ignominy of being asked to play for the Netherlands in the World Cup, only to have the invitation withdrawn.

- In recognition of becoming the first South African to score a Test match triple-century, Hashim Amla was made a member of the Beard Liberation Front. The group – whose members include Rolf Harris and Led Zeppelin's Robert Plant – noted that Amla's unbeaten 311 at The Oval in 2012 was " … **an outstanding example of how a beard can add weight to a sporting performance and make a significant positive impact in the public eye.**"

- While England was victorious over Australia in the 2009 Blind Ashes series, concerns were raised about the degree of disability of one of their top players. A Sydney magistrate, Christine Haskett, whose nephew Mark Haskett was in the Australian team, suggested that Nathan Foy might have had an unfair advantage. But Foy was unperturbed by the accusation, saying: **"I have exceptional hearing which allows me to hear the ball bearings inside the ball even in the air sometimes. Coupled with quick reactions and an amazing skill to know where I am in the outfield, I have become an accomplished fielder without sight."**

- The 100th cricket ground to stage a Test was Sophia Gardens in Cardiff during the 2009 Ashes series. The 101st and 102nd grounds both began operations – the following year – on the same day, a first in Test match cricket. Hyderabad's Rajiv Gandhi International Stadium and the Dubai Sports City Stadium both hosted their first day of Test cricket on 12 November 2010.

- When the Australian government's chief climate change advisor presented a report on the science at a Canberra function in 2011 he was introduced by the MC as the only man to have hit a six on to the roof of Beijing's famous Temple of Heaven. Professor Ross Garnaut is a former Australian ambassador to China, and was captain of the embassy's cricket team.

281

- First-class cricket was played in England in March for the first time in 2012, with a number of university matches beginning on the final day of the month. The Australian-born Sam Robson made history by hitting 117 for Middlesex against Durham MCCU at Northwood, the earliest first-class hundred scored in the UK. Cardiff MCCU wicketkeeper Zachary Elkin (131) also raised his bat by scoring 127 by stumps on the first day of his first-class debut, against Somerset at Taunton, the earliest hundred against a first-class county.

  At Fenner's, three batsmen hit March centuries as Essex bludgeoned Cambridge MCCU to the tune of 506/6 declared. Greg Smith – batting at number six – scored 160, while numbers seven and eight – James Foster (114*) and Graham Napier (100*) – also reached three figures. Surrey's Rory Burns (101*) and Glamorgan's new wicketkeeping captain Mark Wallace (122*) also scored centuries on the same day, for a grand total of seven centurions in the month.

- When Pakistan's Younis Khan fell to Sri Lanka's Thisara Perera in the fourth one-day international at Colombo in 2012, he became the first batsman to feature in a hat-trick in all three forms of international cricket. He was part of an Irfan Pathan Test match hat-trick at Karachi in 2005/06 and was one of the dismissed in a Tim Southee hat-trick in a Twenty20 international at Auckland in 2010/11.

- Two years after he died in 2009, the wife of a former one-day international cricketer claimed that he had faked his own death. Asim Butt, a left-arm quick who appeared in five World Cup games for Scotland, reportedly died in his sleep while in Lahore. His estranged wife, Tara, went public in 2011 saying no record of his death could be found, and that he may have faked his death for financial gain or to assume a new identity. She said: "**I tried to get a death certificate so I could show I was a widow and not divorced. My children were in private school and I needed to prove I was a widow to pay reduced fees. I hired a lawyer but he could not get a death certificate from Pakistan. The authorities say no-one with that date of birth and name had passed away. I've never had a penny from Asim's estate.**"

  On his one-day international debut – against Australia at Worcester in the 1999 World Cup – Butt opened the bowling and snared the prized wicket of Adam Gilchrist for six. He appeared in 29 first-class matches, with a best return of 5-47.

- Peter Siddle, who famously took a Test hat-trick on his 26th birthday, bowled to a fellow birthday boy in the second Australia–South Africa Test at Adelaide in 2012/13. Siddle celebrated his 28th birthday by knocking over Alviro Petersen on his 32nd birthday. Another birthday dismissal took place during the West Indies v India Test at Port-of-

Spain in 1961/62. Jamaica's Easton McMorris – born on 4 April 1935 – was dismissed in the first innings by Bapu Nadkarni, born on the same date in 1933.

- Two of the players in the first-ever Test match were born on the same day in the same city. When Australia lined up against England at the MCG in 1876/77, two of the historic XI – Nat Thompson and Ned Gregory – were born in Sydney on 29 May 1839. Thompson became the first batsman to be dismissed in Test cricket, while Gregory became the first batsman to be dismissed for a Test match duck.

A souvenir from the first Test – Australia versus England at Melbourne in 1876/77

  The Indian-born Victorian batsman Bransby Cooper made his Test debut in the same match, celebrating Test cricket's birth and his birthday. Born on 15 March 1844, Cooper scored 15 on the first day of the Test, 15 March 1877.

- In 1956, a ten-year old boy named Richard Stokes attended the fourth Test against Australia, the match in which Jim Laker made history with the ball. The son of a club cricketer, Richard watched on as Laker took 10-53 in Australia's innings, which, at the time, was a unique feat in Test match cricket.

  Three decades later, Stokes was on a business trip to New Delhi and to mark his birthday went along to the cricket, the second Test between India and Pakistan in 1998/99. Remarkably, he witnessed the second instance of a bowler claiming all ten in an innings, with Anil Kumble taking 10-74. Stokes said: **"I made it to the ground after lunch and Pakistan were very comfortable. Immediately, Kumble got two in an over and I told a friend of mine that I have brought luck to Kumble and India. When he had taken six wickets, I told him about my having watched Laker's feat, and he just said that history was about to be repeated. I merely laughed."**

- In 2012, Gurinder Sandhu became the first male cricketer of Indian origin to play for Australia. The then-19-year-old medium-fast bowler from New South Wales took 2-32 on his debut, against England in the Under-19 World Cup. He said: **"I thought there might have been a couple before me, but obviously not. I guess being the first Indian, some other Indian kids might look up to me, so I'll just hopefully do the best I can."**

In 2001, the Pune-born Lisa Sthalekar had become the first Indian, male or female, to represent Australia when she made her debut in a one-day international against England.

- Jiang Shuyao made a name for himself in 2012 when he became the first cricketer from mainland China to play in an overseas cricket league. Hailing from Shenyang in the north-east of China, Jiang played for the Cleethorpes club in England's Lincolnshire League. Jiang said: **"I like training for one or two hours here. In China we train for four hours, have some rice and then train for another four. And here you can say 'hello' to another player in training. If you do that in China you must run ten laps of the pitch."**

  In 2008/09, Jiang made his debut for the Chinese national team, but endured a wretched initiation with a score of one and two ducks in his first three matches in the Asian Cricket Council Trophy.

- Shahid Afridi was involved in a scuffle with members of the public at Karachi's international airport in 2012 with the Pakistan all-rounder throwing a few punches. Flying in from Dhaka where Pakistan had won the Asia Cup, Afridi was mobbed by fans and had to be restrained by his brother. Afridi said: **"I know what I did was wrong. I should have controlled myself, but I couldn't take it when my daughter was pushed to the ground."**

- India's Virat Kohli was fined half of his match fee during the second Test against Australia in 2011/12 following an incident with spectators on a day that the crowd was reportedly on its best behaviour. Kohli was charged after an indecent hand gesture on the second day and said: **"I agree cricketers don't have to retaliate … the crowd says the worst things about your mother and sister, the worst I've heard."**

  According to cricket authorities, since records began, the second day of the SCG match was the first time not a single spectator had been evicted for unruly behaviour during a Test in Australia.

- A first-class match at Scarborough in 2009 began in bizarre circumstances with proceedings from a funeral beamed around the ground during the opening day's play. The club's public address system inadvertently picked up coverage of a nearby funeral with a number of readings broadcast during the morning session of the Yorkshire–Nottinghamshire match.

- When former Australian Test batsman Marcus North made his first-class debut for Glamorgan in 2012, he became the first player to appear for six different English counties. The West Australian had previously played first-class cricket for Durham, Lancashire, Derbyshire, Gloucestershire and Hampshire.

In North's second first-class appearance for Glamorgan – at Southampton – three other players in the same match had also played for Western Australia. North played alongside Jim Allenby – who appeared in a Twenty20 match for WA in 2006/07 – while Hampshire's XI contained Simon Katich and Zimbabwe's Sean Ervine, who had also played first-class cricket for the West.

- England's wet weather upset a number of fixtures around the country in 2012, with a 50-over match needing 12 days to be completed. A Worsley Cup match at Blackburn scheduled for 9 June finally came to a conclusion more than a month later on 12 July. Playing for East Lancashire (204/6), South African Ockert Erasmus took a hat-trick and 5-21 in an 11-run victory over Enfield (193) in a game played on two grounds – Alexandra Meadows and Dill Hall Lane.

- A Melbourne radio announcer was put in his place by the Australian women's cricket team in 2008 after boasting on air that he could hit a century against them. Keen to prove him wrong, a number of the Australian women's side, including Lisa Sthalekar and Emma Sampson, met up with Nova's Ed Kavalee at a suburban park in Melbourne for a showdown. Kavalee batted against a team comprising four national players, six listeners and a colleague. After copping a number of balls on various parts of his body, he conceded he was wrong after being dismissed for just 34. Kavalee admitted: "**I said repeatedly the girls couldn't throw or bat or field and I could score 100 runs against the Australian women's cricket team. I would now like to retract that statement.**"

- A Kerry O'Keeffe impersonator on Twitter proved to be a huge hit in 2011, sucking in a little under 2,500 followers in just a day. The fake site attracted some big names, such as fellow radio commentator Jonathan Agnew and Australian spinner Michael Beer.

    The ABC radio commentator officially got on board the following year, and had some 6,000 followers on the first day, tweeting: "**No trolls.**"

"I think Glenn [McGrath] wasted his 25 cents there. How much does a tweet cost?"

Channel Nine's Mark Taylor exposing a lack of knowledge about Twitter

---

"I am just too boring. I can't think of anything interesting to say. It wouldn't be useful to me."

Andrew Strauss in 2012, revealing his reluctance to join Twitter

- Champion Russian chess player Peter Svidler is a big cricket fan who borrowed the 'Tendulkar' sobriquet as his nickname in an online chess tournament. The chess grandmaster used the Indian batsman's name on the ICC – Internet Chess Club – website. He said: "**I chose 'Tendulkar' because I meant it as some innocent fun. The intention was to create an illusion. Cricket is not a hobby, it is a full-time occupation. I keep stats, I'm a madman.**"

- When India and Pakistan took to the field for a match at Bangalore in 2012, they combined for the first-ever Twenty20 international played on Christmas Day. Previously, there had been three Christmas one-day internationals – India versus Bangladesh at Chandigarh in 1999, Pakistan against Zimbabwe at Rawalpindi in 1993 and India versus Sri Lanka at Indore in 1997.

  The first first-class match to include play on Christmas Day took place in New Zealand in 1884 in the game between Hawkes Bay and Wellington in Napier. The record for the highest last-wicket stand in first-class cricket was set on Christmas Day in 1928, when the New South Wales pair of Alan Kippax and Hal Hooker added 307 against Victoria in a Sheffield Shield match in Melbourne.

  The first Test to include play on 25 December was in 1951 when Australia hosted the West Indies at Adelaide. The last Test played at Christmas – Pakistan versus India at Karachi in 1982 – featured a five-wicket haul on the day from Imran Khan (8-60).

TESTS WITH PLAY ON CHRISTMAS DAY

Australia v West Indies	Adelaide	1951
Australia v India	Adelaide	1967
India v Australia	Madras	1969
India v England	Delhi	1972
India v Pakistan	Kanpur	1979
Pakistan v India	Karachi	1982

- During Australia's innings loss at the hands of India at Hyderabad in 2012/13, Dave Warner hit a second-innings six which was caught by a former Test cricketer in the stands. Merv Hughes, who was leading a tour group, took 23 catches for Australia in his 53 Tests.

- Opening the batting against South Africa at Durban in 2012/13, Pakistan's Mohammad Hafeez became the first batsman in the history of one-day internationals to be dismissed for a duck obstructing the field. Only the fourth batsman to be dismissed in such fashion in a ODI, fellow Pakistan opener Rameez Raja was the first from his country to go this way, out for a heart-breaking 99 against England at Karachi in 1987/88.

Credits

Books
Wisden Cricketers' Almanack (John Wisden & Co, London - various years).

Newspapers & Magazines
The Age, The Australian, The Canberra Times, Cricket Today, The Daily Telegraph, Sunday Telegraph, The Sydney Morning Herald, The Cricketer.

Websites
www.abc.net.au/news/sport/cricket, www.cricket365.com, www.cricketarchive.co.uk, www.espncricinfo.com, www.facebook.com/askasim, www.facebook.com/asksteven, www.facebook/windiescricket, www.guardian.co.uk/sport/cricket, www.howstat.com.au, www.rediff.com/cricket, www.sportstats.com.au/bloghome.html, www.thecricketer.com, www. wikipedia.org.

Photographs
An Ocean Awaits Records (www.aoarecords.com.au), Akbar Allana, Australian Broadcasting Corporation, David Bartlett, Ashley Best, Bletchley Stamp Art (www.bletchleycovers.com), Boom Cricket, Bunbury Cricket Club, caribbeancricket.com, Neale Castelino, Channel Seven, Charles Leski Auctions, Nat Coombs, Tim Costello, Cricket Foundation (www.chancetoshine.org), D.C. Thomson & Co Ltd, De Montfort University, David Dixson, Eleven PR, Joel Fitzgibbon, Peter Hain, Matthew Hancock, Historic Houses Trust, Frédéric Humbert, Guam Nabis Kari, Andy Kind, Matt King, Graham Lambert, Jasmine Lawrence, Geoff Lawson, Lippy Pictures, Lord's, Netherlands Cricket Team, Nottingham Playhouse, PETA, Office of the Prime Minister of Australia, Office of the Prime Minister of Trinidad and Tobago, Oman

Cricket, Christina Pierce, Eva Renaldo (www.evarinaldi.com), Martin Rowbotham, Rozlyn Khan, Samra Teague, D'Abernon Cricket Club, *Test Match Special*, The Don Bradmans, tonyderbott.com, University of Wollongong, Hendrik van der Merwe, WNBL, West Indies Cricket (www.windiescricket.com), Mandi Whitten (www.mandiwhitten.com).

Every effort has made to identify owners of photographs. If any omissions have been made, acknowledgements will be made in any future editions.

Personal thanks
Julian Abbott, Keith Andrew, Courtney Dawson, Ned Hall, Michael Jones, Marcus Kelson, Geoff Lawson, Connie Liu, Aslam Siddiqui.

Notes
All information and statistics in this book were correct at the time of printing. If any reader has an unusual cricketing story or photograph that could be included in any future editions please forward to email: mdawson@homemail.com.au or cricketbook@hotmail.com. Any item used will be credited.